Gregg Matte is the best new Christian author in America. His latest work, *I AM changes who i am,* is a masterpiece. It changed my life, and it will change yours.

John Bisagno
Author and Pastor Emeritus of Houston's First Baptist Church, Houston, Texas

Gregg Matte, my pastor, is not only a man of God's Word but also a man of prayer. Each Sunday he blesses us not with a sermon about God but with a message from God. Just as we are the beneficiaries of the fruit of his labor on Sundays, the readers of *I AM changes who i am* will be blessed with that fruit on each of its pages! Pastor Gregg is intimately familiar with the heart of God and the power of the Holy Spirit that has guided him to passionately share His life-transforming truths with clarity and honesty.

Mary Ann Bridgwater
President of Pray the Word Ministries, speaker and author of *Prayers for the Faithful*

One thing that you notice in encounters with Pastor Gregg is his passion to see Jesus transform lives. He desires this not only for his own life but also for each life he can touch. *I AM changes who i am* is an amazing journey of seeing the Savior and letting Him transform you—and those around you—with His presence and power.

Ralph Borde
CEO of As Our Own

Gregg's life reveals the impact and kind of power that can only come from relationship with a great God. His leadership showcases the contrast of humility with boldness. When you read this book, you will learn to live the extraordinary life that God intended you to live when He first made you.

Anita Carman
Founder of Inspire Women

I've had the privilege of serving in ministry with Gregg, and when it comes to presenting God's life-changing truths, he is, hands down, one of the best communicators I know. More importantly, he is a godly man with wisdom far beyond his years. Truly, I AM has changed who I am, and as a result, my life has never been the same. I'm excited about this book and the potential it has to change lives.

Vicki Courtney
Speaker and author

Jesus changes everything! Especially you when you choose to follow Him. Gregg Matte shows us how to live the Christ life in a fresh, compelling way that will inspire, motivate and challenge you to live a transformed life.

Jack Graham
Pastor of Prestonwood Baptist Church, Plano, Texas

If you've ever wanted to know who Jesus says He is, *I AM changes who i am* is the book for you. Walking through the miracles and statements of Jesus will help you realize the weight of who our Savior is and who we are in the light of His salvation.

Craig Groeschel
Senior Pastor of LifeChurch.tv and author of *WEIRD, Because Normal Isn't Working*

Multitudes see Gregg Matte as a leader, but I affectionately know him as *pastor*. Rest assured, this man dines on the "I AM" he is serving. Each week I am chiseled into more of the likes of Christ because of his teaching, and I have a hunch the same is ahead for you within this book's pages! Don't read as a spectator; read as a participant. "I AM" longs to transform you.

Tammie Head
Director of Totally Captivated Ministries, speaker and author

From the dirt of a baseball field to the streets of Africa, we desire to live every day with purpose. We do this because Jesus Christ first showed us how, and He challenges us with the life-long task to make an impact wherever we are. This book is a practical and powerful tool that encourages all of us to live out our identity in the great I AM. Gregg Matte illuminates God's Word in a way that captures the attention of readers of all ages.

Clayton and Ellen Kershaw
2011 Cy Young Award winner and All-Star Pitcher of the Los Angeles Dodgers
Co-authors of *Arise*

Gregg Matte is an enormously gifted communicator. In these pages he shows us how a fresh glimpse of the unchangeable God changes everything.

Beth Moore
New York Times bestselling author and Bible teacher

Having taught the nation's largest college Bible study and now leading Houston's First Baptist Church, Pastor Gregg Matte is a proven communicator who speaks to the heart with a twist of humor. His new book on the seven miracles and "I AM" statements of Jesus in the Gospel of John winsomely persuades that the power to fulfill the call of God in our lives comes from depending on who Christ is and what He does. Truly, the great "I AM" longs to change who "i am."

Tony Perkins
President of Family Research Council

I love Gregg's passion for knowing Jesus and making Him known—and I loved this book! Gregg delivers an urgently needed message to the Church today: We need a fresh encounter with I AM. We need to rediscover the power of the gospel and what it means to worship God in spirit and truth. We need to rediscover the miraculous Messiah and how He can transform our lives, our families and our churches. Gregg's book is a must-read for an American Church in desperate need of revival.

Joel C. Rosenberg
New York Times bestselling author and founder of The Joshua Fund

I have personally watched Gregg live an extraordinary life of faith. I love that he has written a book that invites us to join him in the greatest pursuit: the study of the great I AM!

Ben Stuart
Director of Breakaway Ministries at Texas A&M

I am thankful for Gregg's friendship and leadership in my own life. Everyone wants to understand the miraculous Messiah, and in this book, Gregg helps all of us see Him and experience Him.

Chris Tomlin
Worship leader and songwriter

In *I AM changes who i am*, Gregg Matte does a great job of examining excerpts from the life of Christ: seven of His miraculous works and seven of His powerful "I AM" statements from the Gospel of John. Any reader—from nonbeliever to committed Christ-follower—can profoundly benefit from Gregg's keen insight into Scripture, down-to-earth illustrations and practical life applications.

Bryant Wright
Senior Pastor of Johnson Ferry Baptist Church, Marietta, Georgia
President of the Southern Baptist Convention

"Who am I?" is one of the most profound questions you will ever ask. In this book, Gregg Matte gives some life-changing answers to this deeply personal question.

Ben Young
Author of *Why Mike's Not a Christian*

I AM

changes who i am

who Jesus is changes who i am
what Jesus does changes what i am to do

GREGG MATTE

Regal

For more information and
special offers from Regal Books, email us at
subscribe@regalbooks.com

Published by Regal
From Gospel Light
Ventura, California, U.S.A.
www.regalbooks.com
Printed in the U.S.A.

Matte, Gregg.
I AM changes who I am : who Jesus is changes who I am,
what Jesus does changes what I am to do / Gregg Matte.
p. cm.
Includes bibliographical references and index.
ISBN 978-0-8307-6226-2 (hardcover : alk. paper)
1. Christian ethics—Biblical teaching. 2. Conduct of life—Biblical teaching.
3. Christian life. I. Title.
BS680.E84G37 2012
248.4—dc23
2011048753

Rights for publishing this book outside the U.S.A. or in non-English languages
are administered by Gospel Light Worldwide, an international not-for-profit ministry. For additional information, please visit www.glww.org, email info@glww.org, or write to Gospel Light Worldwide, 1957 Eastman Avenue, Ventura, CA 93003, U.S.A.

To order copies of this book and other Regal products in bulk quantities,
please contact us at 1-800-446-7735.

For Kelly

Apart from Jesus, no one has had a bigger impact on my life.
A consistent encourager, you have prayed, supported, loved and challenged
me in enormous ways. I'm so grateful for our marriage and family.
You are a great wife and mother!

"I AM changed who i am" and He used you more than anyone else.
You bless me.

CONTENTS

Acknowledgments 11

Introduction: Contrasts Create 13

1. First Miracle: H$_2$O to Merlot.................................17

2. Second Miracle: Behind the Blinking Light 31

3. Third Miracle: When 2 Plus 2 Doesn't Equal 4 41

4. Fourth Miracle (Part 1): Don't Just Bubble and Squeak By............49

5. Fourth Miracle (Part 2): If We'll Add, He Will Multiply 61

6. Fifth Miracle (Part 1): Time to Sail.........................69

7. Fifth Miracle (Part 2): Pink Canoes and Barbie Dolls 77

8. First I AM: Show, Then Tell 87

9. Second I AM: Flip the Switch...................................101

10. Sixth Miracle: See! 115

11. Third I AM: Some Sheep and a Gate 131

12. Fourth I AM: "Baa" Means Good............................147

13. Seventh Miracle and Fifth I AM: Dawn of the Dead Living..........161

14. Sixth I AM: Partridge Family Praise? 175

15. Seventh I AM: Sprinklers, Pulses and Vineyards....................187

Conclusion: Contrasts Create 201

Appendix I: Thoughts on Drinking...............................203

Appendix II: Why Is John 5:4 Missing in the *NIV*? 209

Appendix III: Tips for Small-Group Leaders 211

Endnotes 215

About As Our Own 219

About the Author...221

ACKNOWLEDGMENTS

Week in and week out, I'm able to stand before tremendously encouraging and loving people—the congregation and staff of Houston's First Baptist Church. Thank you for listening and learning as I teach God's Word. You are a remarkable blessing to the Mattes. It is a joy to follow Christ with you.

Thank you, Ann Higginbottom, for your countless hours of work on this book. I'm glad to team up with such an editor. You possess a great work ethic, insight and writing ability; many great opportunities are ahead of you.

Mary Smith and Joanna Cooke, thanks for all you do in my office. Forty-plus hours a week you handle the details. I'm grateful for your "can do" attitudes and sweet spirits.

Thanks to everyone at Regal. Bill Grieg III and Steve Lawson, thank you for being such a joy to work with. Your care and investment in my writing has been a blessing. Also, please plan more meetings where I need to fly to Regal's office on the California coast!

Research team, what a display of the Body of Christ you are. You did a great job of handing me the fabric from which the garment of this book is sewn. Your study, gleaning and presentation help me to craft the specific message God has while standing on a firm theological foundation.

To Mom, Dad, the Evans, Comfort Crew, my friends and family, you know me as plain ol' Gregg and still love me. Thanks. It is a blessing to be fully known and fully loved.

Greyson and Valerie, you are both an inspiration to me. I'm so grateful to be your father. You are gifts of God, and tons of fun! As you grow older, allow the "I AM" to shape who you are.

Kelly, you are simply the best—best mom, wife, encourager and, most important, my best friend.

Father in heaven, You are the I AM who changed who i am. Thank You! I'm eternally grateful and honored to be Your son.

Contrasts Create . . .

Contrasts create impact. Contrasts can sear images and feelings into the mind's eye: evergreen trees against a blue sky; waves of water lapping up on a hot beach; quietness in a crowd. One Saturday morning, contrast created a memory I'll never forget. The contrast was not of beauty in nature but of a difference in build.

I arrived at the hotel to speak at 9:00 AM, as I had been instructed. Arriving early, and feeling nervous in my starched shirt, I was looking for someone to show me the conference room where I would speak. As I arranged my notes, my listeners filed in—not a smile among them. Stern, serious faces mounted on huge necks sat quietly as I was introduced. *What am I doing here?* shot through my mind, along with, *Dear Lord, help!* Here I was, standing before the Texas A&M football team on game day! Literally, they were almost as tall as me . . . sitting down. Contrast creates impact: them/me; athlete/speaker; tall/short; 345 lbs./145 lbs.; scholarship/"thanks, Mom and Dad"; on the field/in the stands. The room was filled with my exact opposites.

Shying away from any story about when I rode the bench for the Olle Owls eighth-grade B team, I stuck to the Bible. The team didn't laugh at my jokes or wince at the hard truths—they just looked at me. Then it struck me about three-fourths of the way through: They weren't disinterested; they were focused. They were assembled as a team, with no doubt of who they were and what they were to do. Like seated gladiators on a mission set to begin at 7:00 PM, chapel service notwithstanding, they were focused on doing some damage on the field.

The team preached to me that morning about the importance of knowing who you are and what you are to do. They created an impact and indelible memory of what focus looks like when you stare it in the eye. Think about that. Do you really and deeply know your mission? The following chapters are going to allow you to look into the eyes of the one who knew exactly who He was and what He was to do.

Just like the team contrasted with me, He is our exact opposite: Jesus/us; holy/sinful; trusting/prone to worry; free/bound; God/man; Miracle Maker/

miracle takers. Yes, contrasts create impact, and an eye locked on Jesus will recalibrate a person's entire life!

Living the Christian life is difficult, especially in today's culture. Unfortunately, we have left the miracles either with cable TV faith healers or tour guides in the Holy Land. God still wants to do the miraculous today, and He wants to do it in you and me! Therefore, we must realize that the power to fulfill the call of God in our lives comes from depending on who Christ is and what He does. In the Gospel of John, we will see Christ perform seven miracles and proclaim seven "I AM" statements.

Here is our journey clearly stated: By digging into the Gospel of John, we'll discover who Jesus is and what He does, showing us the power to live out the Christian life.

The apostle John starts his gospel account with a big-picture perspective. His book is rich, capable of winning over nonbelievers and encouraging the believer. He begins his account all the way back to the beginning of time: "In the beginning was the Word" (John 1:1). In taking us back to the opening words of Genesis, John reminds us that this "Jesus" is not a new idea, but rather He was there at the beginning of time. John is declaring that God the Father, in His supremacy, has sent a sound wave reverberating through all generations. This sound wave is the Word of God—His Son, Jesus—through whom the Father is making His kingdom known. John 1:14 says that the "Word became flesh and made his dwelling among us." That's Jesus from Genesis, now walking the paths of earth.

For those who believe, we are small surfers on the sound wave of God. What a contrast! John is giving us a "bigger than we could imagine" perspective of who God is through His Son, the Living Word. We will witness that this Jesus performing miracles and making shocking declarations of identity was there at the beginning. He poured the oceans and molded the land. Jesus turned dust into man. Colossians 1:16 states, "For by him all things were created: things in heaven and on earth . . . all things were created by him and for him."

To prepare the way for the coming King, the Father sent a humble servant, John the Baptist, whose purpose was to point to Jesus, declaring that one greater than himself was coming for the salvation of the world. John the Baptist was an arrow pointed heavenward, reminding the people that redemption was on the way. He embraced his identity, knowing that he was not the Christ. In understanding who the coming Christ was, John the Baptist understood more about himself. Knowing who God is transforms the way we see ourselves. When we know who He is, it changes who we are. For all of us, *I AM changes who i am*.

In John 1, we see John the Baptist playing out his role of pointing to the King. The Father used him to prepare the people for Christ, their Deliverer. As the Gospel of John begins, we see a beautiful example of how God uses ordinary people, like us, to accomplish extraordinary things. It has been said that "only small birds sing," and John the Baptist knew he was a small bird. In his humble demeanor but bold approach, he sang of coming salvation. He was meek yet a man of the wilderness, unwavering in confidence that he himself was *not* the Christ, but that the Christ was coming (see John 1:20). Such focus resulted in Jesus' saying, "I tell you the truth: Among those born of women there has not risen anyone greater than John the Baptist" (Matt. 11:11).

John the Baptist showed both greatness and humility in declaring that Jesus is the fulfillment of everything that has been proclaimed since the creation of time (see Gal. 4:4). THIS IS IT! Jesus is on the world stage to perform the seven miracles and declare seven "I AM" statements in the book of John: 7+7=1—1 Miraculous Messiah. Lights, camera, action . . . the one who knows clearly who He is and what He is to do has arrived.

Seven Miracles of Jesus

1. Turning water into wine (JOHN 2:1-12)
2. Healing the nobleman's son (JOHN 4:46-54)
3. Healing of the lame man (JOHN 5:1-17)
4. Feeding the 5,000 (JOHN 6:1-13)
5. Walking on water (JOHN 6:16-21)
6. Healing the man born blind (JOHN 9:1-41)
7. Raising Lazarus from dead (JOHN 11:1-45)

Seven I AM Statements of Jesus

1. I AM the Bread of Life (JOHN 6:35,48,51)
2. I AM the Light of the World (JOHN 8:12)
3. I AM the Door/Gate (JOHN 10:7)
4. I AM the Good Shepherd (JOHN 10:11-14)
5. I AM the Resurrection and the Life (JOHN 11:25)
6. I AM the Way, the Truth, and the Life (JOHN 14:6)
7. I AM the True Vine (JOHN 15:1)

The contrast of His miracles and identity invading our lives and our mundane concerns can only result in change. Keep reading as the discovery map unfolds to show you who He is and what He does. Then you'll be ready to run onto the field with the rest of the team. Your build may contrast with what you think is the super-saint physique, like mine contrasted with those linebackers. But the contrast will create the impact of living out the miraculous Christian life. As we get started, read this next sentence out loud . . . *I AM changes who i am.*

FOR FURTHER REFLECTION AND DISCUSSION

1. Describe a time when you were in contrast to the setting around you. How did you feel? What inadequacy came to the forefront of your thoughts?

2. In what ways are the contrasts between Christ and us encouraging? Discouraging?

3. What "I AM" statement or miracle are you most excited to learn about?

FIRST MIRACLE

H$_2$O to Merlot

Jesus said to the servants, "Fill the jars with water";
so they filled them to the brim.

JOHN 2:7

Seven Miracles of Jesus

1. **Turning water into wine** (JOHN 2:1-12)
2. Healing the nobleman's son (JOHN 4:46-54)
3. Healing of the lame man (JOHN 5:1-17)
4. Feeding the 5,000 (JOHN 6:1-13)
5. Walking on water (JOHN 6:16-21)
6. Healing the man born blind (JOHN 9:1-41)
7. Raising Lazarus from dead (JOHN 11:1-45)

Seven I AM Statements of Jesus

1. I AM the Bread of Life (JOHN 6:35,48,51)
2. I AM the Light of the World (JOHN 8:12)
3. I AM the Door/Gate (JOHN 10:7)
4. I AM the Good Shepherd (JOHN 10:11-14)
5. I AM the Resurrection and the Life (JOHN 11:25)
6. I AM the Way, the Truth, and the Life (JOHN 14:6)
7. I AM the True Vine (JOHN 15:1)

It is a humbling experience when your suitcase catches the attention of airport security, especially when your bag is concealing wine bottles you're trying to smuggle home from a church trip to the Holy Land. It's not like wine would cause harm to anyone in flight—they dole it out in first class. The bottles were just a souvenir idea, certainly nothing worthy of an all-out investigation in the security line. Not to mention the added humiliation of holding up your travel team while security tosses dirty socks and T-shirts aside, digging for the suspicious bottles.

Such was the fate of an unassuming lady who went with her church on a trip to Israel. They saw the sites one is supposed to see when taking a walking tour of the Bible, including Cana, where Jesus turned water into wine. Upon arriving in Cana, the lady decided to haul a few bottles home, commemorating that significant place in biblical history.

Her church was more likely to think the miracle was Jesus turning water into *grape juice*. As a result, the traveler was uneasy about her purchase. So she tucked the two bottles of Cana wine into her suitcase, stuffing them between dirty clothes and other souvenirs. She didn't give it a second thought until arriving at airport security for the flight home. On reaching the front of the security line, she shoved her suitcase through the X-ray machine and waited for it on the other side.

Before her bag made it through, a security officer greeted her. "Ma'am, we've identified two bottles of liquid in your suitcase. We're going to need to open it up and see what they are." *Gulp*. With the whole church group surrounding her, she felt the weight of every eye. "Oh! Don't worry about those. They are just bottles of water. Bottles of water!"

Her hopeless reasoning was unconvincing. "Ma'am, we understand, but we are going to need to open up your suitcase," he replied as he unzipped the bag. He pulled out the two bottles of wine and held them up for all to see. "Ma'am, this isn't water; it's wine."

The lady didn't skip a beat. Holding her hands high, she proclaimed, "Praise the Lord! He did it again! Water into wine!"

It is hard to know where alcohol fits in the context of church and Christian belief. Jesus' miracle of turning water into wine can make some feel a little uncomfortable.[1] Unfortunately, instead of basking in the miraculous, some people spend their days trying to figure out how to turn the wine back into water. We are more comfortable with things that can be easily unpacked and understood. With difficult things in God's Word, we either choose to ignore them or look through the lens of faith to better understand what God is up to. The reality of this passage in the Gospel of John that records the events of the wedding at Cana is that God did something miraculous and beautiful through His Son, Jesus Christ.

At first glance, it may not make a lot of sense; and miracles are often misunderstood and stifled when seen without faith. But when things are beyond comprehension and even understanding, the Christian faith believes that God is doing something bigger than anticipated. In the book of John, we read how the heavenly Father used Jesus to bring forth miraculous work, and we also begin to see that God is able to do extraordinary work in and through us. In His hands we can be used to do great things. When we see the Lord accomplish the unbelievable, our faith grows as we begin to consider what He can do in our lives. In the miracle of turning water into wine, there was a change that challenged all categories of "possible." It is clear that the Father was using Jesus to do something remarkable. He can do the same thing in your life.

Ordinary Brings Extraordinary

On the third day a wedding took place at Cana in Galilee. Jesus' mother was there, and Jesus and his disciples had also been invited to the wedding. When the wine was gone, Jesus' mother said to him, "They have no more wine."

"Dear woman, why do you involve me?" Jesus replied. "My time has not yet come."

His mother said to the servants, *"Do whatever he tells you"* (John 2:1-5, emphasis added).

In our house, the last thing that will ever happen when throwing a party is that we will run out of food. Usually, we have several days' worth of leftovers filling the fridge. If 20 people RSVP, my wife buys food for 25, just to be sure. In biblical times, a wedding was not only the celebration of a marriage; it was also a display of honor and hospitality afforded by the host. Culturally, it was a mammoth *faux pas* to run out of wine. The master of ceremonies would not only be publicly humiliated but could even be legally punished for "breech of hospitality."[2] Thankfully for the host at the wedding in Cana, Jesus was at the party.

In the midst of the lavish festivities, the unthinkable happened and the wine was suddenly gone. A buzz of rumors scattered among the banquet guests. Jesus' mother, Mary, saw the issue and looked to her son to fix the problem. If there were ever a time to pull off a miracle, she thought, this was it. For the sake of the dignity of the host, something had to be done.

Jesus understood that the time for His public glorification had not yet come, and so He responded with a pause. And I snicker at His answer: "Dear woman, why do you involve me? My time has not yet come." Men, give this a try. When you're watching a ball game and your wife gives you a "honey-do," promptly quote Jesus, "Dear woman, why do you involve me? My time has not yet come." You'll probably find out this is a statement only Jesus can get away with!

The People God Uses

One of the deepest desires of every believer is to be part of the plan of God. The compelling nature of the love of God creates a yearning in us to get off of the bench and into the game. On the other side of the coin, God can also use people to further His plan as they go about their day, unaware of how He is using them to further His plan. Being used by God is at times the result of raising our hand and saying, "Here I am," like the prophet Isaiah; or we can look back and see the course God chose to take though we were unaware at the time (see Isa. 6:8). In this moment of need at the Cana wedding, Jesus had an array of characters from whom to choose to remedy the problem. He could have used the master of the ceremonies; his mother, Mary; the disciples; the bride and groom; the servants.

Surely the master of ceremonies, or the wedding party—those with formal titles and standing at the center of attention—would be the ones used to do something great. We often assume that people with social, political or even spiritual status will be God's first choice. But God does not look at the things that people look at. "Man looks at the outward appearance, but the LORD looks at the heart" (1 Sam. 16:7). Often, we assume the boss is the fix-it man. But a formal title or being the most noticeable does not set people apart to be used by God. He is looking for a heart that is willing to serve, not a résumé that proves previous service.

I struggle with this as a pastor and parent. Since I'm the chief of the tribe, I often feel the pressure to make everything right. I need to come up with the great idea or solution since all eyes are looking to my end of the table, whether it's in a meeting or during dinner at home. It's true that a leader is to be an avid problem solver, but God has His own plans. Jesus didn't use the master of ceremonies to solve the problem at the wedding. The ones who possess the formal title or the business card that says "boss" have to trust that God's glory, and not their résumé, is the ultimate goal.

Perhaps Jesus could have used Mary, His own mother. Surely, we would assume that Mary would be a shoe-in for miraculous work. One side of my family is strongly Catholic, and I was baptized as a baby in the Catholic Church. So I can hear my relatives and lineage cheering for Mary to do the miraculous. Many people assume that God uses the family of a spiritual leader to do something great. But not even a family tree dictates those whom God will use. Just being related to someone spiritual doesn't get passed down through the family genes. Remember, God doesn't have any grandchildren, just children. Though we should have great appreciation for our heritage, we all have our own journey with the Lord. No, Jesus didn't use Mary to solve the problem.

Jesus could have looked to His disciples. They had been around Him long enough to know how things worked and what their leader was capable of doing. However, they were in a faith-building time of preparation for work to come. It seems that Jesus understood that His friends needed a season of watching and learning in preparation for a lifetime of ministry.

The disciples symbolize people to whom God is saying, "Not yet." This can be the most difficult group to be affiliated with. These are people who will be used tremendously in the future, but not now. When you are in the "not yet" category of God's plan, two things rise to the surface. First is jealousy. *Why is God using or blessing that person instead of me?* Standing on the sidelines, watching others score the touchdowns, can create thoughts in our mind that we would never speak with our lips.

Jealousy finds its death in humility. The humble heart realizes that God uses different people at different times; they can rest in the fact that they have not been overlooked. The disciples would be greatly used in His kingdom in the future; some would have books of the Bible that bear their names. But for now, they must choose humility over jealousy. The ultimate goal was not that they were star performers in God's every action, but in God's unfolding plan.

I have learned this truth during the last few years. It comes with age, but more so with growth. Multiplying ministry means that you cheer when God uses someone else. Breakaway Ministries at Texas A&M started with a handful of students meeting in my apartment.[3] During the next 15 years, we began to increase in number until there were 4,000 students per week.

Ultimately, we needed to meet in the basketball arena. When I handed the Breakaway reins over to Ben Stuart and took the pastorate at Houston's First Baptist Church, my desire was for greater things to happen under Ben's leadership. And they have.

One Tuesday night, my family and I drove to College Station from Houston to sit in Kyle Field, A&M's football stadium, to worship with more than 8,000 students. As I sat in the stadium with my wife and son, no one recognized me. I just blended in with the crowd, even though I had started the ministry. It was a delight to see God using Ben and his team.

The packed stands forced my wife and son to sit on the row in front of me while I was wedged between two sophomores behind them. This provided one of the greatest spiritual snapshots of my life. This small viewpoint illustrated God's great vision for my life that had been building for decades. I saw my son, my wife and my ministry legacy at A&M singing to the Lord that night. What great joy to cheer on the next generation in ministry! I felt no jealousy, just a deep sense of humility that I had been allowed to play a part. I wasn't being used there at that moment, but God was on the move. His movement, not my direct involvement, was where the joy was found.

Can you relate to the disciples on the sidelines? Do you ever feel like God's will, His hand and His blessing are hitting everyone but you? It's difficult for anyone to be in the "not yet" part of God's plan. Jesus was going to use the disciples, but not yet. This was not their time, and maybe right now it's not yours. But they were mature enough to wait, and so should we.

Surprisingly, to all who were at the wedding, Jesus did the unexpected—He looked to the servants. No pedigree or accolades, just common servants. In using the servants to carry out the miracle, He turned to the ordinary to do the extraordinary. Let that thought refresh you! "Ordinary" is a good description of how I feel. Maybe you peg yourself as someone who fits in the "ordinary" category too. But have you ever considered that God could use you for something extraordinary? In the moment of need, He turned to find servants who were waiting to be used and willing to be taught. Jesus uses those who will slow down and listen up. When we place ourselves in such a position, we are usable in His hands. And when we are willing to be used, God does extraordinary work. Do you have a servant's heart to be used by God for great things? Royal position and family ties don't seem to matter. What does count is a tender heart that is willing to serve and that is sensitive to the needs of God's kingdom.

Miracles meet ordinary needs in unexpected ways. The wedding guests were in need of wine. Amazingly, Jesus not only met the expectations but He also provided abundantly more than imagined. There was no logical avenue to find more wine; so we begin to see that God often works miracles when they are the only way. When we are looking only for the ordinary, God is up to something extraordinary. We wonder how something will ever get done, not noticing that jars are being filled with water and stirred by the Spirit. God is working behind the scenes to meet the need. He is solving the problem when we have only assessed it. He is curing the cancer when we are still trying to pronounce its name, providing the resources as the bills are placed in the mailbox, giving the strength when we are weak.

On a recent "Oh my, I've got a lot to do today" morning, I sat down for my quiet time. I pondered this Scripture passage about the miracle at the wedding and prayed, "Thank You, Lord. You are filling jars to solve problems I don't even know of." God is at work for you. Right now. He is filling what you will be lacking by noon. "Your Father knows what you need before you ask him" (Matt. 6:8).

If we only see the commonplace, we miss the miraculous. We simply see servants filling jars with "well water," but in God's economy, He is setting the stage to shine brightly as Messiah. He chooses to speak to and use those who are willing to slow down and listen up. God is looking for servants with hearts to believe the unbelievable (see 2 Chron. 16:9).

A Walk of Obedience

His mother said to the servants, "Do whatever he tells you."

Nearby stood six stone water jars, the kind used by the Jews for ceremonial washing, each holding from twenty to thirty gallons.

Jesus said to the servants, "Fill the jars with water"; so they filled them to the brim.

Then he told them, "Now draw some out and take it to the master of the banquet."

They did so, and the master of the banquet tasted the water that had been turned into wine. He did not realize where it had come from, though the servants who had drawn the water knew (John 2:5-9).

I can imagine the servants must have thought Jesus' request was odd. I would have too. Turn water to wine? But the servants' position led them to accept the task. God's way shatters our category of what is possible. Jesus looked to the servants and asked them to fill the nearby purification jars with water. People used these jars for ceremonial cleansing of their hands and body before coming inside a certain place. But Jesus had different plans for the jars. He looked to the servants and expected their full obedience as they filled the jars, not just halfway, but to the brim. He wanted the jars filled to the top so that the water dripped over the edge. Without raising an eyebrow, the servants filled the jars until they were brimming with water.

Do we obey Christ completely or just enough to cover our tracks? Obeying Him completely means filling the jars to the brim and declaring, "Lord, I trust You!" It is a moment when we say, "Lord, I'm not just going to go 99.9 percent of the way. I'm going to fill it to the brim. I'm going to follow You and give it all that I've got!" Most of us want our obedience to fill 51 percent of the way and stop. Then we can claim we have surpassed most people and made our best effort, but we have not truly risked in faith.

There must be times and circumstances when His requests don't make sense. In our limited understanding, we don't understand how filling jars with water solves a wine problem. Obedience is not always the result of complete understanding. Many times, it is a matter of trusting the Lord and having faith that He is in control. Faith in His sufficiency can lead us toward obedience.

Bucket by bucket, the servants filled the six 25-gallon jars. It was tedious, tenacious, tactile and time-consuming obedience. The servants followed Jesus' directions precisely. "Now draw some out and take it to the master of the banquet," Jesus instructed them. Can you imagine their walk toward the master of the banquet? The cup they carried contained water for hand washing, not wine for a wedding! They risked a slap in the face and a sentence to the dungeon for such a disgraceful act, but they were trusting the Lord to make the change as they walked. In those moments of walking by faith, the water turned to wine. The ordinary water turned to excellent wine just in time. The master of ceremonies kept his dignity as the finest wine kept flowing. Though many did not realize the source of the wine, the servants knew, and they marveled at the miracle.

Faith and obedience lead to a deeper awareness of God at work in our lives when we don't understand what He's doing. God might call us to walk in obedient faith as we are carrying water but need wine. In that walk of faith, we experience God do something we did not expect. Something miraculous. An act of faith ignites the Father to do something extraordinary.

Some Saturday nights my wife, Kelly, will ask, "How do you feel about the sermon in the morning?" I invariably answer with one word: "Water." I'm thinking about what needs to be heard and then I look at my notes. In that moment, it feels like a cup of water when a goblet of wine is required. This brings me to a crossroads of faith and offers a reminder of the one who meets the needs. I'm the vessel, but Christ is the power. My job is to faithfully walk with a glass of water to the Master of *all* ceremonies. Somewhere in the journey, He'll make the change.

Usually, by noon the next day, Kelly will say one word to explain what happened in our church service: "Wine." My walk of faithfulness unleashed His power to provide exactly what the situation needed. The Sunday sermon was marked with Holy Spirit power, not by my preparation. When I get out of the way and walk faithfully with a servant's heart, God turns water into wine.

Victory over Complacency

The servants' response at the wedding at Cana was compelling because it was so far from typical. We would expect them to respond to such a request, and from a wedding guest, with disbelief and some under-the-breath grumbling. But their availability allowed them to be used by God in a mighty way.

Perhaps you wish you had faith to believe that Jesus could turn something ordinary into something extraordinary. Are you willing to serve and be used even if the path is unclear? When God asks you to do something that doesn't seem practical, remember that His perspective is bigger and filled with more wisdom than you possess. He has something much greater in mind. Victory over complacency begins with a heart that is willing to be used for God's glory.

When the servants came before Jesus with willing hearts to be challenged for the sake of His glory, it placed them in the middle of God's miraculous work. A willing heart opens doors of opportunity to witness Christ doing something we would otherwise miss.

Often, however, we see ourselves as king and God as our servant, and our prayers form a convicting argument to this. When we pray, most of what we take to the door of heaven are errands for God to improve our kingdom, not further His. Desiring more comfort in our corner of the earth, we try to send Him our fix-it list. Instead, we are to pray to the true King about what is needed in His kingdom. Servants are willing to do whatever Jesus asks of them because they understand their role in His kingdom. And if that means walking toward the master of the banquet with a glass of water when wine is needed, they do it.

Pride often keeps us from obeying with complete confidence. No one wants to look ridiculous handing someone water when he's looking for wine. So we don't share our faith; we don't give to a certain cause; we don't take the next step. But the servant goes when the Lord calls. He or she answers yes and then asks for the question. He or she obeys completely, walking in faith because Jesus' commands can be trusted. Are we willing to obey God, but only up to a certain point? True obedience means that we step forward in faith, trusting God's provision for each and every step.

Obedience is simply faith at work, and it gains us victory over complacency. If faith believes that the impossible is possible, then obedience is our faith taking steps forward. The servant works in complete obedience for one simple reason—the issue of who is King has been settled in his or her life. If we have not submitted to the King of heaven, servant-heartedness will be a continual mirage.

The walk of faith can be simultaneously exciting and terrifying. The servants at the wedding must have been aware of both competing emotions, but in the end, faith prevailed. They trusted that the water would be wine by the time it reached the lips of the master of ceremonies.

There will be times in life when you feel that what you are carrying is terribly inadequate. That's when faith becomes real as you trust God to take what you have and make it something better. He is able to do abundantly more than all we could ask or imagine (see Eph. 3:20).

When we come to God with a servant's heart, full of obedience and faith, miracles happen. These qualities seem to be present and ever growing in the people God uses.

Abundant Excellence

Then [the master of ceremonies] called the bridegroom aside and said, "Everyone brings out the choice wine first and then the cheaper wine after the guests have had too much to drink; but you have saved the best till now" (John 2:9-10).

So often we are satisfied with the goodness of God, but we rarely consider His greatness. Though we anticipate provision, we often do not expect abundance. Our expectations are far too low. Big prayers that require a deep measure of our faith bring honor to the Lord. Not only does He answer our prayers and provide for us, but He also does so with overwhelming generosity. Jesus is able to do all that we ask for, and more. His love toward us is extravagant. He delights in God-sized prayers and tasks that would be impossible without Him.

Out of His abundance, Jesus provided more than enough wine for the wedding party. Filling the purification jars with water was hard work! The servants filled each jar with 25 gallons of water—bucket by bucket and step by step. (Christianity is a long faith walk in Christ's direction.) Out of those water jars came 2,500 glasses of water turned into wine—more than enough to satisfy the needs of the banquet.

Not only does Jesus provide abundantly, but He also provides what is excellent. The water Jesus turned into wine was not just cheap house wine to cover the basic needs. He provided the most excellent and choice wine, which the Master of Ceremonies confirmed. Seeing and understanding the extravagance and graciousness of God should lead us to approach His throne with more confidence, joy and assurance.

God loves us, and He provides for us in abundance and excellence. Remember, the jars were used for ceremonial washing, allowing the guests to be pure for the wedding. Through His death on the cross, Jesus provided full forgiveness for our sins—for our cleansing. We are offered forgiveness in Christ; and not just for our sins of the past, but for our sins today and for the inevitable sins of tomorrow. Christ's blood covers them all. In receiving Christ as our Savior, our slate is wiped clean for today and tomorrow. His sacrifice on the cross was more than enough. As a result of the cross, the Father sees us through the excellence of Christ and not through our sins. That gospel is true yesterday, today and forever. The jars that held the purification water symbolize the abundant and excellent transformation we receive in Christ (see Col. 2:13-14). How abundant is His grace toward us!

Jesus' miraculous work at the wedding in Cana reminds us that change and purification can happen in our own lives. Often we are tempted to think that all we have to offer is water. But as we walk in faith, looking toward the Lord, we see our ordinary water turn into wine. The use of purification jars is not an insignificant detail. As the water was changed from within, so our purification comes from within, through Jesus' blood on the cross. Change is possible. Did you think that you were stuck in your sin, condemned to be the same person forever? God loves you too much to let you stay that way.

One reason the Holy Spirit was given to us was to make these changes. He lives in the heart of those who believe in Christ, and He is the power that allows us to make changes for our good and for God's glory. The Gospel of John is a tremendously Trinitarian book, teaching us of the Father, the Son and the Holy Spirit (take a look specifically at John 14 and 17) and that they are working together in the world. The Trinity is one God in three persons, operating in complete unity and shaping us according to His desires, for His glory. Whatever illustration we could construct to describe His character and His work, the triune God is grander and more mysterious.

The change in our lives—our water to wine—is not based on our strength or efforts; it is available as we yield to the Holy Spirit's power. He is God at work in our challenges and within us. Because of God's grace, you can cling to the promise that He is not finished with you yet. Spiritual change is happening every day for all those who look to Christ and desire to be a new person in Him. You are not stuck in the same old shoes. As you walk in servant-hearted faith, your change will begin and you will start to look more and more like Christ.

You can forget the mess-ups of yesterday and even the crass thoughts of today. Being cleansed from your sin is possible. The excellence of Christ's blood washes you white as snow. But you must walk in faith that God is able to do what He said He would do. Miracles do happen. God is in the business of taking the ordinary and making it extraordinary.

In your journey to discover who He is and what He does, let this first miracle set the stage for what God is desiring to do to use you in situations that might not even exist yet. As you realize that all you have is "water," you will grow in faith, trusting Him to transform your water into the best wine. Then your cry will be the same as the lady's at airport security, "Praise the Lord, He did it again."

This, the first of his miraculous signs, Jesus performed at Cana in Galilee.
He thus revealed his glory, and his disciples put their faith in him.

JOHN 2:11

FOR FURTHER REFLECTION AND DISCUSSION

The "I AM" Playlist Pick

Song	Artist	Album
"Our God"	Chris Tomlin	*And If Our God Is for Us*

1. Why is it interesting that Jesus chose to use servants over the wedding party and VIPs for His first miracle?

2. Discuss the obedience of the servants to fill the jars to the brim. Where are you not "filling it to the brim" in your life?

3. The water turned into wine as they walked in faith. When have you seen God make a change or perform a miracle as you walked out your faith? What situation are you in now where you are walking, but the water hasn't turned to wine yet?

4. Jesus provided excellent and abundant wine. Relate that to how He moves today and how your faith should respond. How is that symbolic of the gospel of Christ?

Behind the Blinking Light

On the bed of sickness the Lord ripens his people for glory.
DAVID DICKSON

Seven Miracles of Jesus

1. Turning water into wine (JOHN 2:1-12)
2. Healing the nobleman's son (JOHN 4:46-54)
3. Healing of the lame man (JOHN 5:1-17)
4. Feeding the 5,000 (JOHN 6:1-13)
5. Walking on water (JOHN 6:16-21)
6. Healing the man born blind (JOHN 9:1-41)
7. Raising Lazarus from dead (JOHN 11:1-45)

Seven I AM Statements of Jesus

1. I AM the Bread of Life (JOHN 6:35,48,51)
2. I AM the Light of the World (JOHN 8:12)
3. I AM the Door/Gate (JOHN 10:7)
4. I AM the Good Shepherd (JOHN 10:11-14)
5. I AM the Resurrection and the Life (JOHN 11:25)
6. I AM the Way, the Truth, and the Life (JOHN 14:6)
7. I AM the True Vine (JOHN 15:1)

I entered my house and saw the blinking light on the telephone. I took a deep breath. I knew the message would bring us either relief or concern. Pressing play, I stood back and began to listen. As I heard sobs of sadness and despair, my heart sank. It was Layne and his wife, Erin, dear family members, calling with the test results of why he had suffered a seizure.[1] Kelly and I were expecting the call, but we were hoping to hear the answer to our prayers. Instead, Layne informed us that he had an inoperable brain tumor.

There are moments in life when you are pulled to your knees and all you have to hold on to is faith. Layne's news was a gut punch to our family. We marshaled the strength to face the battle in the only way we knew how—through prayer.

Weeks later, our living room was filled with friends and family surrounding Layne and Erin as we prayed together. We ached for Layne's healing and longed for a miracle. When the odds are stacked against us, a miracle is the only possible solution.

"Inoperable" and "cancerous"—those two words called our faith into question again and again. But there was always hope for a miracle. We prayed together for hours and with such passion that you would expect to see the wallpaper roll off the wall. Praying when there's no other option is incredibly humbling, but desperate prayers remind us of the sufficiency of God.

The unexpected happened. The doctors operated on the inoperable, removing part of the brain tumor and later zapping the rest with radiation. We rejoiced at the news and celebrated for the next five years as biannual check-ups showed no tumor re-growth. However, the cancer did eventually return, and we began to pray with renewed fervor and fear. I believed at that time that if healing could happen once, it could happen again. We prayed for complete healing, but God answered differently than our requests.

When I preached at Layne's funeral, his two little boys sat on the third row. One was wondering where his daddy was; and the other, too young to understand, was fast asleep in the pew. I wanted desperately to answer the congregation's questions. But I also had to address some of my own. I wondered, *Why, Lord? We are godly people who prayed with all that we had.* I thought about how much glory it would have brought the Lord to heal this strong, gregarious, 42-year-old man. Layne was a godly man, who literally never missed a daily quiet time for more than 17 years! Toward the end, he had the Bible read to him on his deathbed. What if the prayer requests for

Layne plastered all over the Internet and emails had been answered with a resounding YES! When I considered how a miraculous healing would have glorified the Lord, His response in taking Layne home seemed confusing. People were watching—believers and unbelievers alike—to see how God would respond to this situation. We needed Jesus to show up in all of His healing power.

When we pray for healing, we do so because we hope and believe that it can happen. When I prayed for Layne, I was certain that God could heal him. Without certainty, my prayers would have been empty and without purpose. If God can heal, surely healing Layne would make the most sense. He was a dad with two young boys—two boys who now have a lifetime ahead of them without their father. As I offered encouragement at the funeral service, I found myself repeating the phrase echoing through my own mind: "We don't understand, Lord. But we trust You."

When you are unsure about the answer given from God's hand, you have to trust His heart. God often brings adversity into our lives—adversity that exposes our helplessness. So we must come to Him as our only Hope, trusting in Him alone. Layne did exactly that. Listen to his trust, in his own words.

From Layne's journal, August 27 (just short of 16 months before he went to heaven on January 19):

Dear Heavenly Father—

Today You, Lord, were in control. Though we had a disappointing time with Dr. Gilbert, You were in control. We found out bad news in that there is a cancerous tumor growing in my head again.

I pray for Your miraculous hand to heal me and free me from this disease. Please, Lord—may Your will be to heal me. May I praise You still for whatever You decide to do. You are to be praised! You are worthy of all the glory.

Lord, I pray for Your intercession. I pray for Erin. What an incredible wife You have blessed me with. I pray for Paxson and Preston. I know they won't comprehend or understand what is happening, but may they someday love You with all their heart, soul, mind and strength. May they know how much I loved them. Please comfort Erin and me through this challenge ahead of us.

Talked to my brothers and Robyn, my in-laws, my mom, Gregg, and Sky. May they pray for me and Erin.

Love – Layne

Sometimes when we pray for healing, we don't see it this side of heaven. But even though there is no physical healing on earth, we can be sure there is ultimate healing in Christ. Jesus heals. But on occasion, it doesn't happen until we see Him face to face. So how do we pray? Does Jesus really heal today, or is that just cable TV charlatan talk to raise money?

In this chapter and the next, we will explore what Jesus says and does in regard to physical healing as we look at two powerful examples from the Gospel of John. Through Jesus' miraculous touch, we will see a God who is worthy of our complete trust. When our faith is in Jesus, we find confidence to face the challenge of understanding healing on earth and ultimate healing in heaven. If you have never prayed for healing, just wait. One day, you will. The reality of our fallen world is that you will need this teaching at some intersection of life's journey.

Desperate for Healing

The majority of miracles we seek today revolve around healing. Just look at your church's prayer list. There is no other type of miracle that makes us feel more desperate. If you have been battling illness or are close to someone who needs healing, you know this. We are touched by the miracle of healing because it pulls at the heartstrings in a way that nothing else can touch. When we are at the end of our rope, with nowhere else to turn, we pray for a miracle.

The Gospel of John highlights seven miracles that captivate our attention and encourage our faith. We need to understand the power of Christ in this. Miracles sand us into His image when we understand the Power behind the wonder. Perhaps more than any other kind of miracle, the healing we see in John 4 and 5 invites us to needed understanding.

A Father's Heart

In John 4, we meet an official who is frantically looking for healing. His son is sick and close to death. If you are, or have ever been, a parent with a sick child, you can probably identify with the official's desperation. When your baby is sick, your world gets rocked. If there is a glimmer of hope that someone can help, you will do whatever it takes to attract his or her attention and mercy. Desperation calls for desperate measures.

Jesus was passing through Galilee on His way back to Cana. Hearing rumors that the miracle worker was in town, the official with the sick child made a distressed attempt to get Jesus' attention. His son's life depended on a miracle. The official took a gamble that maybe this miracle worker could actually do what was otherwise impossible—heal his dying son.

My wife, Kelly, and I have two wonderful children, Greyson and Valerie. One evening, we were finishing a family dinner around Christmas. After adding a farm animal to the Advent calendar and indulging in too many cake balls, I was playing with my kids on the floor. We were wrestling and having a great time together until Valerie let out a shriek; she had bitten her tongue. The amount of blood from one little bite was far beyond a Band-Aid. My head plus her chin equaled a trip to the emergency room.

We all jumped into the car. As the third bloody kitchen towel was held to her tongue, my son asked from the back seat, "Dad, are you speeding?" Slightly panicked, I replied, "Yes, be quiet!" Any parent can understand the stress and mind racing that filled those hours, even though this would only turn out to be a *minor* emergency. But as a parent, I was ready to smash through roadblocks and drive on the sidewalk. An officer who had thoughts of a speeding ticket would actually fit into my plan of a police escort. Thankfully, after a few rolls of gauze and a couple hundred dollars on our insurance, all was well again.

The official in the biblical account was facing something much greater than a tongue bite, and nothing mattered more to him than the health of his son. He was willing to compromise his royal position and reputation by interfacing with a man whom many had questioned. From all that the official had heard, Jesus was a man who claimed a lofty position as the Son of Man. He made bold statements that any normal man would find absurd. But Jesus also had a track record of being a miracle worker. And the official needed a miracle. For those who have been there or find themselves there today, a sick child can bring you to a crossroads where you either believe in God or turn in the other direction. A family in Dallas understands this particular crossroads.

Lucy is a little girl who was born into a large, godly family in Dallas. For reasons that are not fully understood, Lucy has been a cardiac patient her entire life. Lucy's young life has been set on display for many to see. By God's grace, her parents stand as a living testimony to God's great work through their long, difficult journey with their daughter. I was particularly struck with their perspective on healing. As a parent myself, I find it difficult and brave to respond to illness and the hope of healing with such grace-filled boldness.

Lucy's dad responded to the question of healing in a way that beautifully paints the picture of a father's heart that desperately desires his child's healing but wants God's glory even more:

We trust that God's purposes for each of our lives are far deeper than the removal of our "problems." And so, the question is not, "Can God heal Lucy?" Of course He can. Nor is the question, "Why doesn't God heal Lucy?" That has not been given to us to know—either in this situation or in any other. God is always good, and we are in His hands.[2]

The heart of a parent is fierce. But the heart of a believer, rooted in the gospel of Jesus Christ, can weather any storm—even the storm of illness.

Prayer is difficult when we know that God can heal but He sometimes doesn't this side of heaven. If God can heal, why doesn't He do so every time, especially when we are faithful to pray? If the Jesus we read about in the Gospel of John healed an official's son in an instant, why does He seem to remain silent when we ask for the same thing? Lucy's dad offers rare wisdom. He doesn't claim to understand God's reasoning, but he does claim to know and trust his heavenly Father. So how do we pray for healing? We pray, with Lucy's dad, "Lord, we don't know. But we trust You."

David Dickson, a Scottish pastor of the 1800s, stated, "On the bed of sickness the Lord ripens his people for glory."[3] Both the sick and the healthy grow in the shadow of illness. The uncertainty of our lives could leave us paralyzed with fear of illness. This fear would leave us desperate for hope. But, friends, our hope has come! Our greatest problem has been solved. Our worst and ultimate enemy, death, has been defeated. Jesus Christ lives! That hope can buoy us on the raging seas of a sickness. When we are confronted with a human body that is breaking down, the cross gives us hope. Jesus' death brought life, and His brokenness makes us whole. On the cross, He defeated illness and sin. That doesn't mean Christians never get sick or never sin. It means that we have a Savior to fall on when we do get sick or when we do sin. We need to know this because God doesn't always heal in accordance with our wishes. In those times of waiting or grieving, we must cast our questions at His feet, just as we did our requests.

The royal official said, "Sir, come down before my child dies."
Jesus replied, "You may go. Your son will live."

The man took Jesus at his word and departed. While he was still on the way, his servants met him with the news that his boy was living. When he inquired as to the time when his son got better, they said to him, "The fever left him yesterday at the seventh hour."

Then the father realized that this was the exact time at which Jesus had said to him, "Your son will live." So he and all his household believed (John 4:49-53).

Healing Happens in His Timing

The miracle of healing leaves us with questions. Is it about magic or sleight of hand? Fear of our hopes being dashed when the smoke clears gives us pause in trusting the power of God. The work of a miracle and the work of magic, however, are vastly different. When you are watching a magician, there is exterior surprise—something you see and exclaim about. There is a "Wow!" or "How did he do that?" reaction. Magic is about a temporary exterior gasp.

A miracle aims at an interior wow. The goal of a miracle is to point to the work of God and encourage trust in Him. Even more so, miracles declare that God is sovereign over all aspects of our lives and creation. He is not only waiting until the end of days to make things right or show His power. Miracles are His illustrative interjection to say, "I am the one who is and is to come" (see Heb. 13:8; Rev. 1:4). He is present tense as well as past and future tense. The redemption and power are "now" and "not yet." Miracles are glimpses of future heaven and earth in the present. For example, our healing now is to remind us of eternal healing to come. The tension of living in the "now" and the "not yet" is a challenge and a hope at the same time. We know that our loved one will be healed in heaven, but we are also praying for the hospital discharge on earth.

Unlike any power of magic, a miracle shows that God's timing is perfect. In the case of the official's son, the goal was to declare Jesus as God's son. The miraculous work of healing came from an instantaneous declaration by Jesus, and His timing was precise. In the moment Jesus spoke the word, the official's son was healed. Miracles are always about God's timing, power and purpose. More than coincidence, miracles are streaked and stained with God's touch. At times, they cannot be explained, but they can be embraced. The official experienced God's timing and power in the healing of his son in order for God to declare His purpose.

When we struggle with a need for healing, God's timing is both comforting and concerning. We operate on a "need it now" basis, while He seems to be in no hurry. It is beautiful and yet challenging to be wonderfully dependent as we pray, receive treatment and wait. But we can wait with confidence, knowing that His timing is accurate. Even our waiting has an unseen purpose. It allows for tilling the unplowed ground of the heart in search of rich soil (see Hos. 10:12-13). The father in John 4 experienced that the timing of healing perfectly matched the words of Christ.

The Power of a Word

I can imagine that the people around Jesus were looking for signs and wonders. We do the same thing. We want to see a sign that something is about to happen. But in the Gospel of John, Jesus does something different. In an unexpected way, Jesus shows us His mastery over time. He speaks, and in that instant the boy is healed. Not a moment after. As the official runs home, his servants greet him. They inform him that his son is well. It happens just as Jesus said it would. God can speak the word and it's done.

The official took Jesus at His word, believing that what He said would come true. He had nothing to go on other than Jesus' word. That is all the hope he needed. The official took Him at His word not because of signs. He could have been sold a bill of goods for the return home, but he trusted. In his desperation, a word of hope from Jesus was more than enough. The Lord's healing comes in His perfect timing and involves our full trust in Him.

The official didn't see sparks fly or the wind change direction; he simply heard Jesus' voice and believed His words to be true. In our culture today, we love the flash and pop of magic and signs. As a result, we tend to neglect the Word of God. But the more we look for signs, the less we will trust in God's Word. Jesus could have called the official's boy to His presence and done an impressive tribal dance with signs and wonders, making unbelievers believe. And yet, He chose not to. Instead, Jesus spoke the healing into existence from a distance of 20 miles.[4] He wanted the people to believe in Him—the Word made flesh—not just in signs or miracles (see John 1:14). When the official believed in Jesus' words apart from any other sign, he experienced mercy from the very hand of God. The Person and the power is the right combination for our belief.

One of the primary points of my previous book, *Finding God's Will*, is that those who know His Word the best hear His voice the most. God's Word is a powerful sword. The more you truly know the Bible, the more you will know the God of the Bible. Knowing God's Word has the ability to change your life. As you understand what God's Word says, you can make sense of what He does and, therefore, know Him more intimately. The official heard healing from the lips of Jesus Christ in the flesh. Hearing those words changed his life and saved his son's. We hear God's voice in His Word, the Bible, and it has the power to save us. Do you know God's Word in a life-changing way? Rooting His Word deeply in your heart will equip you to face life's challenges and celebrate its joys.

God may want to speak something to you that seems disconnected from your situation but is still significant for your life. When we are in need, we are tender, and God's voice speaks loudly because we are receptive. Tender places are ripe for the voice of the Lord to be heard. Hospital waiting rooms are reminders of the importance of family and friends. Often, those rooms are the places that speak of the worth of life and the pettiness of how most of our minutes are logged. In those moments of waiting, we are reminded of the brevity of life and the eternity of God's love.

Though sickness often acts as a tool opening our hearts to a deeper place, listen for His voice apart from just the issue of healing. The famed evangelist Charles Spurgeon said:

> I venture to say that the greatest earthly blessing God can give to any of us is health, with the exception of sickness. Sickness has frequently been of more use to the saints of God than health has.[5]

It's true that our attention to the vocabulary of God is more acute during trials. Listen closely for His voice in all areas of life. He may want to speak to you in the hospital about your home, or when you are in pain about your perspective. It is human to focus only on the ailment, assaulting it with attention and care. But it is heavenly to allow the ailment to reveal deeper issues of our soul and priorities. What a waste to endure sickness and pain and not arrive at the other side refined in our hearts. Don't waste the trial. Don't waste the sickness. Embrace it for the eternal good He wants to do in you and others.

Ache, pray, listen and grow.

For Layne Cole (1967–2010)

Friend, it was an honor to know you. I'm different because of your influence. Enjoy your ultimate healing and Healer.

FOR FURTHER REFLECTION AND DISCUSSION

The "I AM" Playlist Pick

Song	Artist	Album
"Life Light Up"	Christy Nockles	*Life Light Up*

1. How did the stories of Layne and Lucy impact you? What encouraged you about their faith?

2. Do you struggle to believe that God still heals today? Why or why not?

3. Have you ever experienced God's healing for a member of your family or for a friend? Tell the story.

4. How does healing show that Jesus is the Messiah?

5. In regard to healing, how can the difference between God's timing and ours grow our faith?

When 2 Plus 2 Doesn't Equal 4

*Some time later, Jesus went up to Jerusalem for a feast of the Jews.
Now there is in Jerusalem near the Sheep Gate a pool, which in Aramaic is called
Bethesda and which is surrounded by five covered colonnades. Here a great
number of disabled people used to lie—the blind, the lame, the paralyzed. One who
was there had been an invalid for thirty-eight years. When Jesus saw him lying
there and learned that he had been in this condition for a long time, he asked him,
"Do you want to get well?" "Sir," the invalid replied, "I have no one to help me
into the pool when the water is stirred. While I am trying to get in, someone else
goes down ahead of me." Then Jesus said to him, "Get up! Pick up your mat and
walk." At once the man was cured; he picked up his mat and walked.*[1]

JOHN 5:1-9

Seven Miracles of Jesus

1. Turning water into wine (JOHN 2:1-12)
2. Healing the nobleman's son (JOHN 4:46-54)
3. Healing of the lame man (JOHN 5:1-17)
4. Feeding the 5,000 (JOHN 6:1-13)
5. Walking on water (JOHN 6:16-21)
6. Healing the man born blind (JOHN 9:1-41)
7. Raising Lazarus from dead (JOHN 11:1-45)

Seven I AM Statements of Jesus

1. I AM the Bread of Life (JOHN 6:35,48,51)
2. I AM the Light of the World (JOHN 8:12)
3. I AM the Door/Gate (JOHN 10:7)
4. I AM the Good Shepherd (JOHN 10:11-14)
5. I AM the Resurrection and the Life (JOHN 11:25)
6. I AM the Way, the Truth, and the Life (JOHN 14:6)
7. I AM the True Vine (JOHN 15:1)

After Jesus healed the official's son, John the apostle recorded another circumstance when Jesus caused a scene by healing an impoverished man. The result of healing was the same, but the routes were vastly different. There is no formula for healing. Each path is different, but for the same purpose—to show that Jesus is the Messiah.[2] Two healings; one Messiah. Miracles always reflect God's placement, purpose, timing and power.

When Jesus, who is on the way to Jerusalem for the feast of the Jews, stops at a pool of water where the lame, blind and paralyzed seek refuge and healing, He encounters a man who has been an invalid for 38 years. In front of a captivated crowd, Jesus gives the command, and the invalid is healed. When you cross paths with Jesus, you can't help but walk away changed. I AM changes who i am. This interaction with Jesus demonstrated God's incredible power. Again, His word proclaimed healing: "Pick up your mat and walk" (John 5:11).

2 Plus 2 Doesn't Always Equal 4

Our culture likes things that are predictable, manageable and easy to manipulate. So when it comes to worshiping God, we often want Him to fit within the provided parameters. But God is not easily contained. He explodes the boundaries. As we consider the two healings in the Gospel of John, we notice there is no pattern or formula for how God heals. We can't corner God or obligate Him to heal. Neither can we find the recipe to go around Him. He is sovereign and multifaceted, leaving us with the ingredients of prayer, faith and trust. When we lay each of these at His feet, whether in sickness, health or death, we are declaring the glory of God (see Rom. 14:8).

In John 4, we read that the official went in search of Jesus. He knew enough about Jesus to know that He was capable of bringing new life to his sick son. Often we find ourselves in a position where we know our need for Jesus. In those moments, we chase after our need. The official was desperate to find an answer to his problem, and he knew that answer could be found in a man named Jesus. It didn't matter that the official's son was 20 miles away; Jesus was not limited by distance. He healed the child with a word.

Jesus could easily have healed the lame man we read about in John 5 in the same way. It if worked once, it could work again. However, God does not follow a method and is not constrained by a formula. Jesus found the sick man sitting near the pool. The man was not looking for Jesus. And yet,

God's mercy is seen as Jesus sought him out. God is in the habit of looking for those who desperately need Him, even if they don't admit it. The official knew who Jesus was. However, the man by the pool had no idea that he was face to face with the Son of God. That is a picture of mercy. Before we even know our need for Jesus, He takes a step toward us, with an offer of healing. The Holy Spirit chases after hearts prone to wander.

Jesus commanded the healing of the lame man in front of a crowd of people. Right there, sitting in front of his Healer, the man stands and walks for the first time in 38 years. Jesus didn't heal from a long distance as He did the official's son. He looked at the lame man and said, "Get up!"

The miraculous healings recorded in the Gospel of John remind us that God is bigger than a formula and more concerned about those He is healing. When we look for God in expected ways, we are prone to miss the miraculous.

Let's look at the differences:

John 4:43-54: The Official's Son	John 5:1-14: The Invalid Man
The official was a wealthy man of status	The invalid was forgotten by society
The son was healed at a distance (20 miles)	The man was healed face to face
The official asked Jesus to heal his son	Jesus asked the man if healing was desired
The official knew Jesus' power	The invalid was unaware of who Jesus was
The young son was healed	The invalid, an adult past the life expectancy of that time, was healed

God's formula for healing can't be figured out. Rest and find comfort in seeking the common denominator—Christ. For some, healing is found in the pharmacy, surgery, counseling or a better diet. But these are just tools in the Wonderful Counselor's hands. He is the Healer of all of our needs—emotionally, physically and spiritually. We honor medicine and technology, but we glorify God. Don't get those confused.

When Healing Happens

The healings of the official's son and the lame man bring us great encouragement as believers. Seeing God heal people in the gospel accounts gives us great hope that He can bring healing in our lives too. The reality is that sometimes when we pray for healing, it doesn't happen. And yet, sometimes it does. Witnessing the healing hand of God is humbling because we know it is clearly not something we earn or deserve.

Our God heals to show us His power. He is not a God of odds, and He is not limited by a bad prognosis or by statistics. He defies the odds and has mastery over medicine. Healing brings God glory. As believers, we pray with expectation, hoping that God will do what we know He can do. Whether or not healing occurs, our response should be thanksgiving before God.

He also receives glory from the one who is suffering. The volume of our witness is turned up in sickness. A sick man giving glory to God is vastly different from a healthy man proclaiming Jesus. Both are honoring to the Lord; but when someone with a life-threatening disease talks about the goodness of God, heads start turning.

J. C. Ryles was an Anglican bishop in the nineteenth century. He wrote a paper entitled "Sickness." As you read an excerpt from the paper, don't just read the words. Instead, drink them with the thought in mind that God can use our sickness for the good of our souls and the souls of others. Speaking about sickness, Ryles remarked:

> It is a blessing quite as much as a curse. It is a rough schoolmaster, I grant. But a real friend to a man's soul. . . . It exposes the emptiness and hollowness of what the world calls "good" things, and teaches us to hold them with a loose hand. The man of business finds that money alone is not everything the heart requires. The woman of the world finds that costly apparel, and novel reading, and the reports of balls and operas, are miserable comforters in a sick room. . . . Sickness is a purifier to the heart. Surely I have the right to tell you that sickness is a blessing and not a curse, a help and not an injury, a gain and not a loss, a friend and not a foe of mankind.[3]

Amazing words of how God uses sickness to cultivate and focus our souls! We often busy ourselves trying to squirm out of sickness, when He desires to teach us within it. Of course, it is not wrong to seek health. But realize that sickness is a purifier of our faith, and when carried faithfully, we can shine with Christ. Our perspective moves from earthly to heavenly. Ryles goes on to say:

I earnestly entreat all sick believers to remember that they may honor God as much by patient suffering as they can by active work. It often shows more grace to sit still than it does to go to and fro, and perform great exploits.[4]

As the prophet Habakkuk wrote, "Though the fig tree does not bud and there are no grapes on the vines, though the olive crop fails and the fields produce no food, though there are no sheep in the pen and no cattle in the stalls, yet I will rejoice in the LORD, I will be joyful in God my Savior. The Sovereign LORD is my strength; he makes my feet like the feet of a deer, he enables me to go on the heights" (3:17-19).

When God Seems Quiet

Though my story is different from yours, we have all experienced a moment when healing doesn't happen as we desire. In those moments, the temptation is to feel like God is absent. If God can heal, why doesn't He? I prayed earnestly for Layne to be healed. It made complete sense to me that God would be glorified most by healing Layne from cancer. And yet, my prayers were not answered as I had hoped. God did not heal Layne on earth, but in heaven. In the midst of a situation where healing doesn't happen, we are plagued with the "why" question. Those are the hardest questions to answer. So we must remind ourselves of what we know to be true.

God ordains a different path for each of us. Our culture's perception is that a full life is one that is lived through the sunset years. So we cry "Foul!" when someone passes away at a young age, assuming they have gone too soon. In God's Word, David says, "All the days ordained for me were written in your book before one of them came to be" (Ps. 139:16). Our lives are not one day too long or too short. We live the exact number of days that God ordained. As historian Daniel J. Boorstin once noted, "To those who have the misfortune to die young, history assigns the role of inspirer."[5] Some lives include health and others include illness. Either way, God is sovereign and in control of each day and each life. No matter the path, God can use every life for His glory.

It also helps to remember why God sent His Son. Jesus came foremost for our spiritual healing. True, at times He does bring physical healing, and we praise God. But the Incarnation happened because we were incapable of handling our biggest problem—sin. God is most concerned about our souls, not our bodies. He came near to us because our problem was deeper than a physical illness. It was a sickness of the soul that could only be cured by a Savior. Our heavenly Father cares deeply for those who suffer. But as we face illness, our enemies sin and death are defeated in Christ, and we have spiritual healing. Heaven is the next step for the believer in Christ.

Often, an illness can seem like it is more than we can handle—because it is. On this earth, we will receive more than we can handle (see 2 Cor. 1:8-9). But we will never receive more than we can handle with God's help. When you are facing what seems to be an all-consuming trial, you don't have to handle it alone. God never intended it to be that way. Christ came to save us from ourselves. You are not alone. And you don't have to pretend to be.

When you realize that you are not alone, though you may feel lonely, it is the beginning of intimacy with Christ. Your relationship with Him is not to be at a distance. He is not a high school friend you email occasionally—He is the safest confidant. In the dark of night, when the house is quiet and you are worried about tomorrow, you have the gift of prayer. When you are unsure of the right direction or you're feeling restless, connect with Christ through the Bible. Sharing and receiving from Him at a soul level is the fertilizer for your intimacy with Jesus.

Remember, the Holy Spirit is seeking you too. The Spirit's quest is one of giving, while ours is one of knowing. He already knows all, including us. Even as we are desirous of the gauge to move from empty to full, He is actively loving and filling you as He reveals Himself to you.

Spiritual growth is more than hearing a sermon or attending a conference. Christian programming, entertainment and music are not the essence of intimacy but are intended to offer a vehicle of deeper connection with God. These are tools that leave us at the foot of the heavenly throne with the desire to know more. This is what sickness can do as well. The fluorescent light of the hospital corridor can drive us to heavenly warmth if we direct our soul to Christ. God is seeking the real you—the deep parts that you might not even understand. Scary? No, comforting. Mysterious? Yes, more than we know. The One who loves you wants to heal you physically and spiritually. So yield to Him and surrender and rest in His Spirit's powerful work in you.

Help Me! Heal Me!

One way or another, we all need healing. Maybe it is physical healing or perhaps it is something else. What healing are you looking for? Jesus can heal your relationships, your guilt, your finances and everything else.

One of the biggest areas needing God's healing touch is the area of our relationships. They are constant reminders that we need God's healing hand. The only two things that last for eternity are God's Word and the souls of men, so relationships with people matter! Friends and family have the unique positioning in our lives to build us up or leave deep wounds. If you are looking for healing in your relationships with your friends, family or even in your community of faith, Christ can help. He brings healing between people.

Perhaps you are looking for moral healing. Your life is not playing out in a way that brings God glory, and you long to live differently. The beauty of the gospel is that you have a clean slate today. Your past is wiped clean and the sins of tomorrow are forgiven. If you are looking for a different path, it is not too late. As you move toward God and seek His best for your life, the power of the gospel will change your heart as well. Jesus brings healing.

Don't think you're alone if you need financial healing. The state of our world ebbs and flows based on the economy. Maybe you have more money than you could ever need, and that causes problems. Or maybe you don't have enough to make ends meet. Either way, God can replace your focus on finances with a greater love for Him. Healing can happen when you give God first place in your finances.

The miracle of healing is not just something we read about in the Bible. Because Jesus brought healing to the official's son and to the man by the Pool of Bethesda, we know that Jesus can heal us too.

So, how do you pray when healing is needed? I have found this simple healing prayer incredibly helpful: "Jesus, I know that You *can* heal. I pray that You *would* heal." Remember, it brings God glory when we ask for things that only He can do. When you pray for healing, ask with confidence, knowing that He is able.

While on a trip through Israel, our group stopped at the Pool of Bethesda. The tour leader encouraged our team to take a few minutes to be quiet and pray for someone who needed healing. I asked the Lord to lay someone on my heart. My friend and fellow church member J. J. LaCarter came to mind. J. J. had been diagnosed with ALS, otherwise known as Lou Gehrig's disease. As I walked around the pool of healing referenced in

John 5, I prayed for J. J.'s complete healing. That was in February. By September, J. J. sat in disbelief as his Jewish doctor shared the news, "You have been healed." Seven months after my prayer for J. J.'s healing, he had a clean bill of health. The doctor shared in our astonishment. Since 1982, he had only seen three cases of ALS completely healed. While he didn't acknowledge Jesus, he had to acknowledge that a miracle had taken place. God heard our prayers for J. J. and responded graciously with a miracle.

The Lord is able to heal. We must trust God to be more than enough for us, whether He brings healing on earth or in eternity. Either way, healing will happen. As we cling to the promise that Christ will heal in this world or the next, let's join with J. C. Ryles in this prayer:

> Let us cleave to Christ more closely, love Him more heartily, live to Him more thoroughly, copy Him more exactly, confess Him more boldly, and follow Him more fully.[6]

FOR FURTHER REFLECTION AND DISCUSSION

The "I AM" Playlist Pick

Song	Artist	Album
"Healing Is in Your Hands"	Christy Nockels	Passion: Awakening

1. Why do you think Jesus healed the lame man in such a different way from the way He healed the official's son?

2. There were several quotes in this chapter from the Puritan pastor J. C. Ryles. Which impacted you the most? Why? How did it reshape your thinking?

3. How do the physical healing miracles give us confidence of Christ's ability to spiritually heal us?

4. Who would you like to pray for that Jesus would heal? Share with the group and write the person a note in the next 24 hours.

Don't Just Bubble and Squeak By

If you want your faith to grow, don't shrink back from opportunities for your faith to be tried.
GEORGE MUELLER

Seven Miracles of Jesus

1. Turning water into wine (JOHN 2:1-12)
2. Healing the nobleman's son (JOHN 4:46-54)
3. Healing of the lame man (JOHN 5:1-17)
4. **Feeding the 5,000** (JOHN 6:1-13)
5. Walking on water (JOHN 6:16-21)
6. Healing the man born blind (JOHN 9:1-41)
7. Raising Lazarus from dead (JOHN 11:1-45)

Seven I AM Statements of Jesus

1. I AM the Bread of Life (JOHN 6:35,48,51)
2. I AM the Light of the World (JOHN 8:12)
3. I AM the Door/Gate (JOHN 10:7)
4. I AM the Good Shepherd (JOHN 10:11-14)
5. I AM the Resurrection and the Life (JOHN 11:25)
6. I AM the Way, the Truth, and the Life (JOHN 14:6)
7. I AM the True Vine (JOHN 15:1)

Leftovers. Our refrigerator was so full that we could hardly squeeze another roll in between the casserole dishes. For safety precautions, it seemed a good idea to strap on a helmet before opening the door for a mid-afternoon snack. No telling what kinds of Tupperware and aluminum-foiled treasures would come spilling out.

Most refrigerators work overtime the day after Christmas. A family of 10 sits down for Christmas dinner to a spread of food capable of feeding 50. So, naturally, there are leftovers. At the end of the meal, the table is still overflowing with grandmother's famous stuffing and mom's green bean casserole that everyone claims to love. There is more than enough for another meal . . . or even for meals into the next week. The refrigerator is bursting at the seams. You would think we would learn our lesson to not cook so much the next holiday. But another celebration rolls around, and we pull out the trays and fill them back up again.

The Europeans developed a way of enjoying their leftovers one last time. The day after Christmas is a celebration known as Boxing Day. Part of Boxing Day is a meal that cleverly incorporates the leftovers from Christmas dining. Taking the surplus food, Europeans fill a pot with veggies and potatoes, fry it all in oil and then enjoy it as their Boxing Day delicacy. I'm not sure this vegetable "hush puppy" they call "Bubble and Squeak" would pass muster compared to the authentic Tex-Mex we enjoy in Texas!

Across cultures, leftovers are a natural part of post-holiday celebrations. So far in the Gospel of John, we have seen Jesus provide all that was needed and then some. At the wedding in Cana, He met a need for wine by providing abundantly more than the master of ceremonies could ever imagine. And then with the healing of the official's son and the invalid man at the Pool of Bethesda, Jesus provided life—new life—to those who had forgotten what it would be like to be healthy again. From what Jesus does, we learn more about who He is. The New Testament miracles are God's declaration that Jesus is the Messiah and is sovereign over all.

In John 6, Jesus reveals more of who He is through what He does. The Son of God is doing more than miraculous works. He is causing a stir everywhere He goes. People hear about the miracles and the unassuming man named Jesus. They are intrigued by the reputation that precedes Him. When word spreads that Jesus will be passing through town, the streets begin to stir with frenzy. Beyond seeing this budding celebrity, the people want to see the signs and wonders that happen in His presence.

> And a great crowd of people followed him because they saw the
> miraculous signs he had performed on the sick. Then Jesus went up
> on a mountainside and sat down with his disciples (John 6:2-3).

On one particular day, Jesus and His disciples were reclining on a
mountainside at the far side of the Sea of Galilee. Word traveled quickly,
and soon they were surrounded by thousands of people, anxiously await-
ing a miracle. In the fourth miracle—the only miracle found in all four of
the Gospel accounts—Jesus shows compassion for the people by filling
their stomachs and opening their hearts. It's another example of Jesus providing more than enough.

Our common fear is that He will *not* provide enough. But the biblical
example is that the Messiah always provides *more* than enough. In Christ, we
never lack provision. He provides all that we need and more to live to the
glory of God here on earth.

Vision and Provision

In John 6, we read about an incredible moment in the ministry of Jesus. He
performs the miracle of feeding each and every person in a crowd of thousands. The Scripture declares there were 5,000 men present. This means
there were possibly 10,000 people, including women and children, in the
surrounding crowd. Beyond feeding the multitudes, the disciples collected
12 basketfuls of leftovers. There was more than enough. This miracle prepares us to hear what Jesus will proclaim at the end of the chapter when
He declares Himself to be "the Bread of Life." When we see how fulfilling
the Lord's provision is for thousands of people, it becomes intimate and
personal when He calls Himself the Bread of Life for each of us. The
"whosoever" of the hillside becomes personal with each bite.

Before the miracle took place, the calamity of the day had been building as Jesus and His disciples saw possibly 10,000 people approaching
them as they sat on the mountainside. Not all of the people were coming
to worship Him or declare Him to be the Son of God. Most were simply intrigued by the miracles and the acts of wonder that Jesus was reported to
have done. They were following Jesus, hoping to see a miracle. As the
crowds swelled, the disciples noticed a problem. The people were hungry,
and there was nothing to eat nearby. Jesus looked on the people with great
compassion and instructed them to sit down. The odds—10,000 to 1—were
not in His favor.

In the midst of the chaos, Jesus singled out Philip. Pulling the disciple aside, Jesus began to pepper Philip with questions that were impossible to answer. Throughout the Scriptures, Jesus is known for asking rhetorical questions that are frustrating and encouraging at the same time. In asking questions, Jesus is able to uncover our doubts and fears in a way that is constructive. And He reminds us of His omniscience. He knows all. Looking at Philip, Jesus asks, "Where shall we buy bread for these people to eat?" (John 6:5). Jesus asks the question with the solution already in mind. The perfect response for Philip would have been, "I have no idea! What do You think?" Instead, Philip's response reveals fear and doubt.

God is like that. He asks pointed questions to divulge our concerns. He knows what we need and how we will respond before He even asks the question. But God redeems every opportunity. With each loving question "The Answer" asks, our fears are revealed. And yet the Lord loves us too much to let us stay in our fear.

Are You Asking "How Much" or "Where"?

When Jesus looked up and saw a great crowd coming toward him, he said to Philip, "Where shall we buy bread for these people to eat?" He asked this only to test him, for he already had in mind what he was going to do. Philip answered him, "Eight months' wages would not buy enough bread for each one to have a bite!" (John 6:5-7).

Philip's reply, citing how much it would cost instead of where the meal would come from, reveals something deep. "Philip answered him, 'Eight months' wages would not buy enough bread for each one to have a bite!'" Jesus is asking "where?" not "how much?" which are vastly different questions.

The question of "where" is a question of location. Jesus wanted Philip to see that the Son of God answers the question of "where." Jesus Christ is always the location for our provision; He is the resource for our hunger. "Where" is answered in Jesus Christ, the present tense I AM. When our lives are lined with uncertainty, we can look to Jesus to provide. He is the place we point to when there is a question of provision. When we are plagued with fear, we need to point to Jesus. When we need satisfaction, we will find it in Christ. When we need employment or comfort or strength, Jesus is the answer to "where." Philip should have looked at Jesus and said, "You! You will provide!"

Over and over again, Jesus is the answer to "where." Where will we find enough wine for the wedding? Jesus. Where will the official find hope for his dying son? Jesus. Where will the lame man find strength to walk? Jesus. But before we say, "Philip, get with the program," we need to look at our own hearts. How can we doubt when we've seen God do so much? Yet, we still do. Even after witnessing these acts of wonder, Philip responded to Jesus' question in a way that we can identify with.

Humans—that means you and me—miss the biggest "where" of all time. Like the old country song, we are "lookin' for love in all the wrongs places."[1] Jesus is the "where," and when you understand that, the "How much?" question will take care of itself. Truly, if He is the Creator of the world, He can handle eight months' wages. The right "where" answer, settles the "how much" question.

This is a struggle, particularly for leaders. Part of the leader's job is to ask "How much" in order to keep the organization on firm footing. Certainly, vision becomes reality when we count the costs. But vision can also be squelched when we think the goal is solely managing the costs. There are opportunities for faith that arrive on the leader's desk. These moments are to be seized by faithfully trusting that God is able to meet the cost for the sake of the mission. We lead from the guidance of the Holy Spirit, not just the bottom line of the spreadsheet. This was Philip's moment to jump out of the plane and trust the parachute, but he paused and told Jesus how impossible was the issue of food for 10,000 people.

Philip's (and our) question of "how much" evokes fear of provision. Realizing our apprehension becomes a stepping-stone toward freedom. We are often wound so tight in the anxiety of "how much" that it creates back problems and tightens our shoulders. Just ask my chiropractor. I was laid out for a week after working out too hard and stressing out too long. I had to preach from a stool and sleep on the floor. The simple root of our stress is usually our question of "How much?"

The origin of this pressure for me is when I believe that I am the provider. Often, I assume it is my responsibility to prepare the sermon, raise the kids, put food on the table and lead the team. I convince myself that God is the helper, but in the end, I'm the provider. "If He would just bless my hard work, all would be fine." This is exactly where Philip sat. He was thinking about how man's vocational earnings can supply Jesus' need. However, the gospel, and particularly this miracle, shouts that God is the Provider. There is no question that we are called to count the costs (see Luke 14:28). However, continual fear of the costs will paralyze action and faith. You and I are not the source of provision. We don't create the bread; we serve it. We are the waiters, not the bakers.

Instead of pointing to Jesus and declaring Him to be more than enough, Philip looked at the problem without faith. Practically speaking, it made no sense to try to feed 5,000 men, not to mention their families. That's the point—practical thinking often blocks the path of faith. Faith charts the supernatural path. It leaves room for Jesus to accomplish the miraculous. Faith sees the invisible, believes the incredible, and receives the impossible.[2]

Philip's response was laced with fear and doubt as he told Jesus what it would take to feed such a crowd. Philip questioned God's provision. Even after seeing Jesus turn 6 jars of water into 2,500 glasses of wine and bring new life to those in need of healing, the thought of feeding such an overwhelming crowd seemed impossible. But opportunities for Christ's glory to be seen begin with impossible circumstances. He's the Miracle Maker, the Messiah and the Voice of heaven, calling us to follow Him.

Where are you standing before a hungry hillside crowd, feeling ill-equipped in resources? Perhaps you are a mom with kids, a leader casting vision, or the listening friend trying to give a helpful reply. All of us should feel lacking in this position. Yes, you read that right—we *should* feel lacking. It is in those "Even eight months' wages won't do" moments that *the* Messiah has to be *our* Messiah. Jesus moved Philip from corporate belief to personal belief. He wasn't asking the disciples to find bread; He was specifically asking Philip to find bread. The personal call requires a personal faith. If you step away from the crowd to the lead, you will feel it.

At times, I've found it easier to believe God for other people's provision than to believe in Him for my own. "I know He'll provide for others, but will He for me? I believe that the spiritual super-saints' prayers will be answered, but will mine?" My close proximity to the need allows me to see the rust on my faith and the sandpaper in His hand. I don't feel those same emotions when others' faith is required like I do when my number is called.

George Mueller said it this way: "If you want your faith to grow, don't shrink back from opportunities for your faith to be tried." Jesus wanted Philip to see that He is the location of our provision and that He will provide the bread. Miraculously, unattainable goals are within reach when we trust Jesus to provide.

Live on the Give

The mountainside, once quiet, is now teeming with chaos. Thousands of people are streaming in with circus-like fascination. Hungry people who want to see a miracle make for a tough crowd. With the throngs of people billowing in, it seems only natural that "Team Jesus" would feel overwhelmed by the calamity. However, instead we see Jesus do something far from ordinary. He is most concerned about individual hearts, not just the herd. The Messiah sees with different lenses than man. He counts in ones, not thousands.

> Another of his disciples, Andrew, Simon Peter's brother, spoke up, "Here is a boy with five small barley loaves and two small fish, but how far will they go among so many?" (John 6:8-9).

A beautiful aspect of the Savior is that He sees individual hearts, and not just a mob of people. The story could also be called "The Growing Faith of Phil and a Kid" instead of "The Feeding of the Five Thousand." The individual growth of their faith is a miracle as well. We see this in the way that Jesus spotlights a young boy who is carrying a lunch big enough for only his appetite. Jesus uses a small offering to accomplish an enormous task. The young boy's lunch doesn't even have enough food for two people, let alone 5,000. And yet, Jesus uses the boy as a vessel for provision. I can imagine that the kid was looking forward to his meal—it was just enough for him. But when he was asked to give it up to this man named Jesus, he does so without hesitation. He did not hoard it or try to escape into the crowd. In a moment of intrigue and joyful offering, the boy hands his meal to his Maker. He is living on the give, not the take.

It is a part of our sinful nature to want to hoard the good things. Perhaps it is abundant finances or a God-given talent. We often struggle to give away what is good in our lives. That is yet another sign that we struggle with the fear of provision. All "experienced Christians" will most likely acknowledge that all we have, God has provided. But the level of provision drifts into a level of normality. We are blessed but we don't *feel* blessed, so our unspoken goal becomes the maintenance of existing and the acquisition of more. The game is to keep what we have and fill the blank places. But life blossoms when we give instead of receive. We must move our thoughts past money and stuff and focus more on time, attention and trust. Jesus is saying, "Give me your life, and the rest will take care of itself" (see Matt. 6:33).

Giving to the Lord takes our measly ham sandwich in a Ziploc bag and creates baskets full of leftovers after thousands have been fed. The principle is exemplified in the young boy's willingness to give away what he had. No doubt the boy thought he would rather enjoy his lunch alone. He's hungry too. He was the only one who had the forethought to plan for lunch. But Jesus called the young boy to give away what he had without concern.

Life is found when we trade our plans for His. This has the potential to bring anxiety, fear and questions of "how much." Our resources, talents and gifts are not our own. What do you have to give away in your life that would make Jesus look great? As believers in Christ, we are called to give away to the multitudes of those who didn't plan well, those who have sinned deeply, or even those who were born behind the power curve of blessing. Allow Christ to break through your fears, taking you from the bench to the field.

"Live on the Give" Lived Out

I've seen this exemplified in recent years as I've watched families adopt children. Talk about a "live on the give"! Opening heart and home to biological children requires an incredible amount of time and emotional energy. A family with adoptive children requires even more. I have been privileged to see this style of live on the give firsthand. Two children adopted from Russia live across the street from us and often play with our kids. Also, our church has a strong adoption ministry called Legacy 685.[3] So, having children from different countries and backgrounds in our church congregation is nothing new. It blesses me in the church hallways and my neighborhood streets to see parents willing to share more than their lunch on the mountainside of life.

The adopted children are in need and, for the most part, the adoptive parents are already possessing very busy lives. This makes a tough combination. However, these families aren't asking, "How much?" They are trusting the Lord's provision as they provide for another life. To live on the give is not to hide your lunch box or act like your sandwich is too small. It is to realize that in giving instead of taking, we leave a legacy. Christ looks great through the lives of those who dare to give away more than they receive. Think about how many men were on that hillside. There were 5,000 men. And yet, we are still talking about one little boy. That is a beautiful picture of the faith of a child and giving a mustard seed (see Matt. 17:20).

The Klein family, in our church, is giving more than a sack lunch. For years, Steve and Mary wanted another child. They already had two biological children, David and Anna, but they did not have peace that their family was finished growing. Little did they know how God planned to answer their desire for another child. Adoption was not their plan, but God laid the idea of adoption on their hearts, and they could not let it go. In fact, there was a point in the decision process to adopt when Steve and Mary realized they would not have peace if they walked away from that quiet nudging God had put in their hearts.

Through a period of infertility and the faithful prayers of their daughter, Anna, God continued to lead them to His design for their family. They knew their inadequacies, and at times, fear would grip them. Would they be able to take care of the needs of a girl who had spent the first two years of her life in an orphanage? Would they be able to get past their shortcomings?

Isaiah 43:19 strengthened them for the adoption journey: "See, I am doing a new thing! Now it springs up; do you not perceive it? I am making a way in the desert and streams in the wasteland." At the end of the day, it was God calling them to do something without a guaranteed outcome. As a couple, it was a place they had never been before. It was God calling them to a step of faith—to trust Him to provide and to open their hearts and their home.

After months of praying about all of their questions, fears and inadequacies, they will never forget walking into an orphanage in St. Petersburg, Russia, to meet Catherine. It was a cold and dark place with expressionless faces everywhere. The building was a throwback to the 1930s, with dripping pipes and an obvious odor that infiltrated every room. The children had very few toys, most of which were kept out of reach. A play area that measured 6 feet by 6 feet was coldly set in a corner. Wooden crib slats kept the children contained. Caregivers marched to their routines, whisking by the children as if they weren't even there. In the midst of the filth and stark conditions sat their beautiful daughter, Catherine. With strength that could only come from God, the fear literally vanished, and Isaiah 30:21 came to mind: "Whether you turn to the right or to the left, your ears will hear a voice behind you, saying, 'This is the way; walk in it.'" Steve and Mary stepped out in faith, confidently knowing that Catherine was the child they had been longing for.

The Klein family truly felt blessed beyond measure, and yet God began speaking to their hearts: "What are you going to do with the gift of adoption? Are you going to keep it to yourself or will you be open to what I want to do in your lives, your family and in the lives of others?" After praying about this, Steve and Mary knew that God was leading them to adopt again. This time, they began to consider a special-needs child. In an orphanage in Dongguan City, China, the Kleins met their precious Chinese daughter, Kaylynn, who was suffering from a cleft palate.

The orphanage in China was filled with stark white walls and a silence that was deafening. There was hardly a noise to be heard, even a child's cry. A courtyard play area had been updated but was never put to use. The children all slept in wood-bottomed stainless steel cribs without a mattress, pillow or blanket. Each room was outfitted with 25 to 30 cribs lining the walls and organized neatly in the middle of the room.

Kaylynn would later recall those sleepless nights. She would reach through the wooden slats to hold the hand of her friend in the adjoining bed, comforting each other as they fell asleep. Years later, that hand-holding friend has a home with a family in New York. Kaylynn developed an early comfort with insects because the doors were often left open for outside visitors. To this day, she still has bite marks on her legs—a lasting impression of her days in the orphanage.

Steve and Mary were overwhelmed by the opportunity to rescue Kaylynn out of this life and offer her something new. After several surgeries and four years of speech therapy in the States, the Kleins can't imagine what they would have missed if they had not been open to follow God's path. What if they had said no to adoption? Realistically, it was illogical to adopt—they had two wonderful children and their lives were already busy and full. Yet, they would have missed the incredible miracle of adoption, and they consider it a rich blessing that God did not give up on their doubting hearts. He continued to call them to live on the give until they embraced the blessing of Catherine and Kaylynn.

People often comment on what a blessing this family is to their adopted daughters; however, Catherine and Kaylynn are the true blessings in their lives. The Kleins now understand in new ways that adoption is about what God wants to do in their lives as well as what He wants to do in the lives of their youngest two children. He has taught them so much about their own adoption as children of God, about faith and about His design for children to be raised in families. They are often asked, "How did God confirm that you were supposed to adopt?" Their answer is simple. The confirmation comes each day when their two youngest daughters live new lives and they see the miracle that God brought to their family. They get to be a part of something bigger than themselves.

It was a significant moment of impact when Catherine and Kaylynn fully understood that they belonged in the Klein family in a permanent way. There would be no more changing caregivers. Kaylynn expressed it best one night at the dinner table. After being with them for several months, she went through each family member by name, including herself, and said, "They all family." It was a profound moment, and there wasn't a dry eye at the table.

Perhaps the most incredible moment of impact was when the two girls trusted Christ as their Savior. They both understood the magnitude of God's love for them in a way that pointed them to Jesus. In their own time, Catherine and Kaylynn made the decision to trust in the Lord. Steve and Mary love being able to tell them that they were adopted twice. Adoption changes everything and everyone individually. The Lord is interested in changing one heart and life at a time.

In a crowd of thousands, Jesus set His eyes on a particular heart of doubt in Philip and a willingness to give what he had in a young boy. It is a sweet reminder that though Jesus cares for many, He is particularly interested in *you*. At the beginning of John 6, Philip is set up as a classic pessimist, although it is hard to call him pessimistic when we could easily find ourselves in his shoes! Philip's role in this story is easily overlooked. However, his life was never the same after that day on the mountainside. By the time we read John 12:21, Greek worshipers are coming to him asking to see Jesus. After his interaction with Jesus on the mountainside, Philip assuredly points the worshipers to the Lord.

Philip's response coaches us not to worry about provision when Christ is our vision. When Jesus asks Philip to set his eyes on Him, not on the problem at hand, Philip responds in a way that we can relate to. It's hard to trust God when things seem impossible. But the more we know about who Jesus is, the more we can trust what He can do. Philip learned a lesson that day that we spend our lives figuring out: God is not worried about our personal lack of resources. He is the Resource. God often calls us to things that are bigger than we are so that we learn to trust Him. In a crowd of thousands, Jesus looked for childlike faith.

To Jesus, you are more than just a face in the crowd. He changes a crowd one heart at a time, beginning with you.

FOR FURTHER REFLECTION AND DISCUSSION

1. Describe a meal around the holidays in your family. What dish is always served? Has anyone in the group eaten Bubble and Squeak?

2. How does the feeding of the 5,000 encourage you to remember that God can provide?

3. Why do we ask God "how much" instead of "where"?

4. Discuss the Kleins' story of adoption. What can we learn from their journey?

5. How can you live on the give? Identify two ways you can live on the give this week.

6. What is an impossible "Feeding the Five Thousand" task you think God may be leading you to give your lunch to?

If We'll Add, He Will Multiply

Jesus then took the loaves, gave thanks, and distributed to those who were seated as much as they wanted. He did the same with the fish.

JOHN 6:11

Seven Miracles of Jesus

1. Turning water into wine (JOHN 2:1-12)
2. Healing the nobleman's son (JOHN 4:46-54)
3. Healing of the lame man (JOHN 5:1-17)
4. **Feeding the 5,000** (JOHN 6:1-13)
5. Walking on water (JOHN 6:16-21)
6. Healing the man born blind (JOHN 9:1-41)
7. Raising Lazarus from dead (JOHN 11:1-45)

Seven I AM Statements of Jesus

1. I AM the Bread of Life (JOHN 6:35,48,51)
2. I AM the Light of the World (JOHN 8:12)
3. I AM the Door/Gate (JOHN 10:7)
4. I AM the Good Shepherd (JOHN 10:11-14)
5. I AM the Resurrection and the Life (JOHN 11:25)
6. I AM the Way, the Truth, and the Life (JOHN 14:6)
7. I AM the True Vine (JOHN 15:1)

I imagine the young boy never thought that his small lunch would feed multitudes. The portion was just enough to satisfy his hunger, not the hunger of thousands; we suppose the same thing about our own resources. Our time, money, talents and efforts at encouragement seem like enough to cover the bases, but nothing more. But the Lord does the miraculous with what we have to offer. He multiplies our offering to do something spectacular. If we'll add, He'll multiply. God multiplies humble sums to make extraordinary quantities. The challenge before us is to be willing to give. Even a small tithe given on Sunday morning can transform a mission in a foreign country. God takes what we offer and multiplies abundantly. When we realize that all of our resources are God-given, we are filled with more joy when we offer them back to God to be used for His glory.

Perhaps what you have to give seems insignificant. The young boy probably felt the same way. What could Jesus really do with a few barley loaves and two small fish? When Jesus approached the young boy about his lunch, He knew exactly what He was getting. Five small barley loaves and two small fish were perfectly sufficient in the hands of Jesus to feed possibly 10,000 hungry spectators.

"Live on the give" is about our hearts being changed, not God needing something from us. Jesus could have rained manna and quail like God did in the book of Exodus. He is the Creator and is not overwhelmed by human need. But in His grace, He chooses to include us with our humble lunch. As we trust Him with the little we have to offer, we will grow in our trust that He is able to do abundantly more.

I Don't Have Enough and Never Will

The boy's lunch was unfit to provide for such a number of people in both quantity and quality. At the time, most of the population ate barley loaves, as they were unable to afford anything else. Samuel Johnson described a similar concept in his dictionary. He defined barley as "a grain which in England is fed to horses and in Scotland is fed to people."[1] Barley was food for the poor, but best used as horse feed. Humans only eat food for animals when there is nothing else. Remember the prodigal son and the pig slop (see Luke 15:13-16)? As Mona Stewart notes:

> The poor could not afford wheat bread, so barley bread became their
> staple. The lad's lunch in John 6:9 consisted of five barley loaves

and two fish. The barley loaves were probably flat disks much like small tortillas. Having barley rather than wheat indicated his family's economic condition. The rich preferred wheat bread.[2]

A small lunch suitable to feed a poor boy was fed to thousands to the glory of Christ! Jesus asked the boy for exactly what he had, and nothing more. Jesus, not the boy, changed the quantity and quality of the offering. It is up to Him, not us, to multiply our resources. We add and He multiplies. He is the "where" that changes our "how much."

We are often tempted to believe that what we have to give is insignificant; in our own hands, perhaps, but our lack more effectively shows His glory. The hands that hold the goods change the value. For example, a baseball in my hands is worth $25. But if you slip the same baseball into the hands of the New York Yankees' closing pitcher, it is worth millions.[3] In the hands of Jesus, our offering's size and worth are exponentially changed.

None of us has the deep resources to be sincere, unselfish and God glorifying in our own strength. It only comes through Christ. Lay down the oar of effort and ride the current of grace. The Lord will often ask you for more than you can give so that He can serve as the multiplier. God longs to be your vision and provision. He is able to take exactly what you have to offer and accomplish the unimaginable.

While writing this chapter, a small prayer has grown in my heart. I have found myself feeling like the boy with a small lunch looking at a large task, wondering if I've "got the stuff" to write this book. More than self-defeating thoughts, they are reminders of my true strength in Christ. As a result, I have begun whispering this prayer for the book and my life: "Lord, I'm just a little lad will a small lunch, but I'm willing." Make that your prayer this week and see how God multiplies your contributions. *I AM changes who i am.*

More Than We Could Want

Jesus then took the loaves, gave thanks, and distributed to those who were seated as much as they wanted. He did the same with the fish. When they had all had enough to eat, he said to his disciples, "Gather the pieces that are left over. Let nothing be wasted." So they gathered them and filled twelve baskets with the pieces of the five barley loaves left over by those who had eaten (John 6:11-13).

The loaves and small fish were distributed among the hungry crowd. The apostle John records that the 5,000 people ate until they were full. Jesus provided enough food to not only satisfy the pangs of hunger, but to also show His power. He instructed the disciples to collect the leftover food. In obedience, they spread out among the masses and collected 12 baskets full! Remember, this is an agrarian culture where leftovers were unheard of.

For many people on the hillside, this may have been the first time to see leftovers. Think of your refrigerator after Thanksgiving and then ponder the 12 baskets brimming with food. That is what we experience with life in Christ. He provides more than we want or need. The crowd ate until their stomachs were full. They did not need any more, nor did they want any more. And yet, 12 baskets remained of unneeded, unwanted food. It is the nature of the great God we worship to provide more. God grants infinite forgiveness in a boundless universe for those of us who never run out of oxygen. He is the infinite resource to us—finite human beings.

God is a God of incredible leftovers that way surpass our Bubble and Squeak on Boxing Day. The twelve baskets of leftovers show how God longs to give us more than we could need or want. But our desires are often too small. We desire just enough to satisfy when God intends to lavishly pour out blessing on us. We are satisfied with good when God is offering great. We seek to numb the pain or get by when God is offering soul-satisfying peace instead. When offered peace, we settle for mediocrity.

Why, when God abundantly pours out provision for our needs, do we still feel anxiety in our hearts? Perhaps we don't trust that God can fully provide but only partially. Learning to trust God and walk in faith is a lifetime adventure that has a cumulative effect. It's like a snowball rolling down a hill that collects snow as it goes. The more you believe, the more you believe; the more you trust, the more you trust. Each day's decision to rest in His power and not your own changes you to look like Him. No one masters it in a day. The goal is that Christianity would master us over a lifetime.

For those who walk with Christ for the long haul, a deep satisfaction rises that is not swayed by circumstance. In the struggles, there is hope. In grief, there is even joy. A seasoned believer can celebrate the young boy choosing to be used by God through giving his lunch away. Would he have been more satisfied by hiding his food? Being used by God to accomplish something great or small is without comparison. The believer's preference is to be poured out and used by God rather than give in to fleshly hunger and desire. The boy shared his lunch with thousands upon thousands that day through the power of his Creator, whose voice rang through every crunch of the shared sack lunch. It was far more fulfilling than a solitary lip-licking picnic. It is always soul satisfying to watch the Lord use our small offering for a greater good.

Earthly Dissatisfaction

Post-Christmas morning at the Matte home is a sight to see. It probably looks a lot like your home. Wrapping paper scattered everywhere and children joyfully occupied with their new treasures. The day before Christmas, we had more than enough. There was no list of "dire needs" our lives depended on. However, come Christmas morning, in the gift-opening frenzy, we all open up more to store in our overflowing barns. Sweet "wants" are fulfilled, but usually there is nothing in the "need" category.

Ironically, December 26 marketing ads fill the newspapers with "Day After Christmas" sales. Sure, we just celebrated and opened gifts. But wait, there's more! The reduced prices and "get 'em before they are gone" deals testify to the fact that in our culture people are never content. If we are not physically fulfilled on the day after Christmas, we never will be. Maybe one additional sale item at 50 percent off will do the trick. We have a completed nativity, unwrapped loot and a full belly. Still, we ask the question, "Is there more?" and forget that Jesus is more.

Nothing of this world will completely gratify us. But something of heaven will. We shortchange ourselves on the riches offered to us *in Christ*. In so many parts of our country, people are materially rich and yet spiritually poor. In my part of the world, youth are growing up without sensing a need for Christ, because everything they "need" has been taken care of. As parents, we overwhelmingly satisfy our kids with the world and they have no thought to ask questions about heaven.

In the midst of all that we have, it is a battle to be satisfied in Christ alone. But it is a worthy fight. When you have tasted satisfaction in Jesus, you know that nothing else will do. So how do we deal with our stuff *and* love Christ?

It's a good practice to offer the meal *and* the leftovers to the Lord. Often we hold on to much more than we should for fear that we will one day be in need. However, as we grow in our walk with Christ, we remember that He always provides. Giving to the multitudes in need of a miracle will free us up to trust in the provision of God.

Of course there are necessary tools we need for everyday life. Most likely, to live in the circle where God has placed you, you need a car, a house and appropriate clothing. And it is wonderful to take your spouse to a nice restaurant on a date night. But we shouldn't play "the game." The game is keeping up with others, overspending on ourselves, and finding our security in winning the game. Possess the tools of impact, but don't play the game of coveting. Live on the give, not the take.

It is convicting to me, and we all hate to hear it, but we spend *way* too much on fashionable junk instead of giving to change the world. True life is found in giving your lunch away, not filling the cabinets. Consider radical ways to cut expenses, if needed. For example, cancel cable TV and give another $1,000 away over the next year. How many rooms go unused in your house on a daily basis? Do you really need another shirt?

I don't want you to picture me as a bare-bones zealot. I have a long way to go. I have a nice car, but not as nice as I could have. I have nice clothes—most with brand names—but not as many as I could have. I need the tools of a nice suit and a car with air conditioning to pastor in Houston. Still, it is good to continually assess my life, or I may get pulled into wasting my resources on stuff that breaks. Instead, I want my God-given resources to go toward eternal impact that helps a broken world.

Without judgment, assess your wallet and you'll find waste. Is your lunch box filled with 10 sandwiches? What if you gave away three to someone who needs one? What Jesus does changes what we do. The deeper blessing is in the sharing, not the gorging.

Already King of Kings

Our world begs us to desire more things that leave our souls unfulfilled. Nineteenth-century medical missionary David Livingston was a man who understood the cravings of an earthly focused heart. Ultimately, he decided that life in Christ was far more pleasurable: "I would rather be in the heart of Africa inside the will of God than on the throne of England outside the will of God."[4] If we let it, the world will craft our desires and hopes to long after the material possessions. But the things this world offers will never suit our hearts that were made for heaven.

We fight a worthy battle when we choose to fulfill our heavenly purposes and not slum for the heights of the world. Your God-given calling may be to work as an executive in a high-power company. The business world desperately needs to see people who love Christ. The "up and out" need the Lord as much as the "down and out." Your position is a tool to put you in circles with people to show them and share with them the Miracle Man Jesus. Be grateful for the blessings, and may you use your position to do a mighty work for Christ's kingdom. Share Christ at the country club *and* the second-hand clothes closet. Use the tools the Lord has given you, but don't get sucked into playing the game of finding your self-worth in luxury and earthly success.

Or perhaps you are called to serve as a missionary to the children of Africa. I am confident that you will find no greater pleasure than being in the toughest areas of the continent. Christ's kingdom needs passionate people pouring out exactly where they are planted. Christ, not the circumstance or setting, brings ultimate satisfaction.

Jesus stood on the mountainside and saw the people pouring toward Him. Some in the crowd flocked to Jesus because they were following their stomachs. As loaves and fishes were spread abundantly throughout the crowd, Jesus had in mind to fill their hearts as well. As we continue our journey through the Gospel of John, we will see how all that Jesus says and does points us toward lasting satisfaction in Him. Christ is the only place where we can find satisfaction *and* leftovers. We can eat our fill and trust that in His provision, we have all that we could need or want. So give your lunch away! In Christ, your spiritual fridge is full.

FOR FURTHER REFLECTION AND DISCUSSION

The "I AM" Playlist Pick

Song	Artist	Album
"When the Saints"	Sara Groves	*Tell Me What You Know*

1. What does the phrase "If we'll add, He'll multiply" mean? How can you apply it?

2. How does dining on "heavenly bread" ruin our appetite for earthly bread?

3. What is Jesus trying to teach us by the baskets of leftovers?

4. How can gorging ourselves transform into sharing with others because of this miracle?

5. How can the prayer, "Lord, I'm just a little lad with a small lunch, but I'm willing" prepare you for God's multiplication miracle? Will you begin praying that prayer this week?

FIFTH MIRACLE (PART 1)

Time to Sail

After the people saw the miraculous sign that Jesus did, they began to say, "Surely this is the Prophet who is to come into the world." Jesus, knowing that they intended to come and make him king by force, withdrew again to a mountain by himself. When evening came, his disciples went down to the lake, where they got into a boat and set off across the lake for Capernaum.

JOHN 6:14-17

Seven Miracles of Jesus

1. Turning water into wine (JOHN 2:1-12)
2. Healing the nobleman's son (JOHN 4:46-54)
3. Healing of the lame man (JOHN 5:1-17)
4. Feeding the 5,000 (JOHN 6:1-13)
5. Walking on water (JOHN 6:16-21)
6. Healing the man born blind (JOHN 9:1-41)
7. Raising Lazarus from dead (JOHN 11:1-45)

Seven I AM Statements of Jesus

1. I AM the Bread of Life (JOHN 6:35,48,51)
2. I AM the Light of the World (JOHN 8:12)
3. I AM the Door/Gate (JOHN 10:7)
4. I AM the Good Shepherd (JOHN 10:11-14)
5. I AM the Resurrection and the Life (JOHN 11:25)
6. I AM the Way, the Truth, and the Life (JOHN 14:6)
7. I AM the True Vine (JOHN 15:1)

The disciples were overwhelmed and exhausted, and also amazed. Just a few hours before, they sat among thousands, listening to Jesus. Their personal time with their leader on a mountainside had been interrupted by a crowd of hungry people, curious to see a man who claimed to be the Son of God and who had a growing list of miracles to prove it. God's great miracles can, at first, appear as interruptions. Jesus didn't seem to mind the gathering and, in fact, He welcomed it. Beyond talking to the people, Jesus did something that stopped them in their tracks.

The people came hungry, but Jesus was more than prepared to fill them. It was overwhelming for the disciples to see Him produce food for well over 5,000 people out of a lunch fit for a small boy. It was exhausting to hand plentiful food to the crowd and then collect basketfuls of leftovers. The afternoon left the disciples amazed by their leader and perplexed by His ways. Surely a victorious ride on their shoulders would follow the 5K feast. Instead, shortly after the crowd dispersed, they watched Jesus withdraw to a mountain by Himself. The people seemed eager to worship Him as king, but strangely, He wanted nothing to do with it yet.

The lake was nearby, and the disciples began to make their way there as evening set. As they walked, I imagine they were silent. After a crowd of 5,000-plus, silence was a welcome "noise." It's possible the disciples were unaware that God does great things in times of silence. Nighttime was quickly falling as they hopped in the boat. Jesus was nowhere near, and at His request, they decided to make for the other shore without Him. As the boat drifted out, they finally took a deep breath. A nice, calm ride to the other shore after the chaos of thousands sounded wonderful.

The disciples settled into their journey, their minds on thoughts of the larger journey they were on with Jesus. "Could He be the Messiah?" They had sipped miraculous wine, eaten "wonder bread" and witnessed healings, all dripping with divinity and compassion. They had never seen anything like it. Surely a quiet boat ride would give them time to process the joy and overwhelming experience of following Jesus. What He was doing was slowly changing who they were becoming, and they needed time to muse.

The Beauty and Brawn of the Sea

By now it was dark, and Jesus had not yet joined them. A strong wind was blowing and the waters grew rough (John 6:17-18).

Do you remember the first time you stood on the shore looking out at the ocean? I was young when I first saw the sea. I stood with my toes tucked into the sand, bewildered by the greatness of a giant sandbox that extended for miles. It was a little boy's dream come true to have endless opportunities to dig holes and construct an impenetrable fortress of a sandcastle.

But before I began the day's work of digging, I remember seeing the Gulf of Mexico. I walked to its edge and let the surf rush over my sand-covered feet. Wave after wave came rushing in, splashing the shore. The current went running through my fingers as I reached down and let my hand brush the foam that scattered the tide. Just as quickly as the wave arrived, it retreated, pulling back the water with a tug that shook my balance. The ocean was huge to me—and powerful. I didn't doubt its ability to pull me out to sea with the waves. At a young age, I had a sense that I couldn't control the sea. It was bigger and mightier.

No matter how old you are or how much you grow up, looking out on a vast body of water, it is always bigger than you. I feel smaller when I stand at its shore today than I did as a child. God displays His glory in all of creation. But when you consider the waters—the oceans, lakes and seas—there is an exhibit of power and sovereign control (see Ps. 89:9; Job 38:11). You may harness it with a boat or surfboard, but you can't control it.

The disciples were experts of the sea. They made their livelihood in a boat, fishing and navigating through waters of all temperaments. Day in and day out, they were in their element on the sea. So you can imagine that when a storm blew over the water, they were unfazed. But this storm was different.

I've been to the Sea of Galilee—it's more like an enormous lake. But the topography lends itself to tremendous tempests. Visualize one biblical commentator's sketch:

> The Sea of Galilee lies about six hundred feet below sea level. Cool air from the southeastern tablelands can rush in to displace the warm moist air over the lake, churning up the water in a violent squall. Even today, powerboats must remain docked as the winds buffet the water. How much more could violent storms have wreaked havoc on the wooden boats used in Jesus' time? After rowing about 3 or 3½ miles, the disciples were driven off course and found themselves halfway toward Magdala, where the lake was the widest.[1]

Something was different that night in the boat. The waters, once calm, took on characteristics that were overpowering and terrifying. As the wind picked up and the storm blew in, the disciples' boat was tossed back and forth. The commotion of the storm held their attention until something, or Someone, in the distance caught their eye. It was Jesus. The one who created the seas and commanded the tides was walking on water toward their boat. Panic ensued as the disciples wrestled against practical thinking that no man could walk on water. It didn't make sense.

This storm was different. The essence was not wind and rain, but the voice of God once again affirming the declarations of Jesus. The purpose of this storm was to "whitecap" the disciples' hearts for worship of the Savior who was about to sit in their boat after walking on the waves unassisted. The disciples looked through the storm and saw Him coming.

In a squall, we are pleading for the wind and waves to cease. Instead, we should embrace the rise of water as an opportunity to see Jesus on the horizon. We don't have to like it, but the value of knowing more of Him trumps the pain of the storm (see Rom. 8:18).

This miracle on the Sea of Galilee is a switching point. In all of the other miracles thus far, the disciples have watched Jesus rescue someone else. Now it is personal. Will the cumulative effect of their faith move from God's rescue of others to their personal situation? That's Christ's goal. You can believe for others all day long, but He is asking you to believe for yourself. It is now *their* storm, *their* boat and *their* faith. The first four miracles add up to this application. God's faithfulness in the past is to result in their (and our) trust in the present.

Jesus, standing on the water, speaks to calm their fears. Realizing that it was their beloved Friend and Teacher, they bring Him into the boat. Suddenly, the waters fall silent and their boat hits shore safely on the other side. They passed the test; fear, yes, but also trust.

The reality of life this side of heaven is that there will be mountains of joy and valleys of trial and tribulation. There will be times in life when you feel like you are in the middle of the sea, lost in a storm, like the disciples. As we walk through life, we find ourselves in one of three places:

1. On the shore before the storm
2. In the midst of a storm
3. On the other shore after the storm

When you find yourself in the middle of the sea with a storm whirling from every direction, Jesus is closer than you think. He meets you in the midst of it. You may feel as if the wind and the waves are all around you. The beautiful truth is that Jesus knows exactly where you are in that storm. More than that, Jesus wants to meet you where you are and get into the boat with you.

Calm Before the Storm

The Gospel of John recollects this mid-term examination in the lives of the disciples. The disciples are amazed at the miracles Jesus has performed, but they lack a deep understanding of what their leader is up to. Though they had just witnessed something extraordinary on the mountainside in the feeding of the thousands, they have moved on to the next thought.

We are often just like the disciples. Even though we have seen the Lord do incredible things in our lives, we are prone to forget. We are amazed by all the Lord is doing, and then we immediately get anxious again. This is evident by our apprehensive hearts. When our prayers are answered, we praise the Lord and then move on to the next thing to feel uneasy about. Wayne Cordeiro says we each have a "worry net."[2] Each morning we throw it out to see what we can catch. If no worries are apprehended, we draw the net in only to make it bigger for our next toss. Determined to snag something to concern ourselves with, we increase the size of our worry net until we capture something to stress over.

We constantly live in a state of anxiety because we have convinced ourselves that freedom comes when we are in control. The thought of someone else being in control, even the Lord, is unsettling. We would much rather hold on to the reins ourselves. We have a lack of deep, heart-level understanding that God is good and worthy of our complete trust. As if He has not given us every reason to trust Him through the cross, we constantly ask God to prove His goodness yet again. Our sinful nature asserts that the grace of God is insufficient. If you are living with a worry net, *stop it.* Quit searching for stress, and trust that He is up to something deeper than sinking your boat. He didn't lead you to the middle of the sea to drown you.

The right perspective on trials will free you up to endure even the toughest of storms. Trials purposefully shape us. They build us up to face the next trial with renewed faith and greater trust in the Lord. The disciples have just seen Jesus feed more than 5,000 people with only a sack lunch. And now they are heading to the sea, needing to trust that God will meet them there as well. When trials come, we are faced with two options: We can anxiously bury our heads in the sand and wait for the storm to pass, or we can stand in the Lord, enduring the wind and rain, convinced that He is with us.

When we head into a storm with our eyes on the Lord, a cumulative effect takes place. As we remember the Lord's faithfulness in past storms, we find strength to face the new ones. So when you are standing on the first shore, before the storm, let God's past faithfulness remind you to trust as the rain rolls in. He is worthy of our trust and gracious enough to remind us frequently that He is sufficient, even as a storm is brewing.

Jewish theologian Abraham Joshua Heschel remarked about the stoic faith of Job: "Faith like Job's cannot be shaken, because it is the result of having been shaken."[3] As Job endured the hardships of losing everything he had—family, crops, animals—he found solace in the Lord. Though he could have looked to the comfort of friends and shunned the name of the Lord, Job ran to Him. Job's faith was strengthened *because* the storm raged around him. At the end of it all, Job's faith was unshakable because he knew the Lord was enough. His faith was pressed but never crushed.

God takes us further than we could ever imagine. He is more interested in what is going on in our hearts and souls than anything else. In fact, He even has great intentions. He intends to use it to draw us to Him, where we are safe. C. S. Lewis understood the flood of pain that life often brings our way. In his book *The Problem of Pain*, Lewis talks about our human nature when passing through storms:

> I am progressing along the path of life in my ordinary contented condition, when suddenly a stab of pain threatens serious disease, or a newspaper headline threatens us all with destruction.
>
> At first I am overwhelmed, and all my little happiness looks like broken toys. And perhaps, by God's grace, I succeed, and for a day or two become a creature consciously dependent on God and drawing its strength from the right sources. But the moment the threat is withdrawn, my whole nature leaps back to the toys.
>
> Thus the terrible necessity of tribulation is only too clear. God has had for me but 48 hours and then only by dint of taking everything else away from me. Let Him but sheathe the sword for a minute, and I behave like a puppy when the hated bath is over—

I shake myself as dry as I can and race off to reacquire my comfortable dirtiness in the nearest flowerbed.

And that is why tribulation cannot cease until God sees us remade or sees that our remaking is now hopeless.[4]

God is interested in so much more than our comfort. He is interested in our devotion as well. On the front edge of the storm, there is much uncertainty. But we can be sure that Jesus will meet us in the storm, using every moment to draw us to Him. Tragically, we live with the forgetfulness that God is good. When we remember, we can stand on the first shore of a storm with our feet planted securely. The miracle is not a life without storms; the miracle is a Water Walker who is able to use the storms to strengthen our character.

Stress from the storms can be worn like a garment that we put on in the morning as a badge of importance. We have believed that stress equals significance. We brag of all we have to do today and sprint from the blocks to start the daily race. Today, live differently. Apply the chapter you just read to your day. Allow the Lord to guide you across the sea. What if you trusted Him for the next 24 hours to truly walk on the waters of your stress? When you feel the rain of the storm or the stress of the sea, rehearse in your mind the words, "I'll trust You in the journey." He is able to cross the water, and you are not. Live like that today and see what happens.

FOR FURTHER REFLECTION AND DISCUSSION

1. "In a squall, we are pleading for the wind and waves to cease. Instead we should embrace the rise of water as an opportunity to see Jesus on the horizon." What are your thoughts on this statement?

2. Discuss the idea of the "worry net" presented in this chapter. Do you ever find yourself casting the worry net? How does the miracle of Jesus walking on the water help us from casting the worry net?

3. Discuss the C. S. Lewis quote in the section "Calm Before the Storm." What sentence best explains you?

4. How, and why, does Jesus use the storms in our life?

Pink Canoes and Barbie Dolls

When they had rowed three or three and a half miles, they
saw Jesus approaching the boat, walking on the water; and they
were terrified. But he said to them, "It is I; don't be afraid."

JOHN 6:19-20

Seven Miracles of Jesus

1. Turning water into wine (JOHN 2:1-12)
2. Healing the nobleman's son (JOHN 4:46-54)
3. Healing of the lame man (JOHN 5:1-17)
4. Feeding the 5,000 (JOHN 6:1-13)
5. Walking on water (JOHN 6:16-21)
6. Healing the man born blind (JOHN 9:1-41)
7. Raising Lazarus from dead (JOHN 11:1-45)

Seven I AM Statements of Jesus

1. I AM the Bread of Life (JOHN 6:35,48,51)
2. I AM the Light of the World (JOHN 8:12)
3. I AM the Door/Gate (JOHN 10:7)
4. I AM the Good Shepherd (JOHN 10:11-14)
5. I AM the Resurrection and the Life (JOHN 11:25)
6. I AM the Way, the Truth, and the Life (JOHN 14:6)
7. I AM the True Vine (JOHN 15:1)

Awakened seas create awakened hearts. When we are in the middle of life's storms, we are prone to look around for help. Our hearts are acutely awakened because we are desperate for reprieve. In those moments, the Lord steps in and offers a sure foundation for our unstable stance. Our human tendency is to search for understanding in the middle of a trial. Things seem more certain when we can unpack the details and find clarity in the unknown. A trial is more comforting when there are no hidden enemies. However, in many of life's trials the Lord is asking for something other than understanding.

Obedience is the goal of a trial, not understanding. Yow! If you are like me, you want understanding. Just a small piece of "Why?" or a taste of knowledge to "Where is this heading?" But following the Lord does not always mean understanding His leading. Journeying into the middle of the sea, believing that He is right there in the midst of the storm, is different from understanding. Knowing that God is close by is aimed to be infinitely more comforting than having clear understanding.

Needless fears beset the disciples because they did not trust Jesus' words. If they had just thought for a moment, they would have remembered that He had said, "Let's go to the other side" (see Matt. 14:22). He didn't say, "Let's go to the middle of the lake, become engulfed by a storm and then drown." The disciples should have said to the raging waves, "You can do us no harm, for Christ has declared that we are going to the other side!"

With the focus of obedience, we trust that Jesus will carry us to the other side. Though we might not have any idea where the other side is, we can know for certain that Jesus will pave the way. In John 6, the disciples had to realize that they didn't know much about the journey ahead. Jesus only told them to get into the boat and cross the water. He did not offer details about what the ride would be like or what part of the distant shore was their destination. Life is often like that for believers in Christ. We sense the Lord leading us in a certain direction, but the details of the journey are strategically unclear. The miracle is in God offering us Himself instead of details. Peace is found in listening for His voice, not in looking for His hand. *Awakened seas create awakened hearts.*

Are You Rowing a Barbie Boat?

The Gospel of Mark recounts the same story of the disciples crossing the sea with Jesus following on foot. In Mark 6, the author gives a detail about the disciples that helps us understand their fight against the storm:

He saw the disciples *straining at the oars*, because the wind was against them. About the fourth watch of the night [3 AM] he went out to them, walking on the lake (Mark 6:48, emphasis added).

Jesus saw how his friends were battling against the wind and waves and made His way toward them. When we are in the middle of a struggle, we can be sure that the Lord sees us and times His visual arrival perfectly. When we are in the middle of the sea, it is easy to assume that we're lost without the nearness of rescue. But according to God's plan for our lives, His timing is perfect. Though it is far beyond us to call 3:00 AM a perfect time for anything, God never blinks, much less sleeps. His timing usually seems late to us in the present, but hindsight usually reveals it to be just right. So throw away your clock and lay down your oars.

If you have ever strained at the oars of a boat, you know that it is an exhausting and sometimes hopeless task. The disciples probably felt the same way. Even with years of experience on the water, they were fighting against the power of creation. Straining forward but moving backward is incredibly discouraging. One step forward and two steps back explain many of our days. We are straining and yet still failing: working 40-plus hours a week and still in debt; buying our kids closets full of clothes and stuff, and still seeing greed in them. The ratio needs to be reversed. Be encouraged: two steps *forward* and one step back is still progress. The advance in our vocation or parenting is the result of surrender, not effort. God uses storms filled with emotional winds and relational waves to peel our hands from the oars. Oddly enough, with our hands off the oars the boat travels farther faster.

When Jesus, walking on the water, arrived at the disciples' boat, they quickly arrived on the other side of the storm. The Greek word used in this passage for walking (*peripatounta*) describes an effortless walk over the sea. Their efforts were fruitless until Jesus effortlessly arrived. His presence, not their efforts, carried them across the sea. When I am faced with trial, my innate reaction is to fight harder. But at the end of it all, I find myself exhausted.

Arrival at the destination has nothing to do with how much or how little I strain against the oars; on the contrary, it has everything to do with Jesus. Surrender to God's presence results in the crossing of the sea to solid shore. In your business, in your marriage, in your parenting and in your life, it is His presence, not your effort, that matters. And it's not just a "God is everywhere" kind of presence, but a "God is active in me" presence. This is also important in salvation; His forgiveness, not our efforts, opens the gates of heaven.[1] But in our sin, we often forget what we know to be true. Despite our understanding that Jesus can carry us through a storm, we battle the waves as if it all depends on our strength.

It's difficult to strike the balance between faith and effort. But more than seeking balance, we need to properly prioritize the two. The question is, how do you arrange faith and effort on a typical day? If effort precedes faith, then the result is pressure. I feel a constant pressure when my hard work and planning need to produce results. Enough pressure will actually manifest itself physically through anger, sickness or pain. The pressure is going to get the best of you one way or another.

But, if you prioritize faith first and then effort, the result is peace. The correct order releases the pressure to accomplish and frees you to trust in Him. Not that you will walk perfectly in peace, but you will have peace in His leading of your life. Now you are surfing the waves instead of cursing them.

Don't hunt for the balance of faith and effort. Instead, seek to properly order them. Faith that precedes effort means that you show up and get it done, but you do so with a faithful, not a frenzied, heart. Work hard, be smart, plan, show up early and stay late. But realize that it is not up to you. As faith deepens, your good works will become purposeful. This is the end of arrogance and the beginning of gratitude in the follower of the Water Walker.

When I shared this passage with my beloved Houston's First Baptist Church, I decided to offer a visual example. An executive of a sporting goods store in town attends our church and agreed to lend us a canoe to use during the worship services as a visual aid. I wanted to illustrate the disciples "straining at the oars." So my friend submitted the order to his staff: "Please send a canoe to Houston's First for the weekend." (A few more details might have been necessary.)

Imagine my shock when a *pink* canoe arrived on the doorsteps of the church! It looked like it came from a store in the mall where 12-year-old girls get a free set of earrings with every piercing, not from an outdoors store. I learned that it is always good to specify details such as color. Who knew they make pink canoes!

The color choice was actually perfect, although it initially caught me off guard. Sunday arrived and I explained to the congregation that fighting a storm with our own strength is like floating in a pink "Barbie" canoe. It is a hopeless venture. We overestimate our strength. Trusting in our efforts, and straining at the oars, we will not make it to the other side. Let me put it simply: In your own strength, you are Barbie in the storm. You can battle against the splashing waves and tumultuous wind. But at the end of the day, you are still in a pink canoe more suitable for a Barbie doll than for actual weather. Wise up and lay down the oars—even if you think you're Ken!

In what area of your life are you straining against the oars? It is actually possible to try too hard. Like the disciples, you will stall out and find your own strength to be insufficient. You need the presence of Christ. In Him, you will find that the size of the storm shrinks in the shadow of His protection over you.

If you think you may be paddling too much and not trusting the Lord enough, a good test is to take a look at how hard you are working to stay afloat.

Overworking Is Often Under-trusting

Spending hours at the office and only minutes of prayer each day is a clue that you are sailing in a pink canoe. Your forward progress might be actually sending you backward in the things that really matter. With Jesus, your release of control is the embrace of real movement. Letting go of the oars is the most forward thing you can do. It is safe to lay down the oars when you realize that Jesus is the destination. Believing that He is with you in the storm frees you up to let Him fight for you.

A children's song that we all know was first printed in 1852 and became a schoolyard classic. It is not a hymn, but many use this song as a personal theology for understanding trials. Do you remember "Row, Row, Row Your Boat"?

Row, row, row your boat
Gently down the stream
Merrily, merrily, merrily, merrily
Life is but a dream.

We live as if that song were true. Our rowing creates a dreamy life. Hoping for smooth waters, we believe that floating gently down the stream is the perfect way to live. When trials come and life doesn't seem so merry, we panic. Any adult can tell you this song is bad theology. The stream is not always gentle and the waters are not always smooth. We need something that will buoy us up when life's storms are on the horizon.

At first, the disciples were terrified to see Jesus walking on the water toward them. As He approached, they hesitated out of fear but then let Jesus into the boat, certain that nothing else would work against the raging storm.

Seek Him in the seas. When you are caught in the midst of a storm, let Jesus into your boat. His presence will change the size of the storm in your heart.

There is a cumulative, growing effect in our faith when we trust the Lord in the storms of life. When we have experienced His provision in the past, the next storm doesn't seem so overwhelming.

Walking on water is miracle number five in the book of John for a reason: Jesus was building the disciples' faith. They had to drink the water changed to wine, witness two healings and dine with 5,000 to be ready for the sea. With each miracle and the coming "I AM" statements, they are growing in their faith and trust.

God's goal is to work in ways that are personal. With the feeding of the 5,000, the disciples saw God provide for others in abundance. Now in the midst of a storm, they see God provide specifically for them. He cares for an overwhelming crowd, but He is more interested in each individual heart.

The disciples are on a whirlwind adventure with Jesus. With each new miracle, their faith increases. The snowballing effect will one day mean that they will give their lives for Jesus. Unfortunately, the cumulative effect of a lack of faith can build upon itself too. The less you believe, the less you believe. Make sure your snowball is building speed in the right direction.

Kelly and I have a saying in our marriage to illustrate this increasing effect. It is simply, "The more you talk, the more you talk." Communication is key in a marriage, so we talk about everything. The result is that conversations about the little things as well as the big bundle together to build a relationship in which anything can be shared. For the storms of life, it can also be said that "The more you believe, the more you believe."

Wet, Worn-out and Grateful

As Jesus approached the boat, the disciples were afraid to let Him get in. It can be scary when the supernatural comes into the natural world. Think about the appearance of angels throughout Scripture. Whenever they appeared, they proclaimed, "Do not be afraid!" before saying anything else. Standing by the boat, Jesus speaks into the disciples' fear: "They were terrified. But he said to them, 'It is I; don't be afraid'" (John 6:19-20).

Comforted by His reassuring words, the disciples brought their leader into the boat. Let your existing fear birth your increasing faith! It is difficult when God reaches into your world and the supernatural happens—it can even be frightening. But let it increase your faith to know Him more. The Gospel of John uses supernatural miracles to prepare us for something more—the resurrection of Christ from the dead.

The apostle John prepares our faith to believe that Christ's rising is possible and triumphant. Each miracle builds upon the next. In the chapters to come, John will add the seven "I AM" statements of Christ. These will clarify what He is doing by telling us who He is. The miracles bring the Messiah into focus. "Believe me when I say that I am in the Father and the Father is in me; *or at least believe on the evidence of the miracles themselves*" (John 14:11, emphasis added).

The other side of a storm is a grateful place to be. When we have struggled through the depths of a storm in our lives, landing on the other side seems surreal. The disciples, who landed on the shore of Capernaum, were soaking wet, exhausted and grateful to be alive. Do you feel like that after a tough season of life? By God's grace, you made it through.

There were two miracles wrapped into one in John's account. First, the disciples saw Jesus walking on water. Second, as soon as they pulled Him aboard, the boat miraculously reached the other shore, pronouncing that Jesus was the destination. It always comes back to Him. He is not only the Water Walker, but He is also the destination—the true Omega. When He is in your boat, you are right where you should be. He is not a means to the end; He is the end itself.

Christianity is not the lever to open our personal treasure of relationships or success. The "I AM" is the Treasure. Therefore, we don't look for Jesus to only be our means to marriage or to open the womb, though He can and possibly will. Instead, we say, "Lord, You are my treasure when I'm lonely and the cradle is empty. You are my destination. Therefore I live by Your presence, instead of just asking Your blessing on my rowing or asking You to change the sea."

Working hard to get your "Barbie boat" to the harbor of your choosing is not Christianity. There's a colossal difference between asking God to bless your idea and asking what is His idea. Don't miss how big of a paradigm shift this is: Jesus *is* the destination, not just the means to a personal shore. Trust Him that the voyage is no longer your own. God is walking toward you and rowing for you!

Call Your Dad

During the storm, don't look for understanding. God does not owe us understanding and generally we only see it from the other shore. But He does promise us His presence and power in the midst of it. Often, His presence seeks to change us, not our circumstances. *I AM changes who i am.* He will carry you to the other side. You may be wet and worn-out, but you will see that God is enough to carry you through. A rescued heart is a grateful heart.

Mark Ashton-Smith, a lecturer at Cambridge University in England, was kayaking off the coast of the Isle of Wight when his boat capsized in treacherous waters. Desperately in need of help, he was able to reach his cell phone and call his dad. He had kayaked this area with his father many times before, but at the time, Ashton-Smith's father was 3,500 miles away in Dubai, training British troops. That didn't matter. The 33-year-old made the call for help.

He was able to reach his dad on the phone and tell him the predicament. Without delay, the father relayed his son's location to the Coast Guard nearest to the capsized kayak. Within 12 minutes (yes, 12 minutes), a helicopter filled with rescuers arrived, saving a wet, worn-out, but grateful son.[2] His rescue is an amazing testimony to technology, but more so to fatherhood.

May our first impulse in the midst of a trial be the same as Mark Ashton-Smith's—call your Father, your heavenly Father. He is with you through every storm, whether you are aware of Him or not. He is there. No matter the size of the sea or the power of its pull, He is bigger. God sent more than the Coast Guard to rescue us in our distress. He sent His water-walking Son. You are not in the storm by yourself. The Maker of the seas is in your boat.

FOR FURTHER REFLECTION AND DISCUSSION

The "I AM" Playlist Pick

Song	Artist	Album
"Walk on the Water"	Britt Nicole	*The Lost Get Found*

1. Where are you straining at the oars? How is your "Barbie canoe" holding up?

2. Discuss the proper ordering of faith and works. How does the right order allow God greater freedom to accomplish His will in your storms?

3. How does the phrase "overworking is often under-trusting" show itself in your life?

4. What must the arrival of the Water Walker have meant to the disciples that night? What about to you in your storms?

Show, Then Tell

Faith is believing that Christ is what he is said to be, that he will do what he has promised to do, and expecting this of him.
CHARLES H. SPURGEON

Seven Miracles of Jesus

1. Turning water into wine (JOHN 2:1-12)
2. Healing the nobleman's son (JOHN 4:46-54)
3. Healing of the lame man (JOHN 5:1-17)
4. Feeding the 5,000 (JOHN 6:1-13)
5. Walking on water (JOHN 6:16-21)
6. Healing the man born blind (JOHN 9:1-41)
7. Raising Lazarus from dead (JOHN 11:1-45)

Seven I AM Statements of Jesus

1. I AM the Bread of Life (JOHN 6:35,48,51)
2. I AM the Light of the World (JOHN 8:12)
3. I AM the Door/Gate (JOHN 10:7)
4. I AM the Good Shepherd (JOHN 10:11-14)
5. I AM the Resurrection and the Life (JOHN 11:25)
6. I AM the Way, the Truth, and the Life (JOHN 14:6)
7. I AM the True Vine (JOHN 15:1)

There's great benefit in taking your daily vitamins. Chances are your morning line-up includes a multivitamin and vitamin C. For the more mature readers, perhaps taking two pills is a laughable thought compared to your overflowing pillbox. But for those who aren't breaking the bank on a monthly supply of vitamins and pills, those two simple vitamins can boost your immune system and keep you moving forward in health. Vitamins stimulate your wellbeing, guard against illness and even add a little skip in your step.

In his book, the apostle John gives us two daily vitamins to keep us going forward in our faith: seven miracles and seven statements of identity. They are placed throughout the Gospel account to build toward the climactic finish of Christ rising from the dead. The Gospel of John is intended to be much more than a book of reference for sermons. It's people-talk, not just preacher-talk. Through the miracles, parables and declarations recorded by John, we begin to see who Jesus is by what He does. His actions declare His identity. So far, we have examined five of seven miracles. Miracle after miracle, what Jesus does connects with who He is.

You've heard it said before that actions speak louder than words. We live in a culture where we want to see someone "live it out" before they actually speak. A person's credibility comes from action rather than just talking about it. Jesus does this in the book of John by living out the power of God before He declares who He is through the seven I AM statements.

The Gospel of John has been action-packed with miraculous signs of Christ's power. As we watch these miracles unfold, we are struck with the question, "Who are You, Jesus? Mere man cannot do these things." Blown away by His mighty works, we look at Him in disbelief and wonder, "Who are You . . . who does these things?" Out of the miracles, we begin to grow hungry to discover His identity. In His wisdom, Jesus has been working miracles with power and authority. Suddenly, He speaks into the question we are all asking: "Who is this miracle worker?" And He has our attention. We've seen Him do miracles, and our hearts are prepped to begin to learn who Jesus is.

That You May Believe

The Gospel of John was written with a primary goal in mind. The apostle John had the world on his mind, and he longed for it to know the Savior. John desired for the world to know Jesus. His book is about a believing world. That is his simple goal, clearly stated at the end of his book:

> Jesus did many other miraculous signs in the presence of his disciples, which are not recorded in this book. *But these are written that you may believe that Jesus is the Christ,* the Son of God, and that by believing you may have life in his name (John 20:30-31, emphasis added).

Though John records seven of Christ's miracles, he mentions that there were others. Wouldn't you love to know what they were? But in the seven miracles illustrated in his book, we can be certain that John deeply desired for the world to know Christ. He recorded them in writing so "that you may believe." Throughout his account, John uses the word "world," or Greek *kosmos,* 78 times; and he uses the word "believe," or Greek *pistevo,* 98 times.[1] He was a determined writer with one goal in sight: that the world would believe that Jesus is the Christ. And so John gives us two vitamins—the miracles and the "I AM" statements of identity. He weaves them together to show who Christ is out of the miraculous things He does.

And yet our hearts are prone to skepticism. We want to see it to believe it. The unbelievable truth about the gospel is that Jesus meets us exactly where we are. In John, the miracles are ramping up toward the cross of Christ. Abruptly, there is a change in the action, and Christ makes a declaration that takes our understanding to a new level. Because we have seen His deeds, we lean in to hear what He will say. We want to know more about why He does the things He does. Who is this Jesus?

The integrity of Christ is shown as He makes an "I AM" statement after we have already seen Him in action. Five miracles occur in the Gospel of John before one I AM statement of identity slips from the lips of Christ. So when He speaks of His identity, we listen. The declaration of action is the groundwork for understanding identity. Jesus acts first and then speaks so that our hearts will be prepared for His words.

The same method can be applied to ministry today. Our church in Houston desires to be more than a holy huddle on Sunday morning. We long for our city to know Jesus. But before the people hear us speak the good news of Christ in Sunday worship service form, we aim for them to see us live out the gospel. "The Houston Project" is a multifaceted campaign that illustrates a "see it before you say it" strategy. One hot week each year in July, 1,500 members of our church host 19 sites around

Houston to just love on the children and people, making an impact and an impression. We want to serve the city before we preach to the city. Living out the gospel speaks in such a powerful way. Lord willing, the city of Houston will hear the gospel of Christ because of the hands, feet and mouths of His servants.

Before the July event, several volunteers went out into the community each night to promote the Houston project, sharing the gospel and ministering to others. The Lord did many great things through this effort. One specific story involved three of our volunteers coming across the doorstep of a 76-year-old man who is blind and also being tested for cancer. Our volunteers had deep compassion for this man and prayed fervently for his healing.

After praying, they began to share with him about Jesus and how much Jesus truly loved him. He had grown up going to church and even shared a story from the Bible with the volunteers about the blind man who had received his sight. However, during the conversation, it became clear that the man was not certain whether he would go to heaven when he died.

He mentioned that he had been working very hard to become a better person throughout his life in order to try to please God, and he hoped that God would accept him. He would not say the name of Jesus, but rather would call Him "the Master" throughout the conversation and kept mentioning that he was just trying to "please the Master." The volunteers began to share with him the grace offered through Jesus. As a side note, our prayer team had been praying fervently that folks in the community would be open to hearing the gospel.

The volunteers shared that they felt the presence of God and there was a spiritual shift in the conversation. In that moment, the man was overwhelmed with tears and began to cry deeply. He said he wanted to receive Jesus as his Savior. When he prayed in faith to Christ, he cried more and more. After the prayer, it was as if a ton of bricks had been taken off of his shoulders and he experienced true salvation and freedom. Through his tears, the man began saying over and over, "Jesus is all I need; Jesus is all I need." He said he didn't need any belongings in his apartment; he didn't need the food he has—he just needed Jesus. He once was blind, but now he sees.

At another site in our city, a married couple and a young single discovered that the family they had been ministering to all week had received an eviction notice and had to be out by the following Monday if the rent was not paid. Our people committed to continue serving the family and help them stay in their home. They thought it best to teach the father English so that he could get a job. These people are Iraqi refugees; yet we don't see political lines; we see souls. They have 10 kids—seven in America and three in Iraq. Their apartment was filthy because almost everything they owned had come from the streets. Yet our church members on a mission to our city looked past their nationality and apartment to show the love of Christ, and then they gave a verbal declaration of who was their Savior. Show and then tell. Be the miracle, and then point to the Messiah.

Through seven "I AM" statements of identity, Jesus speaks from the backdrop of His actions to tell us His distinctiveness. Actions declare identity, and Jesus does all these things for the sake of our belief. "That you would believe," Jesus turns water into wine, heals the lame and sick, feeds the thousands and walks on water. And we're not even all the way through the Gospel of John! Two more staggering miracles unfold in the coming chapters. But before we move on, we must lean in to hear what Jesus has to say. We've seen Him "do," now we must hear Him "speak."

The first five miracles declare that Jesus is the Christ. Do you believe it? What He does is intended to change what we do. Now the wind changes, and something new takes place. Jesus speaks. I AM declares who He is, and this truth drastically changes who we are. Read the next sentence aloud and realize that it is true for you: *I AM changes who i am.*

Ego Eimi

Declaring Himself as I AM (*ego eimi*) was a clear echo to Moses' encounter with God in Exodus. As Pharaoh held God's people captive, the Firepower of their freedom spoke to Moses from a burning bush. Sure, he found miracles and plagues, but none were greater than the person of God. Who God is supersedes anything He has created. The power of unlocking freedom for the Israelites was in two key words: "I AM" (Exod. 3:14).

This is the covenant name of God, YAHWEH, that declares He is present tense and self-sustaining. He just IS. Never to be more and never has been less. Like a constant, thunderous hum through all of history, He is. Never refueling, never growing weary, no mood swings, pantry always filled, resources constant, "I AM." So when Jesus declares His identity using this "I AM" tag, it is either 110 percent madcap blasphemy or salvation come to man. R. C. Sproul writes:

In the Septuagint the Greek translation of the name of God, the name Yahweh, which we translate as "I AM WHO I AM" (Ex. 3:14), is rendered by the phrase *ego eimi*, which literally means, "I am, I am." That phrase shows up in each of these "I am" sayings, indicating that Jesus makes a radical claim about His connection with God Himself.[2]

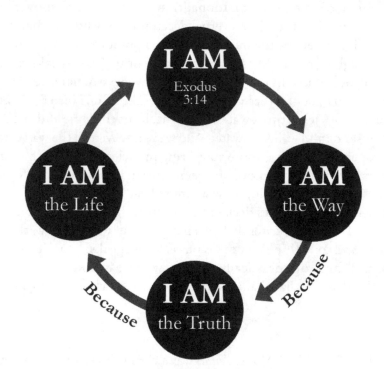

The I AMs of Christ are not accidental or merely descriptive delusions. They are clear, strategic statements unquestionably showing that Jesus is the Son of God. He is one with the Father and sent by Him (see John 8:58; 10:30). I can't overstate how huge this is for the Jewish people to hear a carpenter from Nazareth begin His sentences with "I AM." In order to get a similar shock today, just refer to yourself as president of the United States. In your conversations today, introduce yourself by saying, "Hi, I am President [insert your name]." Now, with that silliness in mind, multiply it by a million and tell a religious culture in biblical times that you are God. That gives you a taste of the significance of "I AM" confidently falling from Jesus' lips in the Gospel of John . . . seven times.

The Old and New Testaments are further connected by what follows the "I AM" in the declarations. Each predicate that follows points back to an Old Testament Judaism motif. Jesus in the New Testament is declaring Himself to be the God of the Old Testament (see John 8:58; 10:30).

Seven Statements of Identity with Old Testament Connections	
1. I AM the Bread of Life	John 6:35; Exodus 16:35
2. I AM the Light of the World	John 8:12; Exodus 13:21-22
3. I AM the Door/Gate	John 10:7; Psalm 118:19-20
4. I AM the Good Shepherd	John 10:11-14; Ezekiel 34:30-31
5. I AM the Resurrection and the Life	John 11:25; Job 19:25-27
6. I AM the Way, the Truth, and the Life	John 14:6; Isaiah 35:8-9
7. I AM the True Vine	John 15:1; Isaiah 5:1-7

Eating Your Fill

"I AM the Bread of Life" is the first of the seven mammoth statements, because we are hungry and He is filling.

There's nothing more satisfying than eating a huge meal and then taking a nap to let it all settle in. Thanksgiving and Christmas Day are prime candidates for that kind of overload. You eat from a spread of all of your favorite foods and even go back for seconds, with Bubble and Squeak the next day, to boot. After the meal, leaned back in your chair, a wave of tryptophan sleepiness leads you toward the couch. You can't imagine the thought of another bite, let alone another meal that day. Ironically, you wake up two hours later and, much to your surprise, you're hungry all over again. Your stomach was satisfied a few hours ago and now you are ready to head back for more. We are prone to return to the place where we find satisfaction, even if that means food!

Jesus and His disciples are safely on the other side of the Sea of Galilee. Despite the harsh weather on the water, they arrive altogether. The disciples are wet and worn from the journey but relieved to be on dry ground. The people on the other side of the water were eager to see Jesus and His friends. Many of them had traveled from the other side. We read in John

6:24 that they were "in search of Jesus." They came because they had seen something extraordinary. Many of the gathering crowd the day before had been among the 5,000-plus on the mountainside. Not only had they witnessed a miracle, but they had also had their hunger satisfied.

Satisfaction

The Lord desires so much more for us than we desire for ourselves. The crowd in Capernaum came to find Jesus because He had satisfied their stomachs. For many, the meal on the mountainside was their first complete meal in a while. Their stomachs were full and they were anxious for more. A full stomach only lasts for a little while. Before long, your body uses the energy of the last meal and you are hungry again. Satisfaction of the stomach is temporary. Jesus is interested in giving us so much more. He wants to satisfy our souls.

In Matthew 5:6, Jesus speaks about our soul-level hunger and His provision when He says, "Blessed are those who hunger and thirst for righteousness, for they will be filled." Jesus is saying that we are to hunger after His righteousness as a starving man hungers for bread, and we are to thirst after Him as a dying man thirsts for water. Do we really do that? If we would, it is hard to estimate how rich in the knowledge and fruitfulness of God we would be.

Jesus knew that the people needed to experience a full stomach to fully understand their need for a satisfied soul. As He was feeding thousands of people, Christ was providing for the satisfaction of the people's stomachs. They had their fill of as much as they wanted. Even after that, twelve basketfuls of leftovers proved the point that Jesus provides more than enough. In filling their stomachs, Jesus was preparing the people to see that He is the satisfaction of their souls as well. While a full stomach lasts only a little while, a full soul lasts beyond a lifetime. In the lives of the people then, and in our lives now, Jesus provides more than our needs. He provides for eternity.

To be satisfied deeply in our souls means that we never run out of nourishment. This is more than spiritual word magic in which something only sounds good. Instead, it means that we have discovered the abiding life of resting in Him. For me, this means seeking the approval of God, not man; and it means desiring righteousness, not praise. It means resting in the irony that my failures are often God's victories because grace becomes more meaningful to me. No longer is perfection the quest as much as faithfulness. I'm not trying to be moral—I trust Him to make me godly. Satisfaction means that I'm no longer searching; I have been found.

Jesus wanted the people who had followed Him to Capernaum to realize that He was offering much more than a meal. He was offering Himself. He arrived on the other shore after the journey across the sea—on foot. His disciples were weary but their eyes told the story of changed hearts and growing faith. Even the disciples, Jesus' closest companions, knew what it was like to be well fed but spiritually hungry. As Jesus began to address the people standing around Him, the disciples leaned in to hear Him talk about a satisfaction that went beyond a full stomach—"food that endures to eternal life" (John 6:27).

Check Your Motives

The people came flocking toward Jesus because He had provided something they were not always accustomed to—a full meal. Crossing the sea to find Him was about more than seeing another miracle. They were not concerned with knowing Jesus or even seeing what He would do next. "Jesus answered, 'I tell you the truth, you are looking for me, not because you saw miraculous signs but because you ate the loaves and had your fill'" (John 6:26). The gathering crowd was most concerned with the next meal following the feast on the mountainside. Jesus had intended for the miracle of multitudes to fix their minds on Him. But the people were looking for something else. They had mixed motives for following Christ. In their simple search for more food, the people were prone to miss the greater blessing—Jesus Himself.

Our culture today is no different. Many choose to follow Christ to fit in with their society. Sadly, in many parts of the country, American Christianity has become more of a pop culture declaration than a saving faith. We are self-focused in our approach to faith—seeking out solutions to our own needs instead of God Himself. Why are you following Jesus? Checking your motives for a professed faith in Christ will bring clarity and focus to your life. Perhaps you have found that knowing the Lord satisfies your daily needs. He is capable of doing that and so much more. Following Christ is life-giving because He brings satisfaction to our souls.

Churches are filled with thousands of people every Sunday morning. It would be interesting to conduct an honest survey about why each person is there. We would learn that the reasons are varied. Many come to church out of habit. Maybe you have gone to church every weekend since you were a kid and wouldn't know what to do on Sundays if you didn't go to church! But attending a worship service has drifted to a habit as a replacement of the longing of your heart to know Jesus.

Going to church also relieves guilt. Perhaps your life is not exactly playing out the way you had hoped it would. You've done things that you're ashamed of, and going to church is just the easiest way to live a life of sin and not feel as bad about it. If you can just make it on Sunday, the sins of the past week and the one ahead don't look quite as ugly. Of course there is also the added bonus that going to church opens opportunities to make a few new business contacts. You might be convincing yourself that swinging a few deals while greeting your neighbor in the pew is a harmless way of climbing the business ladder. Many people do meet their spouses at church, and rightly so. But coming to church on the hunt for a soul mate can get in the way of truly worshiping the Lord.

Maybe beyond all of those reasons to come to church, you are coming because it is incredibly rewarding to know Christ and worship Him with a body of believers. Only Christ can be the contentment of our souls. Everything else will fall short. As the people gathered around Jesus, He knew that a filled heart is vastly different from a full stomach. And He longed to show them that kind of satisfaction.

Working in ministry is an interesting paradox. It may seem that pastors are in the business of souls. But if ministry becomes my industry, then Jesus becomes my product and the church my store. As a result, my lack of intimacy with Christ will morph into a drive to succeed vocationally instead of to honor God's calling. The "industry of ministry" becomes my bread and butter instead of the Bread of life. May it never be.

Any vocation can fall prey to the falsity that Jesus is the means to our personal success, but it is particularly sickening to see it in vocational ministers. Christ purposes to revolutionize a heart at the deepest level. Ministry must be about so much more than filling the pews and feeding stomachs. It must be about knowing Jesus and making Him known. When you begin to work for what matters, loving Him becomes living for Him. A God-glorifying life flows out of a satisfied soul.

The Bread of Life

Up to this point in the Gospel of John, Jesus has been showing His might and authority through what He does—miraculous acts of wonder and change. We learn so much about Christ through how He lives His life and what He does. As we notice the way that Jesus lives, we are given an example for how we should live. We know how to live as believers because Jesus lived His life for all to see. But that is not all He offers. Jesus tells us very clearly who He is. Out of His identity, we can gather who we are. *I AM changes who i am.*

In John 6, Jesus makes a statement of identity. As the people gather on the other side of the Sea of Galilee, Jesus begins to tell them about who He is and how that changes who they are. With a gathering crowd around Him, Jesus addresses their hunger: "Do not work for food that spoils, but for food that endures to eternal life, which the Son of Man will give you" (John 6:27). He continues with a statement that would leave the people silent: "I am the bread of life. He who comes to me will never go hungry, and he who believes in me will never be thirsty" (John 6:35). The day before, Jesus had fed the people bread and fish until their stomachs were full. Now that they have come back for more the next day, He tells them about Himself—the Bread that will never leave them hungry. The one born in Bethlehem, which means "house of bread," now declares, "I AM the Bread of Life." No shock to God, just an unveiling and a connecting of the dots for us. The house of bread was the home of the Bread of Life.

Knowing the Bread of Life—knowing Christ—is so much more than a pastor's profession or a good habit. Many people, myself included, will often run after false gods, thinking that they will find something to gratify their desires. Christ calls Himself the Bread of Life because He knows that everything else will fall short of ultimate fulfillment. Believing in something means that you rest everything on it. To believe that Christ is the Bread of Life is to have faith that He is who He says He is. Charles H. Spurgeon once remarked:

> Faith is not a blind thing; for faith begins with knowledge. It is not a speculative thing; for faith believes facts of which it is sure. It is not an unpractical, dreamy thing; for faith trusts, and stakes its destiny upon the truth of revelation. *Faith is believing that Christ is what he is said to be, that he will do what he has promised to do, and expecting this of him.*[3]

A relationship with Jesus sustains us. We will spend our lives looking everywhere else if we do not realize that fulfillment is found in Christ alone. The prophet Isaiah spoke about our hunger for ultimate satisfaction:

Come, all you who are thirsty, come to the waters; and you who
have no money, come, buy and eat! Come, buy wine and milk without money and without cost. Why spend money on what is not
bread, and your labor on what does not satisfy? Listen, listen to
me, and eat what is good, and your soul will delight in the richest
of fare (Isa. 55:1-2).

We often spend money and time on the things that do not gratify and
only leave us wanting more. The things of this world will clamor for our
attention, claiming their ability to fill us and offer us life. In the end, nothing can hold the weight that Christ carries as King. Being satisfied in the
Bread of Life allows for other things to find their rightful place.

In any marriage or close friendship, there is the potential temptation
to make someone else a priority over the Lord. God never intended for
anyone else to play His role in our lives. A spouse will never be able to
withstand the pressure of playing God. Neither will a dear friend. We were
never meant to be God. But so often we look to other people to fulfill the
role that only He can fill. We see this unfold in relationships as we fight
to remember that another person is not everything. Human beings were
created to worship the living God, not each other. Only Christ can satisfy. People can only play their proper role in our lives when we are not depending on them for too much.

When our souls are deeply content in Christ, we begin to live life as
God intended. Our soul longs to savor what is good. Since Christ is perfectly good, we can spend a lifetime enjoying Him. As we begin to believe
that He is enough, we start to live differently. A life that knows what it is
like to be satisfied by the Bread of Life begins to live and serve others for
the glory of God.

Holding On to Hope

Charles L. Allen wrote a book called *God's Psychiatry*. In this book, Allen offers a staggering illustration. After World War II, the number of hungry orphans that filled Europe overwhelmed the Allied troops. The children were
placed in camps where they could be well fed and cared for. Those who
were left in charge of the children were surprised to notice that despite the
excellent care, the children were not sleeping well. They were overcome
with anxiety and fear. A psychologist finally decided upon a solution and

gave each child a piece of bread to hold after he or she was put to bed. The result of the experiment was astonishing.

There was a drastic change in the children's demeanor as they went to bed knowing for certain that they would have food for the next day. From that day forward, the children slept in peace. The orphans of World War II were anxious because they doubted provision. Holding on to a slice of bread as they slept brought peace to their worried souls.[4]

In a world that offers countless false gods that entice our hearts' affections, only one God can truly fulfill. The Bread of Life will never be taken away from us, so we can sleep in peace. Other things will offer only temporary satisfaction. Only the Bread of Life can completely and forever satisfy our souls.

FOR FURTHER REFLECTION AND DISCUSSION

The "I AM" Playlist Pick

Song	Artist	Album
"I AM"	Mark Schultz	*The Best of Mark Schultz*

1. What does it mean to be satisfied in Christ? How is satisfaction in Christ alone a challenge for you?

2. In what are you tempted to seek fulfillment apart from Jesus?

3. How does Jesus' feeding of the 5,000 first and then declaring, "I AM the bread of life" connect?

4. Remember the story of the WWII orphans sleeping with a piece of bread? What false "piece of bread" do you tuck under your pillow each night to live in peace? How can Jesus be trusted for this provision?

Flip the Switch

I am the light of the world. Whoever follows me will never walk in darkness, but will have the light of life.

JOHN 8:12

Seven Miracles of Jesus

1. Turning water into wine (JOHN 2:1-12)
2. Healing the nobleman's son (JOHN 4:46-54)
3. Healing of the lame man (JOHN 5:1-17)
4. Feeding the 5,000 (JOHN 6:1-13)
5. Walking on water (JOHN 6:16-21)
6. Healing the man born blind (JOHN 9:1-41)
7. Raising Lazarus from dead (JOHN 11:1-45)

Seven I AM Statements of Jesus

1. I AM the Bread of Life (JOHN 6:35,48,51)
2. I AM the Light of the World (JOHN 8:12)
3. I AM the Door/Gate (JOHN 10:7)
4. I AM the Good Shepherd (JOHN 10:11-14)
5. I AM the Resurrection and the Life (JOHN 11:25)
6. I AM the Way, the Truth, and the Life (JOHN 14:6)
7. I AM the True Vine (JOHN 15:1)

The morning dew is thick, and you can feel it splashing the top of your shoes as you make your way through the tall grass. Nighttime is still all around. The blanket of darkness in the early hours before dawn is cold and consuming. You can barely see a step ahead in your walk, let alone what lies farther ahead. There are unidentified noises around you—crunching beneath your feet and the sound of scurrying on either side. The darkness is filled with unknown objects that give way to fears and doubt. There is something unsettling about a dark expanse.

As you continue on your dark stroll, hints of dawn begin to stir all around. Echoes of crickets, once loud and present, slowly fade into a quiet whisper. The midnight melody is replaced with a shrill and confident tune of a songbird sitting in a nearby tree. The morning song begins with a note that pierces through the still night air. Soon, there is a response from another tree—a second bird joining in the morning chorus. Looking down at your dew-covered feet, you notice the shape and dim color of the blades of grass. The chill of darkness is confronted by warmth that precedes the coming of a new day. A pause in the walk opens your eyes to take in your surroundings. A morning glow softens the harsh contours of darkness. Slowly, nature begins to awake as faint colors intensify and cover every corner of creation. You find yourself in the middle of a field.

On the horizon there are dark and looming obstacles that are still unclear. They stand tall and threatening. Suddenly, there is a burst of brightness that slips over the top of the towering object. The morning sun peeks over the edge of the mountain range looming in the distance. As light pours over each peak and into each valley, morning begins to take shape. There is not an ounce of creation that the sun doesn't touch. Nothing is safe from its glare, and everything is exposed. Dawn has come!

Light defeats darkness every time. Even the darkest of nights doesn't stand a chance against the inevitable arrival of another day. The night may be filled with unknown fears and confusion, but morning brings new perspective and clarity. Lamentations 3:22-23 tells us, "Because of the LORD's great love we are not consumed, for his compassions never fail. They are new every morning; great is your faithfulness." The Lord's new mercies come in the morning, filling a new day with light and opportunity. Light changes everything. A dark field filled with noises and ominous horizons is transformed by the sunrise breaking through the shadows. Majestic mountains take shape and color fills every vantage point. Morning light has come with incredible brilliance—and everything is different.

Light makes no distinction. Everything must change. It is a new day in our old mountains.

Another Exodus

Throughout the New Testament, Jesus is careful to define His identity. For most of His life on earth, He avoided conversations that would pinpoint Him as the Son of God. His time had not yet come. The Gospel of John highlights three brief years at the end of Jesus' life when He was bold about His eternal kingship. He claimed to be many different things, including the Bread of Life and the satisfaction of our souls. He continues to define Himself now by claiming to be the Light of the World.

When we consider the effect of light on darkness, we can begin to understand what Jesus meant by this bold assertion. If light changes everything, so does Jesus. Darkness does not stand a chance. If light exposes everything, so does Jesus. Nothing is hidden from His sight.

Jesus and His disciples have just attended the Feast of the Tabernacles. This celebration was to commemorate the faithfulness of God to the Israelites during the 40 years in the desert. During those years, the Lord stayed with His people. The book of Exodus describes the time of exile and the Lord's faithful hand during the exit. The Feast of the Tabernacles was a reminder to the people that God has been loyal.

> By day the LORD went ahead of them in a pillar of cloud to guide them on their way and by night in a pillar of fire to give them light, so that they could travel by day or night. Neither the pillar of cloud by day nor the pillar of fire by night left its place in front of the people (Exod. 13:21-22).

Lamps at the feast were lit to represent the pillars of cloud and fire that accompanied the Israelites on their journey. One biblical commentator describes the scene:

> On certain nights of the ceremony, they would light the four huge lamps in the temple's court of women and there would be an exuberant celebration that took place under the light. "Men of piety and good works" danced through the night, holding burning torches in their hands and singing songs and praises. The Levitical orchestras cut loose, and some sources attest that this went on

every night of the Feast of Tabernacles, with the light from the temple area shedding its glow all over Jerusalem.[1]

The people were encouraged to remember God's presence and protection over the people of Israel. The lights were central to the feast, serving as a clear reminder of the exodus into the Promised Land.

As the celebrated glow of remembrance was being extinguished until next year, Jesus made a bold claim that He is the Light of the World. To declare such a statement at the Feast of the Tabernacles is to say, "I am the fulfillment of the Old Testament exodus and Promised Land. I am your protection and leadership." We read in 2 Corinthians 1:20, "For no matter how many promises God has made, they are 'Yes' in Christ. And so through him the 'Amen' is spoken."

The timing of His "I AM" is as weighty as the statement itself. Jesus is the fulfillment and culmination of the lights described through generations of Judaism. This, along with the other six "I AM" statements in John, is massive in proportion. As author and apologist John Blanchard said, Christ's statements are either cosmic or comic.[2]

Light in Scripture

The use of light throughout all of Scripture is staggering. The Father uses the display of light to reveal much about Himself and His Son. Light serves many different purposes in the Bible. Our first understanding of light comes in the very beginning of time. Before anything else is created, God speaks light into existence. The earth was formless and empty, and darkness covered everything. In a simple moment of declaration, God created light. He is the author and creator of life. Day one of creation, as Genesis 1:3-4 states, "And God said, 'Let there be light,' and there was light. God saw that the light was good, and he separated the light from the darkness."

As we saw in the Feast of the Tabernacles, symbolizing Exodus 13, God used light as protection and guidance for His people, the Israelites. During their exile, He never left them, but set a hedge of protection around them in the form of a cloud during the day and a fire at night. God's light was the provision against harm in the desert.

Let's move to the New Testament. The Messiah's arrival and work is the climax of the Scriptures. The Old Testament looks forward to the redemption and arrival of a Savior, and the New Testament celebrates that

He has come and will come again one day. The birth of Jesus Christ, the Son of God, is a spectacular display of God's grace and glory. It is significant then that the arrival of Christ is announced in a flood of light, to the lowest rung of society—shepherds. The shepherds in a nearby field are told of the Messiah's arrival in a humble manger by the radiant glow of a host of angels. Luke 2:8-9 paints the picture. In the dark of night, the glory of the Lord shows so brightly before them that the angels' first words are, "Do not be afraid" (v. 10). Later in the story, wise men from afar are guided to the nativity by the light of a star in the east.

God's Son, creation's Redeemer, came quietly into the world through the womb of a young virgin. And yet, a glorious light announced the magnificent arrival of the King who would change the world. God used light to proclaim His salvation. John 1:4 would later declare that "In him was life, and that life was *the light* of men" (emphasis added). Jesus' life is a guiding light for all who follow Him. We find who we are to be from who Jesus claims to be. *I AM changes who i am.* The Christian is to shine like Christ.

With just these examples, we see that God likes to kick things off with a light show. The creation of the world, the Israelites' exodus from Egypt and the birth of Jesus all begin with light. Therefore, it makes perfect sense that the ministry of the Messiah would not go too far without involving light. However, this time was different. The light was not a glow from heaven, shining to earth. The Light was now on earth desiring to shine in us. Jesus, the Son of God and man, was the Light of the World shining from earth to show us heaven.

We desperately need light. Our world is filled with darkness and evil, and it is easy to feel downtrodden about the godlessness of our culture. The challenge is to remember that Christ's light has already been victorious. The Light has been shining since the first day of creation. The rays reach from eternity past to eternity future, and we are wonderfully caught in the middle. In present tense, we live in victory over darkness and with the light of God in us. In a world of unknowns, He is completely trustworthy.

When England's King George VI was making a statement to the Commonwealth on his Christmas Eve broadcast in 1939, his country was on the brink of World War II. He calmed the peoples' fears by encouraging them to consider light in the midst of darkness:

I said to the man who stood at the gate of the year, "Give me a light that I may tread safely into the unknown." And he replied, "Go out into the darkness and put your hand into the hand of God. That shall be to you better than light and safer than a known way."[3]

God offers us a light in Jesus that is better than full understanding in dark times. With light, the path ahead can be revealed so that we can live it. God gives us more than light for our path. He gives us His Son, who is the Light of the World.

Following the Light of the World Brings Obedience

I am the light of the world. Whoever follows me will never walk in darkness, but will have the light of life (John 8:12).

One of the 12 disciples fell away from following Jesus and sought out an opportunity to betray his friend and teacher. After spending an evening with Jesus and the other disciples, Judas made a decision that ultimately sent Jesus to the cross. That's why you never went to school with anyone named Judas. No parent from the first century on named his or her child after this traitor. His feet are clean from Jesus' act of service to His disciples a few hours earlier, and his stomach is full from the last supper where he held a seat of honor.

However, as night falls, Judas slips away to hand his friend over to the eager, evil officials. "As soon as Judas had taken the bread, he went out. And it was night" (John 13:30). This is a chilling verse if you connect the symbolism of Judas's duplicity with the phrase "And it was night." The Light of the World has been betrayed for 30 pieces of silver, the price of a slave in those days (see Matt. 26:14-15).[4] Nighttime represented more than physical darkness—it represented a spiritual darkness in Judas. Walking in betrayal is contrary to walking in the Light (see Pss. 82:5; 107:10-11; John 13:30).

Following Jesus offers guidance to those who seek it, but it also requires obedience. Those who long to live for the Lord may be tempted to get weighed down with one more spiritual or moral thing to do. But life in Christ is so much more than a checklist of things to do and things to avoid. Christianity offers Someone to follow—Jesus. He is our guiding Light to show the way. As we walk in the Light, the darkness of sin becomes less attractive. Following and believing in Jesus bring sanctification. Our tastes change. With change comes a desire to obey and follow Christ.

Walking in darkness obscures our vision, and things are not as they seem. When we find Jesus to be who He says He is—the Light of the World—our changed hearts compel us to obey. Obedience flows from a heart that has flipped the switch.

Life-changing Light

When you have an encounter with the living Light of God, you can't help but change. A brush with the Creator is unlike anything else. It is life changing. The Bible is filled with stories of rescue—God taking the hearts and lives of His people and radically changing them. Born-again believers can tell a story of rescue. Each story is unique because God's work in our lives is specific to each one of us and is intimately personal. God saves believers one heart at a time. It seems unfair and irrational when He rescues someone who is living a life of sin, deceit and violence. But that is the gospel—a story of redemption that seeks out hearts that are running aggressively away from the Lord. That is the story of Saul, later to be named Paul.

The book of Acts tells the story of a man who dedicated the first part of his life to seeking out and destroying those who claimed to be followers of Christ. His extreme hatred toward Christians led him to use his power and authority granted by Rome to persecute the Church in its earliest stages. His heart was hard and cold toward the Lord—until the light of Christ broke through.

> Meanwhile, Saul was still breathing out murderous threats against the Lord's disciples. He went to the high priest and asked him for letters to the synagogues in Damascus, so that if he found any there who belonged to the Way, whether men or women, he might take them as prisoners to Jerusalem. As he neared Damascus on his journey, suddenly a light from heaven flashed around him. He fell to the ground and heard a voice say to him, "Saul, Saul, why do you persecute me?"
>
> "Who are you, Lord?" Saul asked.
>
> "I am Jesus, whom you are persecuting," he replied. "Now get up and go into the city, and you will be told what you must do" (Acts 9:1-6).

While traveling on the road to Damascus, a light blinded Saul, and his life was never the same. God changed his heart and his name. Saul, who became the apostle Paul, would later be instrumental in the growth and continuation of Christ's church. When the light from heaven blinded his sight for three days, he was left at the mercy of the Lord, who gave him instructions to follow. Walking in the Light brings life. Paul listened and obeyed the Lord's command in his blindness, and his life was completely changed.

His life before this was dark and full of filth hidden under the veneer of religion. But Light expels darkness. Just like the rising sun chases away the darkness of night, walking with Jesus changes things. Like this murderer turned missionary, when you have a confrontation with Light, darkness has no chance of survival. The Light of the World changes lives. Notice again that light is at the beginning of something great. Paul's ministry grew, and his impact for God would spread around the known world. He would write 13 books of the New Testament. *I AM changes who i am* and what i do (see Phil. 2:14-18).

In Houston, we are close enough to the Gulf of Mexico that hurricanes are a usual threat to our city. We are a part of the U.S. shown on the news that makes people in the Midwest wonder, "Why do people live there?" True, it is plenty hot, and dangerous every so often, but it is the place I call home. As I remember Hurricane Ike that blew through Houston, my most vivid recollection is our street littered with downed trees and power lines. The wind and rain of the storm knocked out the electricity all over our neighborhood. Trashed streets and dark houses had replaced lit windows and people walking their dogs only days earlier.

Powerless houses are hot in the day and spooky in the night. In contradiction to the neighborhood's dark homes, one house stood fully lit a block away. Those particular neighbors were wise enough to own a generator. When the sun went down, they were enjoying air conditioning, and the lights were still on. I wish I could say my first reaction was not jealousy. With the power out all over town, their house shone like a city on a hill.

Light in the windows of that home a block away shined like the dawn to our dark living room. It was a beautiful picture of how we should be as believers in Christ. We should stand out and shine, even through a storm. My envy of a generator turned to conviction and prayer that my house would shine with a different Light.

As the storm raged outside, my house sat in darkness. We needed light, and we were hungry for it. A power outage really becomes inconvenient when nighttime falls. You actually begin to feel the darkness and appreciate any glimmer of light. Learning a lesson from my stormy foe Hurricane Ike, I have created an emergency kit to keep close at hand in case a storm breaks through and we lose power again. Among other random items in the box, my kit is 90 percent filled with light—batteries, flashlights, candles and matches!

Remembering how desperate for light we were in the midst of the hurricane also reminded me how light defeats darkness in our lives as well. When the power lines were fixed and the neighborhood lights surged, there was rejoicing in the streets. Whether or not your lights were back on was the conversation in every office and store. Those still in darkness envied those with light, and those with light gratefully celebrated it. Can you see the Christian application in this? Christ, the Light of the World, is the power enabling our grateful hearts to shine, drawing the envy of a dark world.

Following the Light Brings Clarity

Living in the midst of darkness clouds our vision. Even if you are standing in an open field with mountains on the horizon, darkness conceals what is beautiful and confuses our understanding of what is real.

Sunrise is the beginning of a new day. It is also the end of a long, dark night. Since light overpowers any amount of darkness, a new morning is filled with clarity and perspective. When Jesus claimed to be the Light of the World, He was offering Himself as the one who would bring that same clarity and perspective to our lives.

It is not easy to follow the Light of Christ. But in Him, there is a great clarity. We come to know who He is and, therefore, we begin to understand who we are. We read in Psalm 119:105, "Your word is a lamp to my feet, a light for my path." Darkness clouds our vision, but knowing Christ's Word sheds light into our lives and gives us vision for the path ahead. Sin's darkness also limits our view. When we are chasing after desert mirages, we are like a horse with blinders, only fixated on one idol. Christ's light explodes those boundaries and grants us the ability to see more of the great plan He has in store for us. Clarity comes when you are following the Light. It is a worthy battle.

> The eye is the lamp of the body. If your eyes are good, your whole body will be full of light. But if your eyes are bad, your whole body will be full of darkness. If then the light within you is darkness, how great is that darkness! (Matt. 6:22-23).

Victory over the darkness begins with focus. We are either focused on things of light or things of darkness. The choice is ours to choose the lit route of victory instead of the shadows of deception.

Just as our physical eyes have to receive light to process what is before us, the same is true of the eyes of our heart. The light of godly living is far different from the lust of pornography or the lure of evil posing as good. Eyes that take in the darkness of judgment, pride or lust will lead to a life lacking in clarity. Focused people live in the light. They don't dabble in the dark and call it okay. They distinctly realize that true life is a run toward the dawn's light. If you have been in darkness or even in the shade, dig into your Bible and embrace its clarity. The eyes of your heart will find the Light and keep your focus there.

Following Means Believing

Jesus calls Himself the Light of the World right on the heels of rescuing a woman from a life of adultery. Talk about darkness—she was caught *in the act* of adultery. There were no possible excuses or explanation. Standing in the middle of the temple courts, the naked woman finds herself at the mercy of an accusing and hateful crowd. The people look to Jesus to determine her fate. We read His words in John 8:7: "If any one of you is without sin, let him be the first to throw a stone at her."

The crowd departs, one at a time, until Jesus is left alone with the dejected woman, sorrowful over her sin and yet relieved to be alive. Five verses later, Jesus declares, "I am the Light of the World."

Jesus called her to leave her life of darkness and live in the light. In that moment, the woman's life was changed. Perhaps for the first time, she believed in the one who claimed to be the Son of God. Following Jesus begins with believing. In John 12:46, Jesus declares, "I have come into the world as a light, so that no one who believes in me should stay in darkness." The woman could not stay in a life of darkness because she had encountered Jesus, the true Light.

Our culture is quite comfortable with keeping the acts of believing and following separate. It is socially acceptable to say that you believe in Christ but then live a contradictory life. Following has nothing to do with believing, our world says. We are missing the mark entirely. Saying that you believe and yet not following invites confusion for you and those watching you. It is also impossible in God's eyes to believe without following. The two go hand in hand.

The more you follow, the more you will believe. Likewise, the more you believe in something, the more you will follow it. The two build upon each other. Believing in Christ leads us to follow Him. Following always means believing, and believing always means following (see John 14:23-24).

To believe and follow the Light of the World invites us to discover who He is and what He does. When we commit our lives to that practice of understanding who Jesus is and how He lived, we find great clarity for our own lives. It won't always be easy to follow Christ, but we can rest assured there will be clarity. When my heart is an embattled war zone of worries and fears, I must remember that light defeats darkness. Therefore, Jesus' light conquers my clouds, and the hurricane of my heart is calmed by His Light.

Light Your World

We live in a dark world. By God's grace, He has redeemed it, is redeeming it and will redeem it. But we have made a mess of the world He created. And the world will remain dark unless believers are bold enough to shine the Light of Christ. But you can't shine unless Christ has done a work in your life. Move toward the light right where you are—in your family, in your relationships and in your business. The light of Christ penetrates even the darkest holes and hearts of our world. Light pours from Christians who stay connected to the Source. But walking with the Lord requires discipline and desire.

One afternoon, I went for a run in Memorial Park of Houston, about two miles from our church.[5] There is a three-mile trail that circles the park, and it is continually filled with people who fall into all sorts of physically fit categories. Some are ultra-fit, a ripped specimen of the human physique usually wearing a T-shirt that says "Houston Marathon Finisher 1999–2012." Then there are those, like me, who fall into the "trying to stay fit" category. I've got nothing to prove; I just don't want to die before my time. My group wears whatever T-shirt we can find that's clean. And finally, you see people who are well into the "need to be fit" group. Their shirt says something like, "Sponsored by Krispy Kreme Donuts."

I am most encouraged to see one particular group out on the track. It's not the ultra-fit group. Much of their ability is in the genes. It's not my group of "staying fit." We've got it pretty easy as well. I'm most encouraged by the "need to be fit" group. They are stepping up to the challenge. They might not be fit yet, but they are out there. Every meal is a challenge of choice, and every mile a sweaty pain, but they are moving forward.

Gregg Matte

Staying in shape requires some commitment. There are life-changing results for those who commit to healthy habits and exercises. The same can be said for walking with the Lord. Which category explains your spiritual progress? If your life is on the wrong side of the dimmer switch, take a step today toward change. Flip the switch and scatter the dark.

Jesus presents us light for our path and grace to stay on the track. In giving us Himself, Jesus is offering the Light of the World. Valleys and darkness will come, even for those secure in the Lord. Through the darkest hours, deepest despairs and hottest laps on the track there is a Light. And darkness shudders at its impending future demise.

We started this chapter describing a new day in old mountains to paint a canvas of life. Darkness is so familiar to us; it is our native land. But Jesus' declaration in the second "I AM" statement of John leads us to a newly lit land and a different time of day. He is the Light of the World. He is the Light of creation in Genesis, the exodus to the Promised Land and the shining announcement of Christmas for the shepherds. His Light offers the way to the nativity for the wise men and direction for Saul to become Paul. What light does He want to be for you? Is Christ the Creator of something new, the announcement of the Messiah, your leadership along the path, or salvation for your soul?

Like the dawn in the mountains, Jesus wants to illuminate your life. He is confident enough to reveal the dark corners in need of conviction and kind enough to give you a blue sky of support. In response, be wise enough to yield to the sunrise and welcome the Light of the world to your days.

FOR FURTHER REFLECTION AND DISCUSSION

The "I AM" Playlist Pick

Song	Artist	Album
"I AM"	Kirk Franklin	*Hello Fear*

1. What examples in the Old Testament do you recall where light was important? (See the examples in the section "Light in Scripture" if you need help.) How does Jesus' declaration, "I AM the light of the world," fulfill the Old Testament examples?

2. If you could ask Jesus to turn the light on in one area of your life and the world, what would it be? How could God lead you out of the darkness you are in?

3. How does believing in and following Christ turn on the lights in life?

4. Since I AM changes who i am, how can Christ use you to be a light in your world? (Be specific and do it this week.)

See!

I never would have dreamed that yellow is so . . . yellow.
I don't have the words. I am amazed by yellow.

BOB EDEN
(BLIND FOR 51 YEARS)

Seven Miracles of Jesus

1. Turning water into wine (JOHN 2:1-12)
2. Healing the nobleman's son (JOHN 4:46-54)
3. Healing of the lame man (JOHN 5:1-17)
4. Feeding the 5,000 (JOHN 6:1-13)
5. Walking on water (JOHN 6:16-21)
6. Healing the man born blind (JOHN 9:1-41)
7. Raising Lazarus from dead (JOHN 11:1-45)

Seven I AM Statements of Jesus

1. I AM the Bread of Life (JOHN 6:35,48,51)
2. I AM the Light of the World (JOHN 8:12)
3. I AM the Door/Gate (JOHN 10:7)
4. I AM the Good Shepherd (JOHN 10:11-14)
5. I AM the Resurrection and the Life (JOHN 11:25)
6. I AM the Way, the Truth, and the Life (JOHN 14:6)
7. I AM the True Vine (JOHN 15:1)

Martin Jones lay in a hospital bed after the procedure was finished. As the anesthesia wore off, he became aware of his surroundings. His eyes were closed, so everything was dark around him. But that was nothing different from his normal day-to-day life. He was used to the darkness that comes with blindness. The medical procedure had been performed fewer than 50 times before, so there were clearly risks involved. However, the potential rewards far outweighed the unknowns of such a rare surgery. Voices spoke around him and he could tell that his wife of four years was near. He reached toward her and grabbed her hand. She reassured him that the procedure was finished and the doctors were hopeful.

The hours of recovery were long, and Martin was anxious to know if the surgery was a success. Finally, the moment of truth arrived. He sat up in the bed, waiting for the doctors to remove the bandages from his eyes. Twelve years earlier, he sat in a similar hospital bed after an accident at work that cost him his left eye and sight from his right eye. As the doctors carefully removed the covering, Martin saw light. Things were blurry, as though he were looking through water, but they were visible. A dark figure stood before him. He knew immediately that it was her—he was seeing his wife for the first time.

She was wonderful and lovely, he thought. Nothing could be more captivating than regaining sight to finally see his wife. When the doctors initially told him there might be a chance to see, the first person Martin wanted to see was his wife. When his eyes opened and cleared, she was more beautiful than he imagined. After 12 years of darkness, there was light, color and people. The first car that he saw was a Smart Car, and he couldn't stop laughing. To him it looked like a normal car cut in half. He began to see things as though it were the first time. It is hard to appreciate something like sight until it is taken away.

The thought of vision being restored is phenomenal when you consider how far medicine has come. Martin Jones was the beneficiary of new sight after a rare and risky procedure. The doctors astonishingly utilized part of Martin's tooth to create a new lens that turned on the light for him. The procedure sounds obscure but is a picture of today's pioneering world of medicine. Sight is a gift—an extraordinary gift—especially when returned after blindness.[1]

The apostle John includes in his Gospel account an example of miraculous healing that trumps the story of Martin Jones. Doctors utilized incredible technology and research to heal Jones after an accident. But in

John 9, Jesus used a primitive mixture of mud and saliva to heal a man *born* blind. Considering the modern medicine of today, Jesus' method sounds like a far cry from possible. But God is never limited by the boundaries of possible. Our culture has been infiltrated by technology and "latest, greatest" inventions. The danger is that we can become more amazed by technological advancement than with our God for whom nothing is impossible. We are settling for so much less than God wants to offer us. As consumers, we are blown away by the features on the newest iPhone and captivated by the thought of having a 3-D television in our own home.

When it comes to God and the miracles He continues to do, we tend to put Him in a category of hocus-focus, Bible-times magic. God is boring to us because we believe the lie that the world is whispering in our ear. The world would have us believe that God is holding out on us and that His works are no match for the glamour and fame of our culture. But our boredom with God is because we are far too easily pleased. We have settled for fast food when the Lord is offering a banquet fit for royalty. We are blind to the goodness of God.

Our blind spots block our view of who God is and what He is doing in us and in the world today. We miss truths that are so often right in front of us. It is wonderful when God reveals something we have been staring through. As you consider a man born blind but healed by the hand of Jesus, contemplate possible blind spots in your own life. What do you recognize as joyful or even challenging in other Christians that isn't a part of your life?

Obviously, if it is a blind spot it will be difficult for you to recognize it in yourself. It is like looking at your nose without a mirror. (Go ahead and try it.) Occasionally, a glance at someone whose faith you admire will reveal the hidden area. For example, if you are noticing they are journeying abroad on mission trips and you aren't, pack your suitcase and go. Or if they are connected in a Bible study or serving, follow their lead. Growing people will model the path for those desiring to grow.

I remember many of my friends in high school talking about spending time alone with God each morning; or in college, going on a mission trip; or as a single adult, learning to trust God's timing. All of these were blind spots for me then, and tremendous joys now. At this stage of my life, I'm actively discovering things as a parent and leader that I need to deal with. Admit that your vision can become impaired on this journey and ask for the touch of Jesus to open your eyes. Then deal with it.

Where do you need Jesus' touch in your life? It could be in your relationships, in your perspective of life, or in your physical body. Perhaps, like the blind man in John 9, you need the touch of Jesus to begin to see God's will. Jesus still gives sight for life today. As Jesus and His disciples were traveling along the road, a conversation sparked and they passed by a man who was born blind.

His disciples asked him, "Rabbi, who sinned, this man or his parents, that he was born blind?"

"Neither this man nor his parents sinned," said Jesus, "but this happened so that the work of God might be displayed in his life" (John 9:2-3).

Jesus not only responded to the question, but He also solved the problem. Spitting onto the ground, the Son of God made a mixture of mud and saliva and put it on the blind man's eyes. There was no medicine or highly innovative surgery. The simplicity of mud and saliva in the hands of Jesus restored the man to full sight for the first time in his life.

There are times when the Lord exceeds our expectations. We are looking for the answer to a "what if" question and He offers a solution to the "right now" problem. The disciples wanted to understand the cause of blindness; Jesus wanted them to understand the might of His touch.

Talk Less and Do More

In His compassion toward the blind man, Jesus' actions revealed something staggering about the way our words often do not lead to action. When the disciples saw the man born blind, they were intrigued by his condition, but only to discuss probable causes. Jesus saw more than the condition. When He looked at the man sitting nearby, He saw eyes to heal and a heart to change. As believers, we tend to stop with discussion—we talk too much and do too little. If we know the cure (Jesus) for the world's disease (sin), why are we so slow to share it?

The world is desperate for believers who will allow theory discussion to lead their hearts to ministry action. We talk about missions and even read about celebrities who give to Third World countries and adopt orphaned children. In our talk and fascination with what is going on in other parts of the world, we have lost the vision for what it means to actually go.

There is risk involved in moving ministry into action. As a result, we stay in the comfort zone of discussion.

Even when discussing our salvation through Christ, and faith in Him, it is safer to *talk* about living for the Lord as opposed to actually living for Him. As we think about and discuss the gift of salvation, do we live like we have life in Christ? Our Christianity can so easily become doctrinal conversation instead of life transformation. To debate theology with believers is not as profitable as offering Jesus to unbelievers. Don't misunderstand me. I'm all for iron sharpening iron in biblical debates, but not at the expense of ministry (see Prov. 27:17; 1 Cor. 8:1). Go ahead and sharpen the sword of great orthodoxy, then put it to use instead of back into the sheath. Orthodoxy (right thinking) should always lead to orthopraxy (right living).

The same is true with our faith. It is one thing to proclaim a faith in a God who is loving and good. It is quite another thing to live with feet planted in the Lord's goodness even when a storm blows all around, challenging our faith.

Our comfort with talking has gotten in the way of God-glorifying living. Like the disciples, we see a need and have a theoretical discussion without compassionate action. It is much easier to discuss homelessness and human trafficking than to get into the messy work of changing lives. But Jesus gets His hands dirty with mud, saliva and sin. He calls us to action instead of remaining in the spiritualized avoidance of debating the issue. Entering into such a mess of evil is inconvenient and dangerous. But when God's people see the mess through His eyes, they see the redemption only He can give.

Our church is partnered with one particular ministry that sees children in harmful situations through the eyes of Jesus and takes action. As Our Own is a ministry that fights child trafficking in India, where girls as young as seven years old are exploited in the sex industry. They rescue these girls and care for them their entire lives "as their own" children.

Through God's eyes, As Our Own strives to see these girls as daughters. Such a perspective rescued three-year-old Shanti (pseudonym) from the red-light district, where she was born. Her mom was enslaved in prostitution and dying of disease from this terrible existence. Shanti's future was sure to mirror her mother's. Within a few years, she would be sold to face brutalization by 20 to 30 clients a day. What utter darkness! The As Our Own staff could not allow this to happen to someone they saw as a daughter. By God's grace, Shanti was rescued.

The challenge did not end there, however. The ministry staff understood the messiness that Shanti came from. They patiently and lovingly helped her work through the damage. They nurtured Shanti in a safe environment where she experienced Christ's authentic love.

Today, no one would guess Shanti's beginnings. She remembers life in the district, but it doesn't define her. Her identity is not a girl born in the brothel to a sex slave, nor is it only as a daughter of the As Our Own family, which she dearly loves. God forged a deeper transformation, giving her a strong sense of identity as *His* daughter. As Our Own knows this is the rescue only God can orchestrate—but He calls us to a vital role in this redemptive process. The result is that Shanti is now happily married to a pastor, working alongside him to bring hope to others who are living broken lives.

No matter how messy things are, God is able to rescue little ones like Shanti out of it. But the critical point is that the choice to get out does not belong to a three-year-old. It belongs to the people of God. When His people walk in obedience, He transforms the life headed for destruction into a life filled with light.[2]

So much of our media today is dedicated to talking about sin but doing nothing about it. At any point of the year, there are rallies, protests, and blog posts about the failing efforts of government. We talk politics and scandalous behavior. But how often do we take time to pray for our leaders? Are we praying for ministries like As Our Own? God is not centered on debate and discussion; He is most interested in ministry action. Jesus saw the blind man, saw the desperate need for healing, and did something radical. With the chatter of theory discussion behind Him, Jesus moved toward the man and changed his life by restoring his sight.

Be encouraged: you have moved to action without knowing it. A portion of the proceeds from this book will go to support the ministry of As Our Own. You have helped to rescue through your reading.

Taking Action

Jesus' time on earth was short-lived, but His life fulfilled everything He came to accomplish. His life was not a day too long or a day too short. In perfect timing, Jesus accomplished the Father's will. Time mattered to Jesus. He knew that His days were numbered, so He didn't waste time. He stepped forward in action and set an example for us to live out the plan of God.

As is to be expected, God is doing something so much bigger than performing a miraculous sign for all to see. The healing of the blind man was a declaration by Jesus that He is the Son of God. His action in healing blindness with a mixture of mud and saliva, similar to forming man from the dust (see Gen. 2:7), pointed to the fact that He is the Creator. Prophets and Old Testament accounts prophesized the coming Savior and indicated that He would be known through the healing of eyes:

The LORD said to him, "Who gave man his mouth? Who makes him deaf or mute? Who gives him sight or makes him blind? Is it not I, the LORD?" (Exod. 4:11).

He upholds the cause of the oppressed and gives food to the hungry. The LORD sets prisoners free, the LORD gives sight to the blind, the LORD lifts up those who are bowed down, the LORD loves the righteous (Ps. 146:7-8).

In that day the deaf will hear the words of the scroll, and out of gloom and darkness the eyes of the blind will see (Isa. 29:18).

Then will the eyes of the blind be opened and the ears of the deaf unstopped. Then will the lame leap like a deer, and the mute tongue shout for joy (Isa. 35:5-6).

The Gospel of John points to each one of these references to the coming Messiah. As chapter 9 unfolds, and the blind man is given sight, we know that Jesus is the one who has fulfilled the prophecies of the Old Testament. Jesus steps forward into action and declares Himself to be the promised one they had been waiting for.

As the disciples walk side by side with their teacher and Savior, they have questions about this miracle, and they patiently wait for an answer. Mature people ask a question and then wait for an answer. But it's risky to wait for an answer; that's why we usually keep talking. The disciples, however, found the question worth the risk. Who sinned in this situation—the blind man or his parents? Jesus responds in a way that gives credit only to the Father: "But this happened so that the work of God might be displayed in his life" (John 9:3). God gets the glory, even in blindness.

Who sinned in this situation—the blind man or his parents? We are prone to shift blame to others, and we like for things to have a clear reason. It makes sense to the disciples that a man's blindness is the result of sin—either his own or his parents'. The reality is that the Lord uses circumstances in our lives to bring Him glory. Some illnesses and conditions have nothing to do with determining fault. God is doing something so much bigger. He is interested in using situations in our lives to bring Him glory. There may be something in your life that is hard or uncomfortable that the Lord is using to glorify His name. It's not about you or something that you did. It is about God and what He is doing in you.

Intended for Glory

Every believer's life in Christ is intended to bring God glory (see 2 Thess. 2:13-15). This means that in health and sickness, in joy and sorrow, in prosperity and need, the Lord will use all things to show His strength. It seems more natural that God would use wonderful things in our lives for His glory since we are filled with praise and thanksgiving. Offering thanks to God honors Him. But He is also just as present and glory seeking when things are tough. During the darkest hours of the night, when things are difficult and even sorrowful, the Lord is at work (see Jas. 1:2-4). Those who cling to the Lord through seasons of blindness show Christ's strength to be sufficient.

Consider men and women who have given their lives for the sake and spread of the gospel. Jim Elliot was an evangelical missionary in Ecuador. Along with four others, Jim spent time attempting to share the gospel with the Waodani people. He was killed in his efforts, in 1956, when he was 28 years old. Though Jim's life was brief, his impact and legacy continue to be an incredible inspiration to Christians. God was glorified in the suffering of Jim Elliot. Decades later, Elliot's journal entries encourage those who long to live a brave and bold life for Christ.

In 1949, Elliot wrote these words in his journal about his missionary experience: "He is no fool who gives what he cannot keep to gain that which he cannot lose." He saw the mission field as so much more than a career or philanthropic act. The spread of the gospel was everything to him. It was even worth the sacrifice of his life. God was beautifully glorified in Jim Elliot, who saw suffering, even death, as a worthy price to make Jesus known.

The presence of suffering and illness is evidence of the broken world we live in. This side of heaven, we can be sure that we will all taste human suffering. Perhaps it will not look like the persecution Jim Elliot faced or the situation of the man born blind, but in some fashion we can all relate to the pain of suffering. Commentators on John 9 have discussed the mystery of suffering and why hurt comes to those who don't seem to deserve it. J. M. Boice writes:

> There are no pat answers to the question of human suffering. Consequently, we cannot say, as some do, that it is the right of every believer to be healthy. Or that suffering is always the direct result of personal sin: In some cases, suffering is corrective. It is given in order to get us back on the path that God has chosen for us. In other cases, it is constructive. It is given to build character. In still other cases, as here, it is given solely that God might receive glory.[3]

Sometimes suffering does not make any sense to us; but we can have confidence that God will redeem the hurt and pain of this world. Part of His redemption right now is to use suffering to do something better than we expected.

We can see redemption in the story of the blind man of John 9, whose eyes Jesus touches with mud and saliva. For the first time in his life, the man was able to see. However, even if this man had not been healed, he still could have been used for God's glory. God intended to glorify Himself through the healing of the blind man. But just as easily, He could have received glory if the man remained blind. God will use you exactly as you are. You don't have to be healthy and strong to be used by God for great things.

When a loved one is sick, we pray for God's merciful healing. Certainly a miraculous recovery would make the Lord look great. Healing does bring God glory and it is acceptable to pray for a cure. Because of Jesus, we should approach the throne of grace with confidence, knowing that our prayers reach the heart of God. However, healing is not the only way that God is glorified. Sometimes, healing on our terms doesn't happen. The blind remain blind and the sick remain sick. Is God not big enough to heal? Of course He is. But He is not limited to our definition of glory. Sometimes the most spectacular display of God's glory is seen when the blind man stays blind.

The Blind Leading the . . . Seeing

I had the privilege of going on a mission trip to Venezuela. Our purpose was simple—we went door to door, talking about Jesus. I met a man there who changed my perspective on healing. John was my assigned translator, and he was completely blind. He walked by my side, holding on to my arm as we walked through impoverished neighborhoods. At the end of a street, I said, "John, there is a curb right here." He laughed and replied, "Gregg, I know that. I count how many steps are in a block so I know exactly where the curbs are." I was amazed as I watched him navigate life, without sight, with such confidence.

One afternoon, we came across a field of kids playing baseball. The field was the consolidation of a few backyards with a goat tied to a post in right field and a flattened milk jug for second base. Our group of college students jumped in with them. At one point, we called the kids together and they huddled around John. Using a felt board and fluent Spanish, he explained the gospel to the listening children. Not one piece was out of place. He led countless children to Christ, completely blind. I was amazed at his ability to communicate with such effectiveness and joy.

As the end of our mission trip drew near, I found myself jealous of John's ability to see things that I didn't see. I was the blind one. Without eyesight, John saw things with his heart. His physical blindness absolutely glorified the Lord.

Think about healing in light of circumstances like John's. God can use our illnesses and still receive great glory. He can use healing in the same way. Regardless of whether healing comes or ailments remain, we must continue the work of the Lord with great faith.

Jesus reminds us that the work is not done: "As long as it is day, we must do the work of him who sent me. Night is coming, when no one can work. While I am in the world, I am the light of the world" (John 9:4-5). While it is day, we must get to work on the things to which the Lord has called us. *Carpe diem*—seize the day! God is glorified most in us when we surrender ourselves to the work of His hands. My friend John made Jesus look great. He joyfully accepted his blindness as an opportunity to see in new ways. Through blindness, John saw God at work.

It's All About the Messiah, Not Methods

Restoring sight today is a complex work of modern medicine. So when we consider the unadorned method that Jesus used, it seems impossible. Jesus knelt down and spit into the dirt. He rose again with a mixture of mud and saliva on His fingers. It was that simple. There was nothing special about the dirt. Reaching over to the man, Jesus healed his sight. Life from dirt— a beautiful reminder of when the Creator made man from dirt: "The LORD God formed the man from the dust of the ground" (Gen. 2:7). In John 9, the Lord is using dirt again to bring life, to show that Jesus is the Creator.

Throughout the New Testament, Jesus does miraculous works of healing. Every story has a different method. Healing never happens the same way twice. In Matthew 9, Jesus touches the two blind men and they are healed—touch heals. In Mark 8, He spits on a man's eyes and lays hands on him—saliva heals. In Luke 18, Jesus simply speaks and a blind beggar is healed—words heal. The method of healing changes, but the presence of the Messiah is consistent.

Healing happens in God's perfect timing and according to the authority of His Word. God displays His might in many ways. Among them, healing shows God's incredible power. When our eyes are on the Messiah, we move away from theories and start noticing miracles. The Lord longs for His children to know His heart and then see His ways. So often we get distracted by the methods and miss the Messiah.

The Lord knows our human tendency to focus on a method and miss Him. He understands that our hearts are wayward; He heals in different ways so that our eyes are on Him and not on anything else. As the disciples walked with Jesus from town to town, methods of healing quickly fell to the background as they rested their attention on the one at work.

Every day life is different across countries, cultures and even across the street. Parenting methods differ from home to home. We often fall into the trap of judging the way some parents choose to raise their children. The temptation is to focus on the method and think that one way is right and another way is wrong. Let me interject one common principle: remember that you—not the child—are the parent. In many of today's homes, children are in charge. We worship them instead of raising them. An Englishman once observed, "The thing that impresses me most about America is the way parents obey their children."[4] Two Christian families could look as different as night and day. The important factor is that both families are focused on the Lord. Methods will look different even if our eyes are set on the same goal.

The same thing can be said of churches. It is culturally acceptable in our culture for churches to split over certain arguments. Some are valid disagreements about issues that should be fought for. However, many church splits happen as a result of preference. Some prefer contemporary worship in jeans. Others prefer traditional worship in suit and tie. Some insist on meeting in a church building with a sanctuary and steeple. Others prefer the comfort of a home or rented space. When we get caught up in methodology, we miss the Messiah. A church that is grounded in God's Word and focused on Christ as Savior brings glory to God. Minor differences don't matter.

As a pastor, I notice that most church problems are centered on personal preferences and not theological impasses. Preference is important; you should like your church. But remember that Sunday is not about you. It is about God. By the same token, parenting is not about us either. It is also about God. So, as a parent, a believer in Christ, or a man born blind, are your eyes on the healing Messiah? That's what matters.

Different methods, but the same Messiah.

A Changed Vision Brings a Changed Life

Imagine the blind man the morning before Jesus rolled into town. His day was dark, as usual, and he could not imagine the miracle that would soon take place. He was at the mercy of others for his survival and would beg for food and drink. It was the only livelihood he knew. It only makes sense that when the man's vision was changed, his life was changed as well. Vision changes everything. After a treatment of mud and saliva, the man became a former beggar and a former blind man. He had a past, but now he was leaving it behind and beginning his future. His encounter with Jesus broke through his blindness and began a work on his heart. The man who was *formerly* a beggar now stood by the side of the road with new eyes. A meeting with the Creator will radically change you. You can't remain the same. If you are walking with God, there will be a lot of "past tense" in your life that you leave behind you.

The problem comes when our past tense is still present. This is confusing to those who are watching our walk with Christ. Remember, people find out who Jesus is by watching the lives of those who proclaim Him as Savior. Perhaps no one is asking about your faith or the things you used to do before you came to Christ because there is no past tense.

There should be a big portion of past tense for Christians. Formerly, you struggled with jealousy; now you have a heart that is softening and growing in the Lord. You are beginning to see others as your ministry, not your adversaries. Formerly, you lived in the personal prison of anxiety. But that is no longer true, because you have laid down the oars of your Barbie boat. Or perhaps you are now living with a reckless abandonment as you boldly share the gospel with others. The work of God is evident in your life because you formerly practiced a safe and quiet life. You were blind and now you can see.

When human and Holy collide, there is always a past tense for the human. Change happens because Jesus loves us enough to never let us stay the same. He longs to change us so that we look more like Him. When we are free from the things that formerly held us captive, there is a lot of security in the present. We can trace God's faithful hand in the past, and so we begin to rest in Him in the present. And when there is a lot of security in the present, we will find hope and faith while moving into the future. Change happens from the inside out. God's work in our hearts should alter the pattern of our lives (see Eph. 1:18-21; Col. 1:29).

A+B+C = The Work of God

The blind man had a run-in with Jesus. Suddenly, his life had a past. He was formerly blind, but now he could see. God is never defined by a formula, but it is interesting to see the work of His hands. A combination of inward change and past tense points us toward the work of God. In Christ we are a new creation (see 2 Cor. 5:17). There is a heart change that cannot be denied. And when change happens, there is a past to compare with the present, and also a hopeful future.

The sightless man had probably been sitting in the same dirt that Jesus spit into for many years. Of all people, he knew there was nothing special about that dirt. When his sight was restored, it was all about the Messiah. The work of God cannot be constrained to the methods and rules that we desire in order to make sense of Him. Our understanding cannot fathom His ways or His heart for people. God's work happens so that we may see and believe. He wants to heal us of our blind spots so that we can see more facets of the diamond named Jesus.

Like Martin Jones, whose story was at the beginning of this chapter, Bob Eden was blind. He had nothing to rely on apart from smells and sounds for all of his 51 years. His world was a flat darkness. When a skilled surgeon performed a highly complicated surgery, his eyes were opened to the colorful world around him. Here's how Bob describes his new view:

I never would have dreamed that yellow is so . . . yellow. I don't have the words. I am amazed by yellow. But red is my favorite color. I just can't believe red! I can see the shape of the moon—and there is nothing better than seeing a jet plane flying across the sky, leaving a vapor trail. And, of course, there are the sunrises and sunsets. And at night, I look at the stars in the sky and the flashing light. You could never know how wonderful everything is.[5]

New sight changes everything. It gives the blind man gratitude for the past and joy in the present. Jesus is capable of turning our lives around and giving us new hearts and eyes for Him. What He does changes who we are. Formerly, colors seemed dull. When Jesus comes, our lives explode with brilliant color.

"I would have never dreamed yellow is so . . . yellow."

Jesus heard that they had thrown the blind man out, and when he found him, he said, "Do you believe in the Son of Man?" "Who is he, sir?" the man asked. "Tell me so that I may believe in him." Jesus said, "You have now seen him; in fact, he is the one speaking with you." Then the man said, "Lord, I believe," and he worshiped him (John 9:35-38).

FOR FURTHER REFLECTION AND DISCUSSION

The "I AM" Playlist Pick

Song	Artist	Album
"Jesus Messiah"	Chris Tomlin	Hello Love

1. Have you known anyone who is blind? What did you learn from this person?

2. Why was it significant that the man in John 9 was born blind and Jesus gave him sight?

3. What are some blind spots that God is revealing in your life?

4. Are there any places where you are talking too much and doing too little?

Some Sheep and a Gate

Therefore Jesus said again, "I tell you the truth, I am the gate for the sheep."
JOHN 10:7

Seven Miracles of Jesus

1. Turning water into wine (JOHN 2:1-12)
2. Healing the nobleman's son (JOHN 4:46-54)
3. Healing of the lame man (JOHN 5:1-17)
4. Feeding the 5,000 (JOHN 6:1-13)
5. Walking on water (JOHN 6:16-21)
6. Healing the man born blind (JOHN 9:1-41)
7. Raising Lazarus from dead (JOHN 11:1-45)

Seven I AM Statements of Jesus

1. I AM the Bread of Life (JOHN 6:35,48,51)
2. I AM the Light of the World (JOHN 8:12)
3. I AM the Door/Gate (JOHN 10:7)
4. I AM the Good Shepherd (JOHN 10:11-14)
5. I AM the Resurrection and the Life (JOHN 11:25)
6. I AM the Way, the Truth, and the Life (JOHN 14:6)
7. I AM the True Vine (JOHN 15:1)

In the middle of the night a call rang out across the pasture. It wasn't a cry for help or a warning; it was a specific call intended for one purpose. As the sound traveled across the sleepy plain, the quiet flock jolted awake in unison. The sound was familiar to them—they knew its source and significance. Without pause, the sheep rallied together and took off in the direction of the call. Weapons were no hindrance to them as they scurried past the soldiers in pursuit of the call that was certain to be their master's. The Turkish soldiers of World War I were no match for the shepherds of Jerusalem.

While war raged around Europe, the Turkish soldiers had decided to plunder the unsuspecting Jerusalem shepherds. They made their move in the darkest hours of the night and took the sheep by force. The shepherds, bewildered by the strength of the soldiers' numbers and their daunting arsenal, had no other choice but to relinquish their flocks to the thieves. But they knew they ultimately held the upper hand.

Once the sheep were under the watchful guard of the Turkish soldiers, the shepherds enlisted their greatest weapon to retrieve their lost sheep: a call. The hostage situation was no match for the specific call of a shepherd to his sheep. Though sheep are not known for their intelligence, they know the call of their shepherd. And these sheep came running—past the guards, past the guns and out of captivity. The shepherd's call rang out over all other noises and defeated any other threats. Sheep know the voice of their shepherd, and they follow.

A Hostage Situation

As believers, we bear more similarity to sheep than we'd like to admit. So often, the enemy and his ploys hold us hostage. We are led astray by the things that Satan offers with the same kind of convincing argument he used on Eve. And yet, the powerful voice of our Shepherd speaks. We desperately need to hear from the Shepherd, for His voice calls us out of captivity and into relationship with Him.

By nature, sheep are very simple creatures. They respond best to the voice that cares for them and offers protection. The shepherd is the primary caregiver of his flock. He provides everything his flock needs for life, including food, protection and guidance. When danger is on the horizon, the shepherd stands in front of his sheep, blocking the intruder. He spends his days and sleepless nights watching over the flock. The sheep are his livelihood and his most important charge of responsibility. A shepherd would lay down his life for one of his sheep threatened by danger.

As we understand the role of a shepherd, it is wonderful to hear Jesus' claims to be the Gate and the Shepherd of the sheep (see John 10). The chapter begins right on the heels of Jesus' healing of a blind man. As He continues in conversation with His disciples and the surrounding crowd, the Lord makes a bold claim:

> Therefore Jesus said again, "I tell you the truth, *I am the gate for the sheep.* All who ever came before me were thieves and robbers, but the sheep did not listen to them. I am the gate; whoever enters through me will be saved. He will come in and go out, and find pasture. The thief comes only to steal and kill and destroy; I have come that they may have life, and have it to the full" (John 10:7-10, emphasis added).

We discover who we are when we hear who Jesus says He is. He is the Gate; we are the sheep. So it is noteworthy to us that Jesus calls Himself the Gate for the sheep. As Jesus explains this to the listening crowd, it must have hit home for them. Society in the time of Jesus was mostly agrarian—farmers and shepherds. The people understood the terminology Jesus was using, because shepherding was a profession their culture thrived on. Jesus' claim as the Gate for the sheep held great weight to the people of His time. Even in our modern culture today, knowing that Jesus is the Gate is life changing.

Speaking and Leading Shepherd

Jesus is speaking to the people on their level in John 10. They listen because He is using an illustration that makes complete sense to them: the love of a shepherd for his sheep. Furthermore, He claims to be the Gate, and then the Shepherd. From their level of understanding, the people know that a gate is used as protection for the sheep from any outside invaders. Stationed in the middle of the gate is a watchful shepherd. Nothing can get in or out without his permission.

Sheep respond to the voice of the shepherd without hesitation. They know his voice intimately and follow his guidance. To know the voice of the shepherd changes everything for sheep. Although it is a humbling comparison, we are sheep as well. Like sheep, when we know the Lord's voice, we can discern the path He has for us. Knowing the sound of His voice always precedes discerning His path. It is impossible to walk in the Lord's path for us if we do not personally know His voice. Yet, as we identify the voice of the Lord in our lives, there is an overwhelming confidence found in walking the road ahead. Understanding the path comes with understanding the heart of our Shepherd.

For those of us who have a relationship with the Lord, it is a constant fight to discern His voice. Our culture shouts lies and sells us counterfeits that mimic life while only offering death. Like sheep, we are prone to wander away from God. At times, it is intentional and, at other times, it is because we don't know any better. That is exactly why Jesus came to earth. Lost in our sin, we knew no way out. Jesus came as the Gate for His sheep, and through Him, we have everlasting life.

The fight to keep walking with Jesus looks different with each season as we grow in the Lord. As a young man, I wanted so desperately to fight for my walk with the Lord. With so many choices before me, I found that the best way to think about Jesus during the day was to place a reminder right in front of my eyes. From an early age, I always enjoyed wearing a baseball cap. In fact, I wore one so often growing up that my mom was afraid I would never grow hair on the top of my head. I like wearing a hat, and so it made sense to me to put a reminder right there. On the inside bill of my hats, I would write the reference of a Bible verse that continues to be a great encouragement to me: "Today, if you hear his voice, do not harden your hearts" (Heb. 3:15).[1] I needed that reminder every single day. As I looked up into the bill of my hat, I would mutter that verse to myself. The Lord used that verse in my life in a powerful way. Like a sheep, I wanted to respond to the voice of the Shepherd and not harden my heart.

Blah, Blah, Blah . . . Turn Down the Noise

Think of the last time you experienced complete silence. It has probably been awhile. Even now as you read, you may be surrounded by people and, as a result, noise. People are a noisy brood, but God seems to prefer whispers. Yes, we live in a noisy world. I'll take it a step further. We are addicted to noise and we fear silence. It's the norm to wear headphones when we travel and have the TV on when we are home. To a harmful degree, we like to feel connected to the world we are living in. What if you missed a day of the news? Can you even remember the "News Alert" from last week? Noise, noise, noise is shepherding us.

The things, people and the culture you listen to will lead you. If you listen to Hollywood, you'll be tempted to feel ugly or poor. If you listen to the doom and gloom of the news, you'll fear that the sky is falling. Listen to culture and you'll live for fashionable fads instead of lasting truth. Your ear determines who is your shepherd. Many of us, including myself, have slowly and unknowingly chosen to follow relentless shepherds who are driving us instead of leading us.

In order to mute the cultural shepherds and tune in to the Shepherd of life, we have to move into the correct field. We cultivate the sound of His voice, and He desires us to choose it, call for it and yearn for it. His voice is distinct. Those who are too busy with life risk not hearing it at all. The Good Shepherd speaks to the listener who has pushed away the fattening sound of culture and chosen to feast on spiritually fit food.

I'm not trying to build a case for monasticism or a legalistic disconnect from life. But I do encourage you to acknowledge your false shepherds and embrace your True Shepherd. So ask yourself, *Who do I regularly listen to?* Think larger than a person; think about a perspective of life. Who has your ear for defining what life is about? A worldly culture, or Christ? Cultivate a listening spiritual ear to His voice and let who He is change who you are becoming. These changes may seem to come slowly, so it's good to remember that His time is set on eternity. Fight to live for, listen to and love the good Shepherd—not just an imitation. Find true beauty, wealth and principles to live in the contraflow lane of Christ.

Every believer's fight to know the Lord's voice looks different. Maybe my hat trick would be a good method for you. But perhaps all of us can identify with the fight against thinking that hearing from God is for someone else. The temptation is to reserve that privilege for the "Navy Seals of Christianity"—those who are pastors, teachers or spiritual mentors. We convince ourselves that only the "truly righteous people" hear from the Lord, not the commoners like ourselves. However, the truth of the gospel throughout the Scriptures is that the Lord wants to speak directly to you. The Holy Spirit indwells every believer in Christ to the same degree. One saint doesn't have more of the Spirit than another. Billy Graham and the teenager saved at camp this year have the same power resting in their souls—the power that raised Christ from the grave. Let that settle in. In Ephesians 1:18-20, Paul states:

I pray also that the eyes of your heart may be enlightened in order that you may know the hope to which he has called you . . . his incomparably great power for us who believe. That power is like the working of his mighty strength, which he exerted in Christ when he raised him from the dead.

The voice is the Holy Spirit. The reason we don't hear His words at times is because of our failure to listen, not His lack of speaking. As the earthly shepherd calls to his flock, so the Lord, our Shepherd, longs to speak to His sheep through the Spirit within us.

If we believe that the Lord can speak directly to those who are listening for His voice, we will begin to see the incredible ways that He is at work. "If anyone has ears to hear, let him hear" (Mark 4:23; see also Mark 4:9; Matt. 11:15). There will be moments in life when God's voice is as clear as a bell. Then there will be times when His voice is muffled or even seemingly silent. Understanding how He speaks is essential to our walk with the Lord. And determining the voice of the Lord and how He speaks is the discerning work of a lifetime.

A sure way to hear His voice is by knowing God's written Word, the Bible. God's Word is living and active and the surest guide for how we are to live as believers in Christ (see Heb. 4:12). The Bible also tells the history of redemption—a story of the patient love of God for a people who had gone astray. God's Word not only tells us where we have been as sinners, but it gives us hope for where we are going as those who trust in Christ for salvation.

Desirous Discipline

Knowing God's Word comes down to what I call "desirous discipline." God has placed new desires in your heart through Christ and the indwelling of the Holy Spirit. Your desire is no longer for sin and cheap substitutes. Your tastes are more distinct; your deepest inner desires are for righteous living and Christ Himself. Sinful pursuits will never satisfy a Christian heart. You have been remade, born again for holiness and purity. That's why sin brings an ache to the believer's belly and regret to his heart. You are different now, because of the cross. The gate, as we will see further in the chapter, has swung wide open.

Therefore, you long to hear His voice and know His Word. Though it may not feel like it, as a believer in Christ, your deepest desire is to know

Him more. The problem is the clatter and chatter of other "noises" that stack up against that desire. The things that are set right before you are bills, tasks, responsibilities and what's for dinner. The urgent swallows the important. But as we begin to scrape through the mundane, we find there is a heart beating for and longing toward the streets of heaven. It is your deepest desire, even if it is not your strongest at the time. Let that desire loose.

"Discipline" is defined as "training to ensure proper behavior."[2] For our context, I would like to change it to "training to ensure proper listening." If we hear well, we will live well. Training our ears to hear the Shepherd's call is a recalibration that requires practice. Remember, this training is far from a chore. This is not the part of the book where I preach that listening to God is like eating your vegetables. "Eat your Brussels sprouts; they're good for you." Instead, I hope that you realize that your deepest spiritual desire is to know Him. Your flesh has been crucified and your spirit has been made alive (see Gal. 2:20).

From that place come the discipline and the training to listen properly. Through our deep desires, we open up the pages of the Bible each day.[3] Desirous discipline is different from duty. It is a "want to" instead of a "have to" mentality. Our desire is not an excuse for ambiguity without action. Discipline means writing a verse in your ball cap, memorizing a Scripture verse written on a note card or working through a book of the Bible in a study group or on your own. Discipline is the part of life that gets things done.

Spending time reading the Bible is essential for anyone who wants to live a life for the Lord. God speaks most clearly through His written Word. He will not step over the Bible to speak to us. As we understand the depths of what He has written in the Bible, we come to know the Lord Himself. Like most things that require discipline, sometimes it doesn't come easily. We know that we need God's Word, but sometimes we lack the discipline to read and study. Pray to uncover the desirous discipline that resides in your new heart. God is gracious to respond to those who long to know Him more by cutting through the noise to hear His holy whisper.

Here are a few examples of my personal desirous discipline at work. Each morning, I set the alarm to go off early enough to read my Bible. Usually, I read a book of the Bible several times in a row by reading one chapter a day. Right now, I'm reading through the 14 chapters of Hosea. By looking at a chapter or two a day, I've read Hosea two or three times now.

Then when I feel like I have understood the book and sense the Shepherd's call, I move on to a new biblical field to graze.

My desire to give monetarily to the church is coupled with the discipline of automatic withdrawal. Every two weeks, my bank automatically deducts a percentage of my income to send to the church. It is the best money spent each month. It's more rewarding than the electric bill or credit card payment.

Every month, on the second Thursday, I fast and pray. I had read numerous times about fasting but could never find the time. Now I use the time I would have spent eating to pray, and with every hunger pang, I say, "Lord, I'm doing without to focus on You doing something within."

In discipline to train myself "to properly listen," I put it on the calendar and it happens. Personally, I became weary of my good intentions resulting in sporadic actions. I didn't want my Christian life to be the predictable road of knowing a ton and applying an ounce. Maybe you are in the same place. If that's the case, do something about it. In His strength, make a change. You can live differently. Don't harden your heart; listen instead.

Spending time with God, giving financially and fasting are examples of "desirous disciplines." They require effort and planning, but the blessings far outweigh the cost. By positioning yourself in the fields of obedience, you will hear His voice. We don't enact discipline out of a sense of "ought," but out of our truest desire. The Shepherd has given us spiritual connectors to help us hear His voice. By prioritizing connectors like Bible study, prayer and obedience, we open our ears to hear His Spirit's whisper.

Discerning Ear

Jesus' sacrifice on the cross brought salvation to undeserving people. While He took away our sin, He also left us with the Holy Spirit. The Holy Spirit dwells within the hearts of those who trust in Jesus Christ as Savior. What an amazing thought! The God the universe cannot contain dwells within me. Augustine describes us as "but a particle of Thy creation."[4] Yet this little particle of creation, all five-feet-eight-inches of me, contains the Holy Spirit of the Creator. It is mind-blowing and ear opening, all at the same time. The Shepherd leads me. Yet, even more grand than that—His Spirit lives in me.

When you hear His voice speaking to you, that is the Holy Spirit leading you as a shepherd leads his sheep. Walking with the Holy Spirit requires discernment. We must learn to decipher God's voice. The difficult part is that there are competing, noisy voices, begging for our attention. It is helpful to know how to distinguish the Spirit's voice from any other.

Even though Christ has already defeated Satan, Satan clamors for our attention. As we learn to discern the Shepherd's voice, we can remember that there are some things the devil will never tell us to do. For example, Satan will never tell us to share our faith, give of our resources, walk in greater holiness or make peace with someone. He views tempting toward obedience or reconciliation as basically throwing an interception to God's team. Satan will never tell you to share the truth of Jesus.

To the contrary, obedience, love and reconciliation come from the voice of the Holy Spirit. When you hear that voice, follow it. Simply put, the Good Shepherd speaks truth and leads us to fertile fields. The enemy speaks lies and leads us to barren wastelands. Listen for life, and choose it. When you hear a whisper in your heart, ask if it is truth or a lie; if it's life giving or defeating. Then choose the truth and the life, and you are on your way to delighting in your Shepherd.

We also hear God's voice through His people. The Lord uses Christian community in a powerful way. He speaks through us to one another. We were created to be in community, connecting and ministering to each other. In a community of believers, you never suffer alone or celebrate alone. Remember, shepherds lead flocks. God's design of community is beautiful. In today's society, we have lost the vision for sharing life together. In a way, we are living in "solo Christianity." Our independent world has told us to be autonomous or live in the pseudo-world of the Internet.

God never intended for us to live life alone. He intended our hearts to live together in community. The hearts of believers are interwoven whether we practice it or not, because the Holy Spirit lives inside of us. Our oneness in Jesus crosses lines of denominations, gender and socioeconomic class (see Col. 3:11).

I have travelled to numerous countries and experienced the bond of believers that results from the indwelling Holy Spirit. We are bonded because of our relationship with Jesus. Those who have trusted the Messiah for salvation have been moved from being children of the devil to children of God, and from descendants of Adam to those who are grafted into Christ (see Rom. 11:24; 1 Cor. 15:22; 1 John 3:10).

These are huge theological and eternal destiny shifts. But they also create a different definition of family. Because of Christ, there is a vast depth that connects believers to other brothers and sisters in Christ. It is more than sharing a potluck supper and a laugh—it is a connection of heart and soul under the Father. Jesus prayed in John 17:20-21:

> My prayer is not for them alone. I pray also for those who will believe in me through their message, that all of them may be one, Father, just as you are in me and I am in you. May they also be in us so that the world may believe that you have sent me.

Our present practice needs to catch up to our theological reality. Then, through the community of believers, we will hear God's voice more clearly. Sometimes the words of a friend, spouse or neighbor are the exact words we need to hear from the Lord.

The fight for true community and the fight to hear God's voice are worth it. The more we understand the heart of the Lord and what He has to say, the more our path ahead will make sense to us. We do not worship a silent God who makes us guess at every next move. Our Lord is a gracious Shepherd who guides us with His voice and leads us with His hand.

During my seminary years, I worked at Camp Olympia in East Texas, for three summers.[5] Nestled on the banks of Lake Livingston, it was a beautiful camp and a great place to work. I led a cabin full of teenagers during each term. Sure, it was a noble effort, but it also zapped every bit of energy in me. As a result, a night off was pure gold.

As soon as my few hours of freedom began, I would jump on my mountain bike and ride about a half-mile to my car. Freedom! After late nights and long days with teenagers, nothing hit the spot like the local hamburger stand in town. And that's about all we had time for. My fellow counselors and I would go to the drive-in to get a hamburger and cherry limeade. The hours off always flew by. At the end of the night, we would return to camp and I would hop on my bike to ride back to the cabin. By that time, nighttime had fallen. The Piney Woods of East Texas are spectacular in the daylight but spooky at night. My half-mile bike ride seemed like miles on the way back to camp. The night was pitch-black—so dark that I couldn't see three feet in front of my handlebars. It felt like a scene out of the movie *E.T.*

I figured out that if I looked up, I could see the path of stars through the 50-foot pine trees. Each tiny light pierced through the black night, giving me the perfect path to follow. So in order to get home, I would look straight up. Imagine riding a bike downhill, over unseen bumps, craning your neck to see the sky. A crazy posture, yet one that provided guidance for the ride home.

The same can be said about following the Shepherd. Hey, sheep—just look up! Take your eyes off the dark road and trust Him with the pastures ahead. Look up instead of down and the Shepherd will lead you home. After all, not only is He the Good Shepherd, but He is also the Light of the World.

Gates Change Things

Throughout the Gospel of John, we have noticed specific moments when Jesus makes a bold claim about His identity. So far, He has claimed to be the Bread of Life and the Light of the World. Jesus' third claim as the "Gate for the sheep" is significant, directly preceding His declaration to be the Good Shepherd. The Gate ramps us up and tunes our listening ear to hear His voice. Unless we are in the sheep pen, we don't belong to Him. Our understanding of who Jesus is takes a momentous turn when He claims to be the Gate, preparing us to follow Him as our Shepherd.

Gates change things. When you think about a gate, there is something on one side and then something different on the other side. My wife, Kelly, recently shared a moment with her dad that forever changed his life. And the moment unfolded at the threshold of a gate. The story is a powerful reminder of God's faithfulness and His invitation to know Jesus, the true Gate. No one can tell the story better than Kelly:

> Gates—they were everywhere growing up. Living on a ranch in the Texas Hill Country, gates were just a part of our lives. To go through 10 in a day would not have been strange. They were a necessity to my dad, the rancher, but they were a bit of a nuisance to me, the perpetually designated gate holder. I could do the routine in my sleep—the old pickup rolls to a stop, rumbling in idle, as smells of exhaust compete with the dusty corn and sweet hay in the back. My turn was up . . . again. I didn't need a reminder; I knew my job. I was supposed to hop out and open the gate. I would hold on to it while the truck hummed by, spitting crushed gravel out behind each tire. Then I would latch it up, hop back in, and get ready for the next one. Little did I know at that young age that all these gates would one day serve a higher purpose than

merely dividing fields, securing animals and giving me a chore. They would be used of God to lead my dad to Jesus.

Fast-forward—decades and thousands of prayers later. Buckets of corn jostle in the back of my dad's Jeep as he drives. Sloshing through the low water crossing of the creek where I learned to swim, he makes his way up the wooded hillside. We're talking on cell phones miles apart, but I can almost taste the earthy air and feel each rocky bump on the dirt road. The scene is beyond familiar. I can see in my mind what my dad sees through the windshield. The steep climb begins to level when I say, "I know exactly where you are. You're coming up on a gate." He chuckled and said, "I'm sittin' right in front of it." I sensed the Spirit leading.

"Dad, that's what I want to talk with you about—a gate. You are looking at a physical gate that separates one pasture from another. I want to talk with you about a spiritual Gate that separates one pasture from another." He was unusually receptive, so I continued. For the next five minutes, God used the gate, the one my dad had seen countless times but never like this, to help me illustrate the gospel. I explained that God is holy and created us to know and enjoy Him, but our sin has separated us from having a relationship with Him and honoring Him as He deserves. I shared the good news that God sent His Son, Jesus, to live the only perfect life, take the punishment for our sins through His death on the cross and rise victoriously from the dead. We can be forgiven, rescued from hell and enter into an eternal relationship with God by grace through faith in Jesus Christ. John 10:9 came to mind. Jesus says, "I am the gate, whoever enters through me will be saved."

I asked him carefully, "Does that make sense?" He answered, with a new seriousness toward God, "Yes, it does." Then, with hope, I invited, "Do you believe and want to receive Jesus, trusting in Him alone to be your Savior?" Immediately, he responded with sweet sincerity, "Yes, I do. I really do." We both prayed—a sacred moment I will savor forever. My dad believed, with repentance and faith. God saved, with power and glory.

I'll never see a gate the same, especially not the ones on our ranch. The sheer frequency of them will from now on only remind me of God's relentless pursuit of us. No longer just rusty bars or rugged boards connected to a fence-line, but now vibrant metaphors of God's mercy and grace—constant recollections of His character, calling out that Jesus is the Gate!

Gates make a huge difference. There are gates at stadiums, gated communities, gates at airports and gates on ranches. There is a difference between life with Christ and life apart from Him. Life is vastly different on the other side of a gate.

Jesus capitalizes on this principle and gives a spiritual frame for the illustration. The gate for sheep in and out of the pen is a significant passageway. The shepherd guards it, and nothing and no one is allowed to enter the pen through the gate other than the shepherd. When Jesus claims to be the Gate for the sheep, He is claiming to be the passageway to the Father. Jesus enters our hearts so that we can exit this world, heaven-bound. Because of what He did on the cross, He offers us an exit from sin so that we can enter holiness. Apart from Christ, we would never be considered holy before the heavenly Father. Jesus, our Gate, makes us holy in the Father's sight. He dramatically changes everything.

Exclusivity: The One and Only

Jesus is bold in all of His claims of identity. He does not hesitate in claiming ultimate status as the one and only Gate: "I tell you the truth, the man who does not enter the sheep pen by the gate, but climbs in by some other way, is a thief and a robber" (John 10:1). Everyone else is a thief. In our world of tolerance, many religions are accepted as potential truths. However, Jesus' declaration as the one and only gate offers a much different perspective on competing religions. It is impossible for all religions to be right because they are at their core mutually exclusive. If reincarnation is true, then heaven with God is false. If salvation is by good works, then it is not by grace. If the Koran is the Word of God, then the Bible isn't. If Buddha declared the truth, then Jesus can't be declaring it as well. Any religion worth its salt must be exclusive, because it is claiming to possess the truth, which by nature excludes the rest.

It is far more likely that all religions are false than it is that they are all true. Faith based on the religious symbols spelling the "Coexist" bumper sticker is our generation's conclusion of group hugs, rope course elements and "everyone gets a trophy" upbringing. Only one can be true, and Jesus claims it is Him. He will go even further in His sixth "I AM" statement in

John 14:6 by declaring that He is "the way and the truth and the life. No one comes to the Father except through me." We will look in chapter 14 at that identity statement and give factual reasoning to back up this exclusive claim. It is safe to say that whether you agree or not, Jesus is not mixing words about being the route, the gate and the only path to heaven.

How can He say that? Does this type of statement bother you? It is hard for us to accept that He is the only way to the Father and to heaven. But that's the truth according to Christ. Think of all the ground we have covered so far in this book. Miracle after miracle shows that He is the Messiah; then statements of His identity are a strong follow-up. The goal of Jesus' time on earth was not to keep us confused about the right path to God, but to give us clarity. He is telling us that He is the Gate, and any other way is not. These are not the harsh statements of a bully saying, "The gate is locked"; they are grace-filled statements to give us clarity on the issue of eternity and relating with God.

But we often desire works instead of grace. We want to have control in the situation. So it seems only fair that the measuring stick of heaven would be sincerity instead of salvation. Many people say things like, "If a person is sincere in their belief, then it should count."

Sincerity in the wrong object is worthless. I can sincerely believe that I can fly, but that won't help one step off of the cliff. I need a plane, not stronger arms. Likewise, we need a noticeable Gate, a visible Shepherd to act on our behalf. Sincerity in the correct Object results in a relationship with God. Sincerity in a random object or religion of our fancy does not.

I wish all roads led to heaven and everyone was headed on that path. I'm a kindhearted guy who doesn't want anyone to be left out, especially from heaven and knowing God. But that is not how the Scriptures set forth Jesus. Therefore, I have to lay down my wishes, personality and disposition at the feet of Jesus' claims. I'm either going to trust in His view of eternity or trust in mine. It is safe to say that my views are frail and skewed at best, while His are barreling through the hallways of time with certainty.

The study of Christianity is unlike any other religion. Jesus matches the description of every single Old Testament prophecy given centuries before His time. The words of King David, Isaiah, Jeremiah and others are perfectly displayed in the birth, life, death and resurrection of Christ (see Ps. 132:11-12; Isa. 11:11; 53:2-5; Jer. 23:5-8). He fits every description. In the Gospel of John, Jesus is narrowing the focus of who He is. We do not doubt who He says He is because it matches who the prophets said He would be. The thread is weaving the garment through time, and the colors match perfectly. His gentleness doesn't negate His precision of saying, "I AM the Gate." The surprise we find in Jesus is that He is more gracious and merciful to us than we could have ever imagined or expected.

Jesus is not ambiguous in His statement of who He is. He makes an exclusive and strong proclamation. But this truth's exclusivity is open for acceptance to all races, creeds, social statuses and backgrounds. He is the one and only Gate—the one way to the Father. As we move through the Gate, we move toward salvation and also toward the new things the Lord is calling us to. Out of who Jesus says He is, we discover who we are and how we should live. Knowing the true Gate changes our perspective. Once we know Jesus as Savior, the other side of the gate looks vastly different.

He Is All There Is and All We Want

A little boy could hardly wait to get home after Sunday School. After climbing into the car after church, the little boy's mother asked him about his time in class that morning. The boy was elated to tell his mother the new Bible verse he had learned with his classmates: "The LORD is my shepherd, I shall not be in want." Proudly, he proclaimed his version of Psalm 23:1: "The Lord is my shepherd, *that's all I want.*" His mother looked into the rearview mirror and smiled proudly at her son. She didn't correct his paraphrase, but replied, "Perfect. That's exactly right." The young boy learned something about his Shepherd that day that many will spend a lifetime figuring out—the Lord is our Shepherd and He is all that we could ever want.[6] That understanding reflects the heart of a youngster who has stepped through the Gate to discover the Shepherd worth listening to for life.

FOR FURTHER REFLECTION AND DISCUSSION

The "I AM" Playlist Pick

Song	Artist	Album
"I AM"	Nicole C. Mullen	*Redeemer*

1. What does "desirous discipline" mean? In what area do you have the desire but not the discipline? How can you change that?

2. How will desirous discipline help you follow the Good Shepherd's voice?

3. What is the most dramatic change you have experienced going from one side of a gate through to the other?

4. How do Jesus' miracles prove He's the only gate?

5. Are you sure you have walked through Jesus as the only gate of eternal salvation? If not, here's a prayer to guide you: Jesus, I know that I have sinned against You so many times. I'm sorry and ask for Your forgiveness. I believe Your death on the cross was to pay for my sin. I believe You are the gate of salvation. I place my belief in You as my Savior and Shepherd. In Jesus' name, amen.

"Baa" Means Good

I am the good shepherd. The good shepherd lays down his life for the sheep.
JOHN 10:11

Seven Miracles of Jesus

1. Turning water into wine (JOHN 2:1-12)
2. Healing the nobleman's son (JOHN 4:46-54)
3. Healing of the lame man (JOHN 5:1-17)
4. Feeding the 5,000 (JOHN 6:1-13)
5. Walking on water (JOHN 6:16-21)
6. Healing the man born blind (JOHN 9:1-41)
7. Raising Lazarus from dead (JOHN 11:1-45)

Seven I AM Statements of Jesus

1. I AM the Bread of Life (JOHN 6:35,48,51)
2. I AM the Light of the World (JOHN 8:12)
3. I AM the Door/Gate (JOHN 10:7)
4. I AM the Good Shepherd (JOHN 10:11-14)
5. I AM the Resurrection and the Life (JOHN 11:25)
6. I AM the Way, the Truth, and the Life (JOHN 14:6)
7. I AM the True Vine (JOHN 15:1)

Sheep are predictable creatures. They are followers by nature, so you will always find them in a flock. They know the voice of their shepherd, and that's about it; no tricks like shaking hands, sitting or begging. But as we saw in the last chapter, the shepherd's call outweighs soldiers' guns and a noisy world. Life is spent in the pasture for these creatures, so there are no fragrances named "Eau de Sheep." They are also creative about how to get into trouble. When you combine all these traits with their lack of intelligence, you've got a problem. Sheep don't go looking for trouble, but they have a predisposition to find it.

To be compared to a sheep hardly sounds like a compliment when you consider such a list of characteristics. In fact, it is a humbling comparison. And yet, we find ourselves best defined as sheep. The beauty of being called sheep is that we have the opportunity to have a unique relationship with the Shepherd of our souls. The shepherd knows his sheep intimately. They also have the opportunity to know the shepherd, understanding his voice.

For those who know the Lord, the Great Shepherd, we share that same privilege. Our pleasure is to know and be known by the Shepherd. But we also have a tendency to follow the flock into trouble, don't we?

In Yorkshire, England, shepherds were debating methods of safety to keep their flocks within a pen. They came to the conclusion that utilizing a contraption similar to a cattle guard would keep the sheep in and danger out. For the readers outside of my home state of Texas, a cattle guard is simply an iron grid that lies on the ground in front of a gate. Animals such as cattle and sheep cannot pass over the guard without their legs slipping between the bars. It was the perfect solution, or so the shepherds thought.

Rarely does a sheep outsmart a shepherd, and yet it happened. One sheep approached the cattle guard and simply laid down and proceeded to roll across the bars of the cattle/sheep guard—an easy escape! Stop, drop and roll. The watchful flock took notice of the lead sheep's exit and followed right behind, one by one. Finally, the entire flock had creatively copied their way out of the pen and none of the local residents' flowers were safe. In a matter of minutes, the shepherds had been outwitted and the flock stood proudly on the other side of the pen. Of course, the sheep never considered the danger outside of the protection of a pen.[1]

For the sheep to simply stay put and enjoy the protection of the pen would have been much easier. However, they sought greener pastures on the other side. As humans and believers in Christ, we are perfectly compared to sheep. For us, peace comes in obeying God, but we try to roll out of His will and go into other pens. We are no better than sheep. The sheep in Yorkshire did not understand the purpose for a pen. While it offered safety and access to the shepherd's provision, they saw it as nothing more than a hindrance to their desires. We do the same thing. The Lord, our Shepherd, has our best interest at heart. And yet we try to roll in a different direction, hopeful that we will find excitement elsewhere.

Crayon Color: Worldly Green

The lie of the ages is still told: "The grass is greener on the other side." Adam and Eve thought the deeper green lay in the wrong tree; David thought it was in Bathsheba's embrace; King Saul thought he could find it in power. Most of us could probably relate to a biblical character few have taken notice of. His name was Demas, and his tiny portrait in Scripture tells us that he succumbed to the "greener grass" lie too.

I bet you never went to school with a kid named Demas, and it probably never made your list of possible baby names. Demas was a classic example of one in search of greener pastures. He was known for leaving his post in search of something better. He is mentioned in Philemon 24 and Colossians 4:14 as one of Paul's "fellow workers." He is also mentioned in 2 Timothy 4:10, where he is said to have deserted his responsibility. In the closing verse describing Demas, the apostle Paul says, "Demas, because he loved this world, has deserted me and gone to Thessalonica." Fade to black.

The sheep named Demas ceased to follow the Shepherd and struck off in search of greener grass. If the wandering were a crayon, it would be named "Worldly Green," the color voted "most tempting" by the flesh of humans. Before we judge, we should admit that we have the potential to follow Demas's path instead of Christ's. The world is alluring and it calls out to our hearts, promising power, beauty, comfort, ease, accolades and identity. Demas, whose name means "popular," took the bait to head to the party town of Thessalonica.[2] Now, thousands of years later, he is a footnote of what *not* to do.

I can be a lot like Demas too. The world is a falsely comforting place. The praise of man and the taste of success can lead us all astray. But instead of rolling over the "sheep guard" of wisdom to get outside the sheepfold, we are to walk with the Good Shepherd. We are to follow His voice by walking away from sin and into His plan. Though He sometimes seems to move too slowly, and He often leads from silence, the wise follow what they already know to do in order to discover what they need to know next. The Lord shepherds His people with incredible kindness. When we know how great the Shepherd is, we will never want to leave Him.

In John 10, Jesus continues His illustration of the sheep and shepherd. He offers us access to the Father through Himself—the Gate of the Sheep. The Scriptures are filled with shepherd illustrations. For example, David was a shepherd, and God was Israel's shepherd. Jesus saw the crowds as sheep without a shepherd, and the Pharisees and religious leaders represented what bad shepherds look like. Jesus capitalized on this theme by announcing that He is the Good Shepherd, showing us the greater extent of His love (see John 10:11).

The relationship of the shepherd to the sheep is one of love, protection and guidance. A shepherd dedicates his life to caring for creatures that cannot care for themselves. Our Lord is a Shepherd far different from the pharisaical leadership the people were accustomed to. As Jesus describes the shepherd's love for his sheep, He is giving us a metaphor to better understand God's love for His people. The more we understand how a shepherd loves his flock, the more we will be amazed by the Lord's love toward us.

Life!

Jesus sets up His claim as the Good Shepherd in an incredible way. He begins to paint a picture of what a shepherd's love looks like. The Lord's love for us is extravagant, much better than anything else someone could offer. This side of heaven, we will face the temptations and the real and powerful work of Satan. And yet it does not compare with the power and finality of the work of the Lord. The thief's plan stands in stark contrast to the Shepherd's plan: "The thief comes only to steal and kill and destroy; I have come that they may have life, and have it to the full" (John 10:10). Jesus offers life, and Satan offers death, which is sometimes cleverly disguised as life.

Jesus came into our world to show us the immeasurable riches of life in the Lord. He knew that He would satisfy our hearts and desires as our Good Shepherd in ways that nothing else could. In Christ, we have abundant life. The Father sent His Son to be our Shepherd and guide to point us heavenward. It's about life—soul-satisfying life—in Christ. Like sheep, if left to our own devices, we would look for life everywhere else, even in the hand of the thief. But God's love pursues the wandering and the lost sheep. We have a Shepherd to follow who will lead us to life.

Not Going Anywhere

A shepherd's love for his flock is not contingent on danger or circumstance. It is grounded in a deeply rooted affection for the sheep. Jesus longs for people to understand this kind of love.

> I am the good shepherd. The good shepherd lays down his life for the sheep. The hired hand is not the shepherd who owns the sheep. So when he sees the wolf coming, he abandons the sheep and runs away. Then the wolf attacks the flock and scatters it. The man runs away because he is a hired hand and cares nothing for the sheep (John 10:11-13).

At an early sign of danger, a hired hand will run for cover. He loves the wages, not the sheep. So a conflict with a wolf or any other threat is far above his pay grade. Without a moment's notice, the hired hand takes off. He is more concerned with the blessing and ease of a job than the wellbeing of the flock.

The shepherd remains. He is invested in the flock and cares for their every need. The shepherd does not go anywhere, but stands between danger and his sheep. If anything threatens the flock, it first threatens the shepherd. Jesus is giving us an understanding of His love. As the Good Shepherd, He is willing to lay down His life when danger approaches. The most staggering and beautiful example of this love is seen in the shadow of the cross. The guilt of sin stood in the way of our relationship with the Father. But Jesus, the Good Shepherd, took our place, having the wrath of God fall upon Him instead of us.

It is incredibly comforting to realize there is nothing we can do (even as ignorant sheep) to scare God away. The Lord can never love us more or less than He does right now. Throughout Scripture, we can see His faithfulness play out in the lives of others. Ashamed at their disobedience to His instructions, Adam and Eve did their best to hide from God, but He would not leave them to their sin. Instead, God went toward them, seeking them out and longing to restore relationship with them (see Gen. 3).

The Good Shepherd does not run from peril. In fact, He does the exact opposite: Compelled by love, He runs toward His people's trouble. God does not run from our sin. He runs toward it, cleansing us and offering new life. Neither does He run from danger. In 1 Samuel 17, the young shepherd David meets his greatest challenge in Goliath. The Lord moves toward the danger with David, not in the other direction. He does not shrink from adversity, but faces it head-on. Our God cannot be frightened away. As the Good Shepherd of his flock, the Lord stands guard as a protective pastor.

What a challenge for pastors, parents, leaders and anyone else in a shepherding role! The word "pastor" is the Latin word for "shepherd." I feel the joy and the responsibility in my role as a pastor, but in all honesty, there are times when leadership means that you are the "tip of the spear." Everyone else can run from the wolves, show up late or be unprepared. But the leader sets up, gears up and then evaluates. Some Sunday mornings, I wonder what it would be like to just show up as an expectant sheep instead of the prepared shepherd. It would be far easier, I am sure, but it would also leave my gifts on the sidelines and remove one of the greatest blessings from my life. Leading our church is more than an occupation for me—it is a gift.

Yes, the challenge is greater for those who shepherd in teaching or other serving capacities, but the rewards are greater too. Where there is little responsibility and challenge, there will also be little impact and reward. Love, not ease, is our catalyst in leadership.

Are You Driven or Led?

A shepherd knows his flock. If one goes missing, he is able to identify it and begin the search. His sheep are more than a flock to him; he counts each head at the end of the day. He knows his sheep's tendencies and the call they will understand. To gather in the flock, the shepherd lets out a call that is heard and understood by the sheep. They know his voice and come running when they hear the call.

The Lord desires to know His sheep as a shepherd, but He also wants us to know Him. He desires a two-way relationship. God already knows you personally. In Psalm 139, David talks about the intimate way that we are known by God.

For you created my inmost being; you knit me together in my mother's womb. I praise you because I am fearfully and wonderfully made; your works are wonderful, I know that full well. My frame was not hidden from you when I was made in the secret place. When I was woven together in the depths of the earth, your eyes saw my unformed body. All the days ordained for me were written in your book before one of them came to be (Ps. 139:13-16).

As our Creator, the Lord knows the number of hairs on our heads. He knows our deepest joys and understands our greatest struggles. To be fully known by the God of the universe should be a humble reminder that He is interested in knowing every part of us. But He is not satisfied with a one-sided relationship.

He desires to make Himself known to us. Life-change takes place when we begin to know Him too. He already knows us—but do we really know our Creator? Dallas Willard said, " 'The Lord is my Shepherd' is written on many more tombstones than lives."[3] The Lord invites us to pursue a personal relationship with Him. Things will begin to change in our lives when we feel led by the Lord and not driven by Him. A life led by God is one of confidence. We know His call and understand His voice. As a result, we feel pulled forward in life to live for the Lord in new and brave ways.

Many people feel more driven by religion than led by God. They feel like God is behind them calling *for* more instead of in front, leading them *to* more. God looks more like a driving, two-a-day athletic coach on a hot summer day. To the contrary, the good Shepherd and an unsatisfied taskmaster are worlds apart. Yet that is how we project our thoughts on God, which hampers our growth in Christ.

A story is told of a trip to the Holy Land in which the tourist group saw a flock of sheep being driven through town. As they watched, with digital cameras flashing, one sightseer asked the guide, "I thought the shepherd led the sheep from the front. Why is he in the back?" The guide simply replied, "Sir, that's not the shepherd. That's the butcher."

That's Satan's position. He drives and shoves us from the rear with reminders of our past, fears of our future and uncertainties in the present. He pushes through people and situations to lead us to the slaughter. Satan is the thief that comes to "steal, kill and destroy."

Perhaps you feel driven by the Lord instead of led. As clear as I can put it—that's not the truth. He is not driving you. You might be driving yourself or listening to someone else, but Jesus is a good Shepherd, not a butcher. He is a leader, not a prodder. A life that is driven feels pushed and will result in bitterness and guilt. If you live feeling driven long enough, you will not be able to tell the difference between your guilt and the Lord's call on your life. You will begin to act out of guilt or obligation instead of love. Religion *about* God will replace relationship *with* God. Pastor and author Wayne Cordeiro said, "The road to success and the road to burnout is the same road."[4] If we busy ourselves feeling driven and not led, we will burn out and lose our joy in this journey with God.

Whether you are being led instead of feeling driven is based on whose voice you are listening to. Obviously, Jesus' voice is the right answer. But what false shepherds are calling you to follow? What is the noise clogging your ears? "Today, if you hear his voice, do not harden your hearts" (Heb. 3:15).

By nature, my personality can lead me to the wrong pastures. Gregariousness and a desire to connect with people can lead me to say "maybe" when I should say no. But if you are an introvert, you may avoid the opportunity altogether. You may unintentionally live a life of "no" and miss out on the joy of saying "yes" every once in a while. Continually allowing other people to set your agenda will result in losing your identity, your time and, ultimately, your impact.

The point is this: How we are wired is wonderful and God-given. So, be who you are. But when your flesh or other people's expectations combine with your personality, the Good Shepherd leading you has often been replaced by a butcher driving you. An examination of your yeses and your noes will identify which shepherd you're listening to in a very practical sense. When we have too frequently said yes to our personalities, our peers and our parents, the unintended consequence is saying no to the Good Shepherd. His leadership gets thwarted because we have left His sheep pen on an errand for someone else.

Acknowledge the weaknesses of your personality or the strength of another's voice and lay them down at His feet. Allow the Spirit to give leadership instead of the flesh. Follow instead of being driven.

Following the Lord is natural to the redeemed heart and should be like water to a fish. God has re-created us in salvation to be shepherded. We can be certain that following the Shepherd's lead will cause us to have a growing desire for Him. The more we know about the Good Shepherd, the more we will want to stay by His side and follow His every move. Knowing the Shepherd and being known by Him changes us. *I AM changes who i am.*

Bringing Unity

The Good Shepherd does so much more than create relationships and guard the flock. He also breaks down walls and brings unity. Jesus leads us out of "isms" and into oneness in Christ. For example, He leads people out of paganism, communism, individualism, denominationalism and materialism. Out of all of the "isms," the Lord takes our lesser allegiances and focuses our attention on a higher, greater allegiance. There is only one Shepherd and Leader; therefore, Jesus wants to set our eyes on God. As our collective focus gathers on the Lord, not on any other allegiance, there is unity. Everything that once caused division can find unity in Christ.

Unity in Christ also affects ethnicities and backgrounds. I witnessed an incredible picture of unity at our church. As usual, a baptism took place during a Sunday morning service. It is always a beautiful thing to watch a baptism. But this one in particular caught my attention. The man coming forward to be baptized was an African American who had a story to tell. At the age of four, he was forced to pick cotton and was abused. His testimony sounded more like a person from the early 1900s in the Deep South than modern America. Once off the farm, and after years of drug use, he was thrown into prison.

But God knows no boundaries. He got hold of this man's heart. The other man in this story was the one performing the baptism. He was an Anglo man from the suburbs of the city and previously served as a police officer before coming on our staff as the children's minister. Two very different worlds came crashing together during that service when a young Caucasian former police officer turned minister baptized an older African-American ex-convict. This circumstance rang with the truth. Jesus breaks down walls of race, ethnicity and lifestyles. Though the two sheep had vastly different life stories, they shared the unity of knowing Christ as Shepherd. Racial diversity shines with the truth that the Shepherd is leading. If we are really following the Shepherd, there should be diversity in the pen.

Jesus unites. The Good Shepherd brings unity to a flock that is different in every aspect. Jesus, as He was talking to His flock, reminded them, "I have other sheep that are not of this sheep pen. I must bring them also. They too will listen to my voice, and there shall be one flock and one shepherd" (John 10:16). In the traditional application of this verse, Jesus is offering salvation to the Gentile (non-Jewish) people as well. In Christ, we are one. Color, gender, background, language or church denomination does not matter. What matters is that the flock follows the same Shepherd.

Voluntarily and Vicariously:
The Shepherd's "Yes" on Our Behalf

Being a shepherd is a selfless job. During the day, the shepherd leads his flock from pasture to pasture in search of good grazing. At night, he stays awake as the sheep rest quietly in the pen. He does not leave his post, but keeps a steady eye on each head and a watchful eye on his surroundings. In many ways, the role of a shepherd is a thankless profession.

Jesus, our Good Shepherd, laid down His life for us voluntarily; it was not taken from Him (see John 10:17). The Shepherd was a willing sacrifice for our sins. He was willing to pay the highest price so that we would live forgiven and in right standing with the Father.

The cross also shows that sin was paid for vicariously. Jesus had no sin of His own to carry to the cross. His shoulders were burdened by the weight of others' sins—our sin. He died in our place. The death that was ours became His. The Good Shepherd was willing to lay down His life for us. It was His decision to pay for the sin that was not His own. Jesus' sacrificial love is still remarkable to ponder centuries later.

There is no doubt that Jesus is the Good Shepherd. But it doesn't end there. God is using this "I AM" statement to ramp up for all of eternity. Jesus is referred to as a Shepherd three times in the New Testament. Each time, a different adjective precedes the word "shepherd." Watch as the adjectives grow in stature.

1. "I am the *Good Shepherd*. The good shepherd *lays down his life for the sheep*" (John 10:11, emphasis added). Here, the emphasis is on His voluntary and vicarious death. He is good because He leads us and willingly lays down His life.

2. Hebrews 13:20-21 takes it a step further: "May the God of peace, who through the blood of the eternal covenant brought *back from the dead* our Lord Jesus, that *Great Shepherd* of the sheep, equip you with everything good for doing his will, and may he work in us what is pleasing to him, through Jesus Christ, to whom be glory for ever and ever. Amen" (emphasis added).

   Now the emphasis has shifted from the cross to the resurrection, "back from the dead." While Jesus doesn't cease to be good, the empty tomb declares Him to be great. Many good men can give their lives unto death—soldiers, police and firefighters; but only one could give His life and then rise again. The grave could not hold the greatness of God's Son. He is able to lead His sheep past death into eternal life.

3. Finally, 1 Peter 5:4: "And when the *Chief Shepherd* appears, you will receive the crown of glory that will never fade away" (emphasis added). The capping emphasis is not on good or great. He is the Chief Shepherd because He is returning; and upon His return, Christ will reward the faithful. Those who have fulfilled His plan, followed His voice and not their flesh or personality, will receive the crown of glory that will never fade. As a result, the Chief Shepherd finalizes His shepherd descriptions.

Jesus is good, Jesus is great and Jesus is the undisputed Chief Shepherd for all of eternity. Listen and follow His self-sacrificing love.[5]

A Mother's Love Shows Our Father's Heart

Jessica Council was a young woman of 30 whose life illustrated the gospel truth of sacrifice. Jessica was pregnant with her second child when she was diagnosed with cancer. The doctors recommended immediate action in the forms of chemotherapy and radiation. However, they could not promise that the baby would not be harmed. So the Councils said no. Next, the doctors suggested abortion in an effort to save Jessica's life.

However, with each medical offer of assistance the baby's life would be endangered. Jessica and her husband, Clint, declined all efforts to slow the cancer at the risk of the baby. They decided to give the unborn child every chance to grow and remain healthy, no matter the toll it would take on Jessica's body. At the expense of her own health, Jessica battled cancer and kept the child. Unexpectedly, on February 5, Jessica went to sleep with a headache and never woke up again. Though her soul had passed into eternity, her womb still held a child. Clint said, "She knew she was going to die anyway. She didn't share that with me until almost when she died. But I think she knew, and she was thinking she was going to give this baby every chance she could."

Quickly, the doctors performed a C-section to deliver the baby at 23-and-a-half weeks, the threshold of viability. Jessica fought to remain alive until the moment when the baby was viable for life outside the womb.

Death a week earlier would have meant death for both the mother and child. Little Jessi, weighing only one pound and three ounces, came into the world because of her mother's bravery and God's timing. The all-knowing Good Shepherd had led Jessica to heaven and Jessi to earth.

Listen to the words of Clint, husband and father, less than two weeks after the death of his wife and birth of his daughter:

> God is to be praised, my friends. Do not doubt God; do not be angry with Him for me. I am privileged to have had a wife who was so full of the love of the Father. Rejoice with me, brothers and sisters. God has blessed Jessica in taking her to a place of perfect peace and no pain. I must be thankful for the time that I had with her rather than ungrateful for all the things we never got to do together. We must give thanks in all things for this is the will of God in Jesus Christ. Grace and peace to all.[6]

That sounds like a man with a good, great and Chief Shepherd. Why would we ever roll out of the sheep pen of trusting Him? Even in death, the greenest grass is in His pen. A mother lay down her life for the sake of her child. As parents, many of us can testify that we would do the same thing for our children. That is also the kind of love that Jesus has for us. He lay down His own life that we might live forever in Him.

Our God in heaven is a Good Shepherd. He is able and willing to do whatever it takes to teach His sheep the sound of His voice. And He longs for more than a wave across the room. Jesus longs for a vibrant, growing relationship with us. He is also the Gate that changes everything. Through Christ, we have abundant life. *Our Shepherd is good.* He is willing to lay it all down for His sheep. *Our Shepherd is great.* He conquered death on the cross and equips us with everything good for doing His will. Above all, *our Shepherd is Chief* over all of creation. He has come and He is coming again.

Knowing Christ as the Good Shepherd of our souls begins a work in our hearts that will continue until we are complete in Jesus. The Shepherd brings change into our lives by the Holy Spirit; and as a result, we begin to look more like Christ. I encourage you to call on Jesus, the good Shepherd, in your prayers today. I have found such comfort praying along these lines: "Good Shepherd, lead me today. Guide me and reveal to me the path. I'm an unwise sheep in need of guidance. You are the wise Lord who is my Shepherd. I want to follow You. Lead me."

FOR FURTHER REFLECTION AND DISCUSSION

The "I AM" Playlist Pick

Song	Artist	Album
"I AM"	Ginny Owens	*If You Want Me To*

1. How can a feeling of being driven in life instead of led cost us in the long run?

2. Do you feel driven from behind or led by the Spirit? Why? In what ways?

3. How does the sacrifice of Jesus for you change your view of His leadership?

4. Discuss the amazing progression of good, great and chief Shepherd. How does this progression give you hope for today and the future?

Dawn of the Dead Living

Now a man named Lazarus was sick....
"Lazarus is dead."... "Lazarus, come out!"
JOHN 11:1,14,43

Seven Miracles of Jesus

1. Turning water into wine (JOHN 2:1-12)
2. Healing the nobleman's son (JOHN 4:46-54)
3. Healing of the lame man (JOHN 5:1-17)
4. Feeding the 5,000 (JOHN 6:1-13)
5. Walking on water (JOHN 6:16-21)
6. Healing the man born blind (JOHN 9:1-41)
7. Raising Lazarus from dead (JOHN 11:1-45)

Seven I AM Statements of Jesus

1. I AM the Bread of Life (JOHN 6:35,48,51)
2. I AM the Light of the World (JOHN 8:12)
3. I AM the Door/Gate (JOHN 10:7)
4. I AM the Good Shepherd (JOHN 10:11-14)
5. I AM the Resurrection and the Life (JOHN 11:25)
6. I AM the Way, the Truth, and the Life (JOHN 14:6)
7. I AM the True Vine (JOHN 15:1)

Here is a sobering truth: Your life will end in death unless Jesus returns to earth first. How is that for an encouraging way to start a chapter?

Across cultures, backgrounds and lifestyles, death is the most undeniable and inevitable experience we will all share. No one is exempt from death. Eventually, our time on earth will come to an end. There is no one who will escape that reality. Sickness, grief and death are all a part of life. Whether it is your story or the story of someone you love, we will all be faced with the sureness that our time on earth is not forever. But that is not the end of the story for those in Christ. We have so much more ahead. God does not leave us with lingering questions about life after death. He gives us a firm foundation to plant our feet upon.

Our unbelieving culture looks at death with hesitation and a reluctant pause. After losing her husband and sister within a few years of each other, former CBS news anchor Katie Couric began to ponder what it would look like to face death through faith. She offered these words:

> I'm very interested in exploring a more spiritual side of me, and I'm in the process of doing that, both formally and informally. I really envy those who have a steadfast, unwavering faith, because I think it is probably so comforting and helpful during difficult times.[1]

Similar to Couric's perspective on death, actor Jack Nicholson shared his thoughts during an interview before the release of his film *The Bucket List*. Reflecting on his own personal life, Nicholson stated:

> I used to live so freely. The mantra for my generation was "Be your own man!" I always said, "Hey, you can have whatever rules you want—I'm going to have mine. I'll accept the guilt. I'll pay the check. I'll do the time." I chose my own way. That was my philosophical position well into my fifties. As I've gotten older, I've had to adjust. . . . we all want to go on forever, don't we? We fear the unknown. Everybody goes to that wall, yet nobody knows what's on the other side. That's why we fear death.[2]

The world should look to Christianity and consider the comfort that comes with an unwavering faith. To face death or illness while standing firm in Jesus is a beautiful testimony to a hurting world. That doesn't mean that Christians are immune to pain, but it offers the world an example that there is so much more ahead.

John 11 hits us between the eyes. Jesus' dear friend Lazarus is sick to the point of death. Having seen Jesus heal the blind and cure the lame, it startles us that Jesus lets Lazarus die. It is unsettling, since we have seen the mighty works of Jesus. After all His "I AM" declarations and miracles, we expect that Jesus would surely heal a friend.

Remember, the miracles of Jesus have been building upon one another throughout the Gospel of John—water to wine, healing of the official's son and the lame man, feeding of the 5,000, walking on water, and healing the blind man. With His seventh and final recorded miracle in John, we hit the pinnacle. Christ began with a secretive change of water to wine and concludes with publicly raising Lazarus from the dead. This final miracle is perfectly placed before the miraculous resurrection of Jesus Himself. Seeing a resuscitated Lazarus walking the streets, through Christ's power, is just another step to believing in Jesus' coming resurrection from the dead. The healings, feedings and water walking are building the disciples' faith and ours to believe that Jesus is the great "I AM" of the Old Testament in the flesh.

His miracles and I AM statements are the non-fictional script of the Miraculous Messiah. He will defeat death and give us new life. Don't miss the significance of raising Lazarus as His final miracle and declaring, "I am the Resurrection and the Life" as the final I AM statement. He is setting us up for the cross and the empty tomb.

Yet, with all this momentum, His friend dies and the people are devastated. Why doesn't Jesus do what we expect and hope for Him to do? Isaiah 55:9 reminds us of a central truth to our faith: "As the heavens are higher than the earth, so are my ways higher than your ways and my thoughts than your thoughts." By letting Lazarus die, Jesus was accomplishing something bigger than we could envision. In preparing us for His own resurrection, Jesus showed His victory over death when he raised Lazarus from the dead.

As believers, this passage holds incredible hope for us. Death is not the final straw. In John 11, Jesus makes a claim about Himself that brings reassuring peace to souls in the midst of death and illness. The fifth "I AM" statement in John is a bold one: "I am the resurrection and the life. He who believes in me will live, even though he dies; and whoever lives and believes in me will never die" (John 11:25-26). In the shadow of Jesus, death becomes a bee without its stinger. The stinger will be lodged in Christ on the cross, leaving humanity's historic foe powerless, as He rises on our behalf. Death is inevitable. But for those in Christ, death is not the ultimate end.

Purpose or Pointless?

How you think about death determines how you live your life. A life driven by purpose has joy and freedom because we know what lies ahead. This is our reality as believers in Christ! Because we have confidence in an everlasting life with the Father, our lives are full of purpose. Purpose drives us to live in such a way that others would see and know the hope that we have in Jesus. A purpose-driven life is a life planted in the assurance that there is more than what we see this side of heaven. C. S. Lewis once remarked:

> If you read history you will find that the Christians who did most for the present world were precisely those who thought most of the next. It is since Christians have largely ceased to think of the other world that they have become so ineffective in this.[3]

In sharp contrast to purpose is a pointless existence. When there is nothing to live for beyond this life, your days will be void of purpose and filled with pointless activity. Sure, you will be busy, but the busyness has no culmination; it is more like a hamster in a wheel instead of a thoroughbred in a race. Life will seem pointless now because there is nothing to anticipate later. Possessed earthly rewards cannot anchor us like coming eternal rewards.

This is more than telling a child, "We are going to the beach this summer, so do your homework." It is not akin to anticipating a trip or a good meal. Looking toward heaven puts life today into proper perspective. We are meant for more than amassing trinkets and trips. We are eternal creatures pausing for a brief earthly existence. This paradigm-altering thought shapes our lives to live for more than sensory pleasure. Instead, we live for God, and we live in the power of new life in Him.

With this perspective, the people we interact with move from being machinery to meet our needs or scenery to surround our activities, to ministry opportunities with an eternal destination.[4] We want to meet their needs in order to point them to the eternal Messiah of their souls. Hence, a proper perspective on death is crucial in determining how to live life. Jesus gives us great purpose for today because we know what tomorrow holds.

Throughout history, people have thought about death in many ways. Peter Kreeft's book *Love Is Stronger Than Death* outlines the various perspectives on death as history has unfolded:

The ancient pre-Christian mind was death-accepting (and fatalistic); the medieval Christian mind was death-defying (believing in the resurrection); and the modern post-Christian mind is death-denying (looking away from death as a stranger). This explains our fear of silence. We need noise to distract us from the knowledge of our ignorance of life and death. Life is ultimately meaningless to us; but if there is enough noise, we never need hear this terrible silence.[5]

We look at death as an enemy and do whatever it takes to avoid the inevitable. Our society has created so much noise that there is no time to even think about the silence of death. In many ways, we have attempted to make death a spectator sport. Through action movies and media, we are entertained by death, like watching gladiators fight in an arena. Death has become a sport in the hope to replace its reality. Kreeft addresses this as well:

The denial of death is one reason for our tolerance of violence. We watch violence on a TV screen or in movies detachedly, from a distance, as the Romans watched the gladiatorial contest. What we watch is not ourselves. Turning it into an object exorcises it from our inner being. We are not involved, not responsible; we are spectators, not participants. Death becomes tolerable when it happens to others. But when we have made death a spectator sport, we have made life a spectator sport. To be detached from our death is to be detached from our life.[6]

Those are powerful words. Life is discovered when death is faced, and faced victoriously. Enter Jesus stage left. With the miraculous résumé still being written, He will stand before Lazarus's tomb and declare victory—a strong victory to prepare us for the ultimate victory. The stinger is lodged in Christ through the cross and death-conquering Easter.

The story of Lazarus gives us parameters for how to think about death in light of Jesus. Jesus is showing us His mastery over death and also the life that He offers for those who are seeking. In a world where our culture tells us to deny the existence of death, Jesus invites us to consider a life full of purpose because of the assurance we have in Him. Let's watch it play out.

Testing Your Faith

John begins his account of Lazarus with a startling statement: "Now a man named Lazarus was sick" (John 11:1). That simple phrase, which we often pass over, is a gut punch to those who know and love Lazarus. His sisters, Mary and Martha, are overwhelmed by the reality that their brother lies sick to the point of death. At some time in all of our lives, we will encounter such a sentence. Depending on whose name is in that sentence, it will be a gut punch—the closer the name, the harder the hit. Perhaps even more difficult than facing an illness yourself, watching a loved one suffer is an incomparable trial. If the sentence holds the name of your spouse, parents, kids or close friend, the punch will drop you to your knees.

In this life, our faith will be tested by sickness, grief and even death. That is the nature of our broken world. Just a few chapters later in John 16:33, Jesus speaks directly to our pain: "In this world you will have trouble. But take heart! I have overcome the world." Jesus came to earth so that sickness and death would not have the final word in our lives. We see this incredible truth in the story of Lazarus. Though he lay dead from illness, death did not have the final word; Jesus did, and He raised His friend from the dead.

When we face such trials, we have a choice of how we will respond. In our sinful nature, perhaps the most natural reaction is bitterness. The news of an illness or even the passing of a loved one can birth a strong bitterness toward the Lord. Shaking your fist at God, you find it hard to believe that He who claims to be good would allow such pain. Our bitterness shows a faith built on the foundation of sand. When the waters rise and the wind blows against a house built on sand, the foundation does not hold. But he who builds on a rock will not be shaken (see Matt. 7:25).

Another natural reaction to pain is bargaining. We try to strike a deal with God: "If you will heal my friend, God, I promise I will . . ." In a desperate attempt to change God's mind, we slip into the temptation of thinking that we have a better plan than He does. We are willing to up our church attendance or godly obedience if He will just fix the problem. Hospital waiting rooms become places of high stakes negotiations. "God, I will do *X* if You will do *Y*." Obviously, God doesn't broker deals like that. But some good can come from this. A loved one's sickness can reveal our distance from God. It brings to the surface why we feel so helpless. Trials remind us that we have drifted. A Puritan pastor once wrote words that are still true today:

> Vague, and indefinite, and indistinct religion may do very well in time of health. It will never do in the day of sickness. A mere formal, perfunctory Church membership may carry a man through the sunshine of youth and prosperity. It will break down entirely when death is in sight. Nothing will do then but real heart-union with Christ.[7]

Though we initially move through both responses of bitterness and bargaining, the aim is to land in a place of brokenness. Brokenness means hitting your knees before the Lord in surrender to His will. The beginning of this may be tears and emotions stemming from the loss of your will. Brokenness is resting in our inability to handle the situation. Hopefully, we surrender before a battle with God, not just as the result of losing a battle with God.

At times, beginning with brokenness seems unnatural at hearing tough news. But whether we begin there or eventually end there, brokenness is the place where the Lord begins to stretch us and grow our faith. The point of brokenness is when we realize the Lord's sovereignty, even in the midst of trial. We have not resigned ourselves to unending pain, but a broken heart before the Lord is a cry for His strength to carry us.

In such a place, we find ourselves in David's shoes as he wrote, "Create in me a pure heart, O God, and renew a steadfast spirit within me. . . . The sacrifices of God are a broken spirit; a broken and contrite heart, O God, you will not despise" (Ps. 51:10,17). In our brokenness, the Lord begins a masterful work of redemption and restoration.

The faith of Mary and Martha is tested with one simple phrase: "a man named Lazarus was sick." More than a seasonal cold, Lazarus is sick unto death. Seeing that the situation is worsening, the sisters send for a dear friend and healer, Jesus. "Lord, the one you love is sick" (John 11:3). Mary and Martha knew how much Jesus loved their brother. They were also confident that He could heal him. As they reached out to Jesus, they began their journey of trusting God with the testing of their faith.

Delayed for the Sake of Dependence

Sometimes God waits. By our human calculations that is a perplexing thought to understand. Hearing the plea from the sisters, Jesus does something that makes us uncomfortable. He waits. Even knowing the grave situation that Lazarus is in, Jesus takes His time in showing up. When we wait on God, we grow in our dependence of Him. Though we are certain that we know what is needed, God's ways are higher than ours. Our limited minds cannot fully comprehend what He is doing in our lives as we wait.

Jesus' delay is a calculated move toward what is most glorifying to God, not what is physically preferred for Lazarus or emotionally preferred for his family. God's eternal preference is always His glory. We might as well settle it right now: Our preferences will always be trumped by His glory. Though He knows His friend is suffering and his death will cause much pain, Jesus is focused on bringing God glory. There will be countless times in our lives when God's glory supersedes our convenience, change of circumstances or comfort. In those moments, it is a battle to depend on God. But His strength is sufficient for those who lean heavily upon Him. God is radically God-centered. At the center of everything He ordains for our lives, the Lord is decidedly fixated on His glory. He is glorified in us when we depend on Him.

Is God Ever Too Late?

Lazarus dies before Jesus arrives. Death shows that sin has consequence. Romans 6:23 reminds us, "The wages of sin is death." We all die because we all sin. Subsequently, we can take it a step further and say that death was not a part of God's original plan. That's why it is such a punch in the gut! Death of a loved one feels like a tearing away because it is a rip of sin in our fallen world. One day, there will be no more death and the sin-damaged world will have passed; but we are not there yet.

Giving illustration to this point, John uses an interesting Greek word to describe Jesus' reaction to Lazarus's death. In John 11:33 the Word says that Jesus was "deeply moved in spirit and troubled." The word for "deeply moved" is *embrimaomai*, which has the connotation of snorting (in animals).[8] Thus, Jesus is not shown here to express empathy or grief, as He will when He weeps over Lazarus's passing. He is facing His imminent encounter with and assault on death. Jesus "snorted," if you will, at the outcome of sin. Lazarus was dead because he had, like all humans since the

Garden of Eden, sinned. Consequently, he died. This is not what Jesus desired in creation; and therefore, He took no joy in its reality.

As a result of our sinful nature, there is separation from God. Death shows what we deserve to receive because of our sin. In John 11, however, Lazarus's death gives us great hope in revealing that Jesus has defeated death as the last enemy. It no longer has mastery over us. The bee no longer has a stinger—it has been lodged in Christ. Jesus has come and death has lost its grip.

D. L. Moody, the famed evangelist of the 1800s, scanned the Gospels of the New Testament when asked to preach his first funeral message to see what Jesus did at funerals, but to no avail. Jesus never attended a funeral. Any time Jesus and the dead came in contact, the dead came back to life.[9] Jesus and death are in opposition, and Jesus always wins. To take this a step further, the New Testament often refers to the death of believers as having simply fallen asleep (see Mark 5:39; John 11:11; Acts 7:60; 1 Cor. 15:51; 2 Thess. 4:13).

Lazarus's kin might not realize it, but his "falling asleep" is setting the stage for a miracle. Believers make God look great when they are growing through hard times. Even in the middle of tumultuous pain, those who trust in Christ can look to Him. The direction of their gaze is a powerful testimony to all who are watching. Mary and Martha fall to the feet of Jesus. Their Shepherd was 100 miles away from Lazarus when He received the news. Upon His arrival, Lazarus had been in the grave four days. In a hopeless situation, Martha runs toward Jesus. His delay has created her dependence on Him. Weeping at His feet in true brokenness, Martha looks to her friend and Savior. She is dependent on the work of her Lord. That is a snapshot of what brokenness is to look like.

Grieve Toward God

Grieving looks different for everyone. Therefore, the process of moving through grief varies depending on the circumstances and person. But trying to identify normality in the fog can be helpful. Elizabeth Kübler-Ross offers five stages of grief:

1. Denial—"No, not me."
2. Rage and anger—"Why me?"
3. Bargaining—"Yes, me, but . . . ?"

4. Depression—"Yes, me."
5. Acceptance—"It's all right."[10]

Across the board, however, the temptation is to recoil in our grief. In a fast-paced world, we find busyness as an escape from pain. A quiet house is tough on a grieving heart, so we easily fall into the trap of thinking that a full schedule will leave little room to ponder the reality of death. Pastor Bill Hybels gives testimony of this tendency:

I didn't grieve well when my father died; I replaced pain real fast. I think I missed only four days of work. And I just replaced the feeling of loss and disappointment with a frenzied ministry schedule. In short, I ran from grief. That was a bad move for me and for people around me. I wonder how many of us do that. Is anybody running from pain today? Are you trading in your pain prematurely for some other feeling? That's not God's way.[11]

Instead of dealing with the emotional journey of moving through grief, many find relief in drinking, overworking, sulking or just giving up. Our culture tells us to push away grief and charge forward to something else. In the rush of "moving on," the casualty is a heart that has not reckoned with death or found comfort in the Lord. We are drifting backward instead of growing forward.

Believers in Christ have an incomparable hope. We have opportunity to grieve toward eternity. Our hope is secure in the resurrection and the life of Jesus. Distraught by her loss, Martha sees Jesus approaching and runs toward Him.

"Lord," Martha said to Jesus, "if you had been here, my brother would not have died. But I know that even now God will give you whatever you ask."

Jesus said to her, "Your brother will rise again."

Martha answered, "I know he will rise again in the resurrection at the last day."

Jesus said to her, "I am the resurrection and the life. He who believes in me will live, even though he dies; and whoever lives and believes in me will never die. Do you believe this?" (John 11:21-26).

Martha looks to Jesus for comfort in her loss. She is *grieving toward God*, though she lacks understanding. Believers share a hope that we step into heaven upon our passing. Edd Hendee, a friend of mine whose son was killed in a skiing accident, said, "A believer's death is not a finality."[12] We were made to glorify God in this world through faith, and in the next through sight (see 1 Cor. 13:12; 2 Cor. 5:7). We will see Jesus face to face. Death does not have the final sting.

In grieving toward God, we are making a conscious choice to be healed by the one who allowed the dark clouds to roll in. This can be incredibly difficult. However, the challenge of coming to a sovereign God in the midst of pain is also the epitome of trust. Grieving toward God requires strength in Him, to come to Him. Though it can feel like God has us in some sort of a spiritual cul-de-sac, where He wounds in order to heal, it is actually the on-ramp to depth. Taking our grief to Jesus produces a depth of the soul and spiritual understanding that only comes in the darkness of night. Though it doesn't give me joy to say it, depth comes from pain.

When death is properly handled, we grieve toward God instead of running from Him. Our perspective is forced to be heavenly because the pain on earth is too great.

Knowing that Jesus was able to heal the sick and the blind, Martha looked to Him for peace. Jesus claimed to be so much more than she anticipated. He declared that He is "the Resurrection and the Life." Who Jesus is changes everything for us, including who we are. Death no longer has mastery over us because we know the one who is the Resurrection and the Life. As the Lord works those truths deep into our hearts, we are freed up to walk with others through grief. Knowing the end result—eternity with Jesus—gives us strength to face the hardships with grief for ourselves and for others.

Run to Community

The battle for perspective in the midst of a trial such as an illness or death involves fighting against our culture's recipe for dealing with loss. Everything in our culture tells us to grieve alone. But as believers, we have a community to grieve with us. Brothers and sisters under the heavenly Father and indwelled by the Holy Spirit share grief from the soul, not just the emotions. We are not alone in suffering, as our world tells us. Rather, in Christ we have been surrounded by a cloud of witnesses—other believers to point us to Jesus when we can't see past the end of our noses (see Heb. 12:1). Do you know that kind of community when you are in the midst of crisis? Are you aware of brothers and sisters in Christ who need you to surround them? God never intended for His people to face life alone. He gave us a community of believers called the Church. Furthermore, He gave us Himself.

The ministry of presence is a powerful opportunity. Many friends and family surrounded Mary and Martha at the time of their brother's death (see John 11:19). There is no magic bullet for grieving with someone. You don't have to know what to say or even what casserole dish to bring. Compassion is about being present; just being there makes an impact.

A little girl once lost her playmate who lived down the street. She told her mom that she was going to her friend's house to comfort the grieving mother. After an hour or so the little girl returned. Her mom curiously asked, "What did you say to make her feel better?" The girl replied, "Nothing. I just crawled into her lap and cried with her."[13] As loved ones face the gut punches of life, the most important thing you can give them is yourself.

I often feel the pastoral pressure to say the right thing in the midst of grief. However, I have learned that they won't remember what you say, but they will remember you were there. In moments of grief, the greatest thing you can do for someone is act as an arrow pointing to the Lord for the short and the long haul.

A Sure Foundation

Jesus' words to Martha—"I AM the resurrection and the life"—changed everything for her. In a moment she was reminded that life wasn't over for her brother. This statement of identity changes life and death for us as well. He is "the Resurrection and the Life." That gives us freedom to live life with purpose and know that because of Jesus, death does not have the last say. Jesus' declaration is our foundation. Everything changes.

What a scene to witness that must have been! Jesus stands before the tomb and cries out, "Lazarus, come out!" If He, the Resurrection and the Life, didn't specify the name, the entire graveyard would have emptied. I imagine it would have looked like Michael Jackson's *Thriller* video or a bad horror movie. Instead, armed with a specific purpose for a specific person, Jesus calls Lazarus forth, and he appears. Were there cheers of family and friends echoing off the rocks, or stunned silence? We'll never know. But what was unmistakable was the fact that Jesus is more than a mere man. Something is radically different and otherworldly about the one from Nazareth. Lazarus is back . . . from the dead.

Raising Lazarus from the dead is about more than one man's life. Remember, Jesus is preparing us for the cross and His resurrection. He is able to conquer the death of another man and then triumph over His own death as well. Jesus is intentionally personal. In talking to Martha, His conversation turns from a true doctrinal statement to one that is very personal. By using the word "resurrection," He is not talking about the end of time. He is talking about Himself—the true Resurrection for Lazarus, Martha and for us.

A relationship with Jesus offers life instead of death. As we trust in Jesus, we find grace and strength to face things like illness, grief and death with an eternal perspective. Calvin Miller said:

> Death is not a threat to genuine life. It is but a paper tiger that is no longer free to terrorize us once we know the truth about the outcome of the cross. Death is but a temporary inconvenience that separates our smaller living from our greater being.[14]

Because of the resurrection of Jesus, death is a passage to the next world. Like a multistage rocket, we lose a stage that propelled us to the next one.[15] It is not the last chapter, but the beginning of an eternal one. When Lazarus is raised from the dead at the command of Jesus, we find great hope. Jesus Christ, the Resurrection and the Life, conquered death completely and for all time on the cross. A heart that truly understands the magnitude of who Jesus is—the Resurrection and the Life—cannot help but live differently with such a sure foundation.

A wounded soldier knew that he was close to death. Reaching inside his pocket, he pulled out a worn Bible. Flipping through it, he landed on John 11 as he drew his last breath. When the soldier's buddies found him, his blood had stuck his finger on John 11:25: "I am the resurrection and the life." That is a picture of the hope we have in Jesus.[16]

Grieve toward God, knowing that He is the Resurrection and the Life. As you do, living life here on earth will sing a beautiful song of His faithfulness. With our eyes turned heavenward, life has great purpose because there is a great and sure eternity in Jesus.

FOR FURTHER REFLECTION AND DISCUSSION

The "I AM" Playlist Pick

Song	Artist	Album
"Jesus"	Kirk Franklin	*The Fight of My Life*

1. How does properly facing death bring us purpose in life? What negative results can come from denying death?

2. How can Jesus use the "punch in the gut" of a loved one's death to grow our faith? Describe a time when you have experienced or seen this type of growth.

3. Discuss the phrase "grieving toward God."

4. What is the primary thing you learned in this chapter about Jesus' use of grief for His purposes?

5. How does Jesus' raising Lazarus prepare us for the resurrection of Christ?

Partridge Family Praise?

Either Christ was God or He was an imposter.
DR. WILLIAM EVANS

Seven Miracles of Jesus

1. Turning water into wine (JOHN 2:1-12)
2. Healing the nobleman's son (JOHN 4:46-54)
3. Healing of the lame man (JOHN 5:1-17)
4. Feeding the 5,000 (JOHN 6:1-13)
5. Walking on water (JOHN 6:16-21)
6. Healing the man born blind (JOHN 9:1-41)
7. Raising Lazarus from dead (JOHN 11:1-45)

Seven I AM Statements of Jesus

1. I AM the Bread of Life (JOHN 6:35,48,51)
2. I AM the Light of the World (JOHN 8:12)
3. I AM the Door/Gate (JOHN 10:7)
4. I AM the Good Shepherd (JOHN 10:11-14)
5. I AM the Resurrection and the Life (JOHN 11:25)
6. **I AM the Way, the Truth, and the Life** (JOHN 14:6)
7. I AM the True Vine (JOHN 15:1)

Evidence that we live in a religiously confused society shows when worship is based on the famed Partridge Family. Centered on the American television sitcom of the 1970s, the Partridge Family Temple celebrates the tunes and lyrics of the Partridge Family music and holds the show's characters in highest esteem. Partridge Family member David Cassidy is more than a heartthrob of the 1970s; he's worshiped as a spiritual being.[1]

This is a staggering picture of what post-modern religion looks like. Although the Partridge Family Temple is most likely (and hopefully) someone's sense of humor leaking onto the Internet, we live in a postmodern world where we can believe whatever—no rules or limitations. Everything—every belief and thought—is acceptable. In our world, 2+2 doesn't always *have to* equal four. There is a high acceptance of vastly different beliefs as being equal. In a Google search for religious practices, at last count 37,177 beliefs popped up. There is no limit to the spiritual possibilities in our culture.

Times have certainly changed. Even as recently as a few decades ago, our culture practiced more of a generational religion. People followed the tradition of their family. So Christianity was passed down from one generation to the next. Today, people are asking the question, "Why?" In a new age of skeptics, people are prone to reject the faith of their family, whatever that may be, and set out in search of "new" meaning. The cultural characteristics of independence and individuality have created new thoughts and new religions that contradict the Christian faith.

Today, "anything goes." So how can Christians actually think that our way is right? With so many contradictory theories and religions, doesn't it sound arrogant to assume that Christianity is the only true way? Understanding the depth and validity of our faith is essential if we long for the assurance that Jesus is the one and only way to the Father. It is important to understand the lines of debate. Almost everyone believes that a good man named Jesus existed historically. The debate is now centered in His authority, not His existence. The doubt is whether or not Jesus is the Son of God. So the lines of dispute are clear. People rarely doubt Jesus' existence, but they do call His Kingship into question. Those are the battle lines to consider in defending our faith.

So, how do we live and speak with confidence? In the Gospel of John, we have seen Jesus perform miracles and declare authority through the "I AM" statements. He is bold and confident in His declarations, leaving no room for thoughts of other ways to spend eternity with God. In John 14, we will see Jesus' unwavering assurance in His authority as the Son of God.

How can we live and speak with that same confidence, knowing that Jesus is who He says He is? And what about defending our faith against other beliefs? Is it really possible to stand up against opposing ideas and claim that Christ is the only true way?

In our "tolerant" world, Christians can expect opposition. It seems the only belief that is not tolerated today is that Jesus is the lone path to salvation. Our faith will be called into question, as there are many others who believe differently. However, we have something and Someone that others do not. We have the Word of God and His Son, Jesus Christ. It is possible to attest that Jesus is exactly who He said He is. As we unpack the truth of God's Word, as revealed through the life of Christ, we will find a firm foundation for our faith.

Bold and Exclusive

So far in the Gospel of John, we have seen and heard that Jesus is not one to mince words. He makes clear statements of identity that cause a stir and also give us stepping-stones of faith to believe He is the Son of God. In John 14, Jesus has a conversation with His disciples. He is comforting them with the thought that eternity waits for those who trust in Christ. Jesus is also preparing them for the inevitable—His death on the cross.

> Jesus answered, *"I am the way and the truth and the life*. No one comes to the Father except through me. If you really knew me, you would know my Father as well. From now on, you do know him and have seen him" (John 14:6-7, emphasis added).

Jesus makes a bold statement that gives an answer to our question about His authority. The previous I AM statements have ramped up to this one. He claims to be the Way, the Truth, and the Life . . . the ONLY Way, Truth and Life. This statement shouts exclusivity, leaving no room for other beliefs. Even for Christians, this statement can make us squirm in our seats. Perhaps it makes us uneasy because we are so aware of our culture. Millions of people believe in something totally different. And many of them have conviction that their way is right. So how can we be certain that Jesus is speaking the truth? He claims to be the only way to the Father. As we stand back for a clearer perspective, we see biblical footholds that give us reason to know for certain that Jesus' claims are true.

First, Jesus perfectly fulfilled the Old Testament prophecies. The entire Old Testament contains the story of God's work leading up to Christ. Prophets described the coming Savior's birth, life, death and resurrection in detail. Jesus matched every single description. When the Messiah appeared, He was just as had been prophesied.

Old Testament Prophecies of Christ[2]

Topic	Prophecy	Passage
Christ's lineage	Virgin birth	Genesis 3:15
	Lineage of Shem	Genesis 9:26
	Lineage of Abraham	Genesis 12:2
	Lineage of Isaac	Genesis 17:19
	Lineage of Jacob	Genesis 25:23; 28:13
	Lineage of Judah	Genesis 49:10
	Lineage of David	2 Samuel 7:12-16
Christ's birth	Manner of birth	Isaiah 7:14
	Place of birth	Micah 5:2
Christ's life	His forerunner	Isaiah 40:3
	His mission	Isaiah 61:1
	His ministry	Isaiah 53:4
	His teaching	Psalm 78:2
	His presentation	Zechariah 9:9
	His rejection	Psalm 118:22
Christ's death	A painful death	Psalm 22
	A violent death	Isaiah 52–53
Christ's victory	His resurrection	Psalm 16:10
	His ascension	Psalm 68:18
Christ's reign	As sovereign king	Psalm 2
	From exalted Jerusalem	Psalm 24
	With governmental authority	Isaiah 9:6–7
	In peaceful justice	Isaiah 11
	For joyful restoration	Isaiah 35:1–10

The prophets spoke these words and many more long before Christ was born. They were declaring the coming Savior. When Jesus was born to the Virgin Mary in the tiny town of Bethlehem, Jesus began fulfilling every single prophecy. Statistics state that there is a 1 in 100 million billion (that's 17 zeros) chance to fulfill even eight prophecies. But Jesus is not limited to statistics. He fulfilled more than 300![3] The "I AM" statements of the Gospel of John are also the fulfillment of the Old Testament prophecies.[4] Jesus is claiming to be who the prophets said He would be.

Second, Jesus claimed to be God in at least three ways.

1. In John 14:7, we see that Jesus and the Father are one: "If you really knew me, you would know my Father as well. From now on, you do know him and have seen him." This claim bellows His authority as God. If you have seen Jesus, you have seen God. "I and the Father are one. Again the Jews picked up stones to stone him" (John 10:30-31).

2. Jesus also declares that He is eternal and predates Abraham, the father of Judaism. As expected, this doesn't sit well with some of the listeners in John 8:57-59: " 'You are not yet fifty years old,' the Jews said to him, 'and you have seen Abraham!' 'I tell you the truth,' Jesus answered, 'before Abraham was born, I am!' At this, they picked up stones to stone him, but Jesus hid himself, slipping away from the temple grounds." Christ was born but never created—mind-blowing but true. He is eternal and unchanging (see Heb. 13:8 and Col. 1:15-17).

3. Further showing Jesus' belief that He was equal to God the Father, He received worship from His followers. Paul, Barnabas and Peter refused the worship given them in Acts 14 and Acts 10, but Jesus received people's adoration. In Matthew 14:32-33, when Christ and Peter stepped back into the boat and the wind ceased, "Those who were in the boat worshiped him, saying, 'Truly you are the Son of God.' " Also, directly following Jesus' ascension to heaven, the Gospel of Luke tells us, "Then they worshiped him and returned to Jerusalem with great joy" (Luke 24:52).

As William Evans notes, "The homage given to Christ in these scriptures would be nothing short of sacrilegious idolatry if Christ were not God. There seemed to be not the slightest reluctance on the part of Christ in the acceptance of such worship. Therefore either Christ was God or He was an imposter. But His whole life refutes the idea of imposture. It was He who said, 'Worship God only'; and He had no right to take the place of God if He were not God."[5]

Jesus was not just a human teacher; because of His claims and miracles, there are only two options—Jesus was either a raging lunatic or truly the Son of God. He fulfilled prophecy, declared Himself to be God and welcomed worship. This leaves Him either a cracked pot or the eternal firm foundation.

Finally, the empty tomb is a staggering proof of the risen Christ. Three days after Christ's crucifixion, the disciples found an empty tomb, just as Jesus had forewarned them. The authorities were desperate to prove that a resurrection was impossible and went to great lengths to prevent the body from being stolen. The rock was massive, the tomb sealed and guards at attention. But Jesus was gone. If the Romans had only been able to produce the body of Christ, Christianity would have ended in a fizzle. The turning point of our faith is that Christ was crucified, buried and rose again. Because of the resurrection, there was no body to be found—at least not a dead one. He was alive again. The disciples would later give their lives to defend and spread the cause of Christ. Why would they die martyrs for a known lie? They wouldn't! No, the tomb was empty. That is certainly convincing evidence that Jesus Christ, who defeated death, is King.

After Christ's resurrection, more than 500 people gave an eyewitness testimony that they had seen the risen Christ. Hallucinations don't happen in groups. The testimony of more than 500 people makes Jesus' claim of resurrection far from absurd.[6] His bold statement claiming to be the Way, the Truth and the Life finds validity in the perfect alignment of God's Word. We can have confidence that Jesus is exactly who He says He is.

The Way, the Truth and the Life

More than any other "I AM" statement, John 14:6 stops us in our tracks. Jesus claims without exception to be the Way, the Truth and the Life. In the original language of the New Testament, this statement has more going on than in English. The countless times I read this verse, I thought it was just a 1, 2, 3 listing. However, the Greek language's richness is shown in the cyclical statement in which the previous word is the foundation of the next:

> **I am the WAY BECAUSE I Am the Truth and Life:** The structure of this statement is such that Jesus was not giving a string of descriptive terms. He was not saying, "I am: (A) the way, (B) the truth, and (C) the life." Rather, this statement is in an elliptical form, so that Jesus was saying: "I am the way because I am the truth and because I am the life. I am the way to the Father because I am the true manifestation or revelation of the Father. I am the way to the Father because I alone have the power of eternal life" (Acts 4:12; 1 Tim. 2:5; 1:14).[7]

By unflinchingly claiming to be *the* Way to the Father, Jesus is saying He is our payment. We have sinned against the eternal God; therefore, we have eternal consequences. Not only is God eternal, but He is also Holy, which we are not. So how will sinful humans satisfy a holy and eternal God? The holy and eternal Christ paid the debt for us. For humans covered in the filth of sin, there is only one way to be cleansed. And that is through Jesus. It can't be through good deeds, it must be by grace. He is the Way, the only Way.

One day, I had parked my car in a parking garage. After my meeting, I paid for my parking ticket at the lobby meter. Heading back to my car—ticket fully paid—I ran into a friend. After 20 minutes of great catch-up conversation, I proceeded to my car and pulled into the exit line. I arrived at the attendant booth and handed over my redeemed parking ticket. The attendant shook his head and said, "Sorry, you ran over the 15-minute grace period to exit the garage after paying for your ticket. You'll need a new ticket." By this time, there was a long line of cars behind me. It is a humbling experience to ask a line of agitated drivers to back up. Aggravated, I returned to the lobby meter to purchase another pass to get out of the garage, as my "grace period" had evaporated.

If we were to receive God's grace based on our works, how long would grace really last? We would run out of time and find ourselves returning to the meter, attempting to purchase another way out. Jesus is the way to the Father. There is no other. And His payment is once and for all. There is no need to worry that we'll run out of time. He already has us covered.

One of the many incredible qualities of Jesus—the Way, the Truth and the Life—is that He is personal. He's a relationship, not just a religion. His call is to individuals, not to crowds; to individual sheep, not whole flocks. We don't go to heaven in groups, but as individuals.[8] He knows our past and present while at the same time desiring to be our future. Through Christ, our personal relationship with God is possible. God desires relationship, not just spiritual action or morality; He wants to talk with us as friend.

Mamie Adams was an elderly lady who would frequent the post office and time after time wait in line to talk to the friendly attendant behind the counter. She did this regularly, so the postal staff knew her. One Christmas, she went to buy stamps and found herself at the end of a long line. Someone pointed out that she could easily go to the machine in the lobby and avoid the wait. "I know," Mamie responded, "but the machine won't ask me about my arthritis."[9] She preferred conversation to convenience because relationships matter. The beauty of the gospel is that Jesus is personal. He knows our aches and joys intimately.

Jesus offers personal relationship to everyone, even unschooled and ordinary men. In the book of Acts, the apostles Peter and John are standing before the rulers, elders and teachers of the law, defending their faith in Christ. Their testimony was filled with such confidence the leaders were astonished.

> When they saw the courage of Peter and John and realized that they were unschooled, ordinary men, they were astonished and they took note that these men had been with Jesus (Acts 4:13).

Jesus is for everyone. I once heard Melvin Graham, brother of the famous evangelist Billy Graham, remark on the personal love of the Savior. He said, "I'm just a nobody telling everybody that there is Somebody that can save anybody." Jesus can change lives, and He can do it with anyone, anywhere. He is the Way, the Truth and the Life for all who call upon His name.

This declaration of identity is a huge statement. Jesus claims to be *the* Way, Truth and Life. By all accounts, we find confidence in knowing that He is exactly who He says He is.

No Doubt About It

The Lord's statement makes us somewhat nervous because we know the world we live in. Our world is one without absolutes. Postmodern truth is relative, saying there is no such thing as God-given truth. It's up to every individual to determine what is true. That is the water we are swimming in. So when Jesus confidently makes such an absolute statement, we must investigate more. The culture says there is absolutely no absolute truth. *However, to say there is no absolute truth is an absolute statement.* It would be like walking into a Spanish class proclaiming, *"No hablo una palabra en español."* Saying, "I don't speak one word of Spanish" in Spanish completely refutes the point. Obviously, I speak some Spanish, or I could not have spoken the sentence. It sounds absurd. So does the statement, "There is no absolute truth." It is an absolute statement, which contradicts the skeptic's argument.

In our world, we accept absolutes in many things. In math, we accept that 3+3=6. In science, we accept the law of gravity. In regard to traffic law, we stop at red lights, go at green lights and slow down on yellow. Unwritten social rules such as waiting in line are never questioned. Out of the many things we accept, we struggle to accept absolute statements in religion, morals or ethical ways, mainly because it is too personal for our tastes. We prefer to judge according to the situation instead of principles. As we consider absolute truths we follow, it is clear that society would break down without them.

Charles Colson presented a lecture at Harvard University, wittingly titled *Why Harvard Can't Teach Ethics.* His audience's response after the class was worthy of note. He expected a riotous group of students, full of questions and intelligent refutes. To his surprise, however, the students sat in silence during his 45-minute discourse. He later recalled this time at Harvard:

> I left Harvard worried. What would happen to these students when they became leaders of American business? One of the students at Harvard during that period was Jeffrey Skilling, the now-discredited former Enron CEO. Enron's collapse exposes the glaring failure of the academy. Ethics historically rests on absolute truth, which these institutions have systematically assaulted for decades. You see, ethics, classically, are unchanging standards, which derive their authority from a transcendent Authority. Well, the problem is if you teach permissive ethics, you'll turn the best and brightest into permissive businessmen who cut corners and think they can get away with it. . . . But we'd better learn a lesson

well. When you fail to teach right and wrong, don't be surprised when people do wrong.[10]

Society crumbles without the structure of Absolute Truth. On our search, we find two things—Absolute Truth does exist and can be found in the Bible. God is Absolute Truth and is discovered through Jesus and His Word. The Gospel of John is filled with declarations that point to this living Truth (emphasis added):

- John 4:23: "Yet a time is coming and has now come when the true worshipers will worship the Father in spirit and *truth*, for they are the kind of worshipers the Father seeks."
- John 8:32: "Then you will know the *truth*, and the *truth* will set you free."
- John 14:6: "Jesus answered, 'I am the way and the *truth* and the life. No one comes to the Father except through me.'"
- John 16:12-13: "I have much more to say to you, more than you can now bear. But when he, the *Spirit of truth,* comes, he will guide you into all *truth*."
- John 17:17: "Sanctify them by the *truth*; your word is *truth*."
- John 18:37-38: "'You are a king, then!' said Pilate. Jesus answered, 'You are right in saying I am a king. In fact, for this reason I was born, and for this I came into the world, to testify to the truth. Everyone on the side of *truth* listens to me.' '*What is truth?*' Pilate asked. With this he went out again to the Jews and said, 'I find no basis for a charge against him."

Firm Foundation to Stand On

Strong pillars support the Christian faith. Our faith has been tested from every angle, and yet it has stood. It stands because it is based on absolute truth resting in the absolute authority of God. As we grow in this confidence, we are equipped to defend our faith and rest assuredly in Christ. Learning to defend our faith is part of growing in the Lord.

We will talk further about this in the next chapter as well, specifically addressing design versus chance in regard to creation. Rest assured we are defending bulletproof Truth. Jesus is who He said He is; Jesus is also who the prophets said He would be. His claim is absolute and He offers no other option. He *is* the Way, because He is the Truth and He created Life. When something is absolute—even proven with evidence—it is worth sharing and defending. *The Partridge Family* can have the reruns, but it cannot have the worship.

If you know Jesus as the Way, the Truth and the Life, share the gospel with others. It is a firm foundation that our hurting world desperately needs to hear about. This world needs more believers who are certain that Truth—the Savior, Jesus—is Absolute.

> Jesus answered, "*I am the way and the truth and the life*. No one comes to the Father except through me" (John 14:6, emphasis added).

FOR FURTHER REFLECTION AND DISCUSSION

The "I AM" Playlist Pick

Song	Artist	Album
"Jesus Savior/Doxology"	Breakaway Ministries	*Breakaway/Live*

1. Why is it such a problem for today's world to accept that there is only one way to the Father and heaven?

2. Jesus' declaration, "I AM the way, the truth and the life," is bold and exclusive. Does this bother you or comfort you, or both? Why?

3. Which examples mentioned in the chapter are the most convincing to you that He is the only way to heaven?

4. Why is it important to be crystal clear that the path of salvation is Christ alone?

5. How does knowing facts of the truth help your heart trust God more deeply?

Sprinklers, Pulses and Vineyards

By declaring Himself the "true Vine," Jesus took the place of Israel,
claiming to be the authentic, healthy vineyard the nation failed to become.
CHARLES SWINDOLL

Seven Miracles of Jesus

1. Turning water into wine (JOHN 2:1-12)
2. Healing the nobleman's son (JOHN 4:46-54)
3. Healing of the lame man (JOHN 5:1-17)
4. Feeding the 5,000 (JOHN 6:1-13)
5. Walking on water (JOHN 6:16-21)
6. Healing the man born blind (JOHN 9:1-41)
7. Raising Lazarus from dead (JOHN 11:1-45)

Seven I AM Statements of Jesus

1. I AM the Bread of Life (JOHN 6:35,48,51)
2. I AM the Light of the World (JOHN 8:12)
3. I AM the Door/Gate (JOHN 10:7)
4. I AM the Good Shepherd (JOHN 10:11-14)
5. I AM the Resurrection and the Life (JOHN 11:25)
6. I AM the Way, the Truth, and the Life (JOHN 14:6)
7. I AM the True Vine (JOHN 15:1)

Standing in line at the grocery store becomes an entertaining place to people watch, work on your patience and discover the latest gossip. Typically, tabloids and entertainment magazines dishing the latest scoop flank you. They beg for purchase so you will be in the know. The tabloids that create the most outrageous rumors and false accusations always entertain me. The front cover stories are so absurd that I often wonder how anyone could find them to be true. Here are a few examples that made it to print:

- ELVIS IS ALIVE AND PRETENDING TO BE AN ELVIS IMPERSONATOR
- PACK OF WILD COCKER SPANIELS TERRORIZES WYOMING
- WEREWOLVES SUNK THE TITANIC!
- WOMAN DELIVERS OWN BABY WHILE SKYDIVING!
- VEGAN VAMPIRE ATTACKS TREES
- HOUSEWIFE EXPERIENCES HALF-RAPTURE . . . and gets stuck in the dining room ceiling![1]

In many ways, these headlines represent our culture's view on truth. Don't let the truth get in the way of telling a story; just make the sale. In the world's eyes, truth is relative, as we discussed in the last chapter.

Our world does not hold truth high. In fact, we mock it. So if we want to understand truth, we'll be swimming upstream. But the quest is worth it. The Bible and our faith are far from tabloids. They are unshakably grounded and true to the core.

Every day we need to confront and sift through what is true and what is false; what is worthy of attention and what is just noise. These daily forks in the road guide our understanding of truth, which in turn influences our hearts. What we know in our minds affects what we understand at a heart level. And what we understand at a heart level lays a foundation of truth that allows us to become passionate worshipers of the one who is Truth.

Christian worship is a quest for people of truth, not fallacy. The more we know with certainty, the more our hearts will be freed up to worship Him. But worship involves more than just a heart-level understanding.

Many people worship the Lord primarily from emotions; therefore, their foundation is feeling and not fact. By all means, we are to passionately sense His presence among us, but the feelings should originate in the facts. For example, Jesus is alive, fact. Now I will praise with feeling. Those who don't worship with their heads as well as their hearts are likely to burn out. Feelings ebb and flow, but facts remain.

A beautiful symphony of a worshipful life is composed when the heart, mind and soul are in harmony. Facts and feelings don't in the least negate faith in the least. Faith is the locomotive that pulls the cars of facts and feelings. Having security in the truth of the "I AM" brings great change to who i am.

In the beginning of John 15, Jesus holds out the truth to us. As a crescendo to His statements of identity, He claims, "I AM the True Vine." He doesn't reference other vines, but claims to be the only true one. We might be tempted to ask ourselves, "Is He really the True Vine?" Plenty of other people who don't rest their hope in Jesus believe that He is "a vine" but not "THE TRUE Vine."

The precise declaration of being THE TRUE Vine seems like an over-confident statement. But these types of statements have been made by and about Jesus before in the book of John. In John 1, He is "THE TRUE light," echoing the first chapter in Genesis where God's first declaration of creation was "Let there be light." In John 6, He is "THE TRUE bread," reminding us of the use of the manna in the wilderness of the Exodus. Now Jesus says, "I AM THE TRUE Vine," meaning that He is the replacement of Israel, which was symbolized in the Old Testament by a vine (see Isa. 5:1-7). Relationship with God is no longer found through a nation, but through a Person. As Chuck Swindoll states:

> Israel was to flourish as a living example of how obedience bears fruit of righteousness. Moreover, the Lord promised to bless Israel as the nation's relationship of trust grew stronger. But Israel failed. By declaring Himself the "True Vine," Jesus took the place of Israel, claiming to be the authentic, healthy vineyard the nation failed to become.[2]

The Old Testament is fulfilled in the New Testament. Jesus is the light of creation, the bread of provision and the vine of Israel! Like the first six I AM statements, declaring Himself to be the True Vine is a hefty statement.

Other religions in our culture practice values that are similar to those found in Christianity. In fact, many hold Christianity's fruit of the Spirit as noble attributes to attain: love, joy, peace, patience, kindness, goodness, faithfulness, gentleness and self-control (see Gal. 5:16). The Bible teaches that these attributes are like nine colors God uses to paint the face of Christ and Christians, for a watching world. Yes, Islam, Hinduism and Hollywood's "religion du jour" appreciate similar verbs and adjectives, but they don't stem from the same noun of our God. Different religions possess similar moral adjectives but different deity nouns, and similar values vocabularies but different theological dictionaries.

Our culture blurs the lines when it comes to religion. In fact, many people take the "best of" each religion to create a "Mr. Potato Head" faith that is tailored to the desire of their flesh instead of their spirit. This personally preferred "greatest-hits play list of religions" creates ambiguity and causes confusion. No wonder our world is baffled on the subject of truth.

The True Vine

"I am the true vine."

JOHN 15:1

In a world filled with religious confusion, Jesus makes a statement that brings clarity. He claims to be the True Vine. How can we be certain this is true? If you remember our chapters about Jesus as the Gate and the Way, we arrived at the conclusion that He truly is the only path to the Father.

Perhaps we need to take a step back. Jesus claims to be the Son of God. And by all accounts, we are invigorated to believe this is true. However, if you are asking, "But wait, is there even a God?" taking that big step backward will only affirm what we know and add to our foundation as intelligent worshipers. In our world, plenty of people will claim that this whole thing called "life" just happened.

They don't look for a Creator, let alone a loving God who orchestrated it all together. To those people, the evolutionary math is simple: time + chance = order. The theory of evolution is similar to tossing a puzzle into the air over and over, expecting it to assemble its pieces. It would be a complete disaster. If time and chance can't put cardboard together, how can it possibly put the complexity of our world together? Even if billions of years of tossing pieces in the air produced a completed puzzle, where did the pieces come from in the first place? It just doesn't add up.

Arguments of design vs. chance can be found in plenty of conversations of textbooks and classrooms.[3] Parts of our culture seem fixated on solidifying the argument of chance. But perhaps they have never considered the beauty and brilliance behind the signs of design. Think of the following four scientific facts, asking if they are the result of chance or design:

1. The sun sits in orbit 93 million miles away from our earth, burning at 11,500 degrees Fahrenheit. By the time its heat reaches the surface of earth, the temperature has reached an average of 72 degrees. A change—50 degrees hotter or 50 degrees cooler—would cause life on earth to cease to exist. How can 11,500 degrees arriving to earth at 72 degrees be random?

2. Evidence of creation continues. . . . The earth's rotation is overwhelming to consider, rotating at 1,000 miles per hour. If the speed were to slow down by even a tenth, we would either freeze or burn up like a rotisserie chicken. Its rotation is perfect for the existence of human life.

3. Not only that, but there is great intentionality in the earth's elliptical orbit. We are moving at 64,800 miles per hour. If that speed were to reduce by one-third, we would burn up. Our globe's rotation and orbit are precise. Can you doubt there's a design?

4. Finally, the moon sits 240,000 miles away from earth. If it had been placed one-fifth of that distance closer, the tides of the oceans would cover the continents twice a day.[4]

The Creator's hand was gentle and meticulous. The evidence of such creative design is absolutely astonishing. Our earth and solar system are filled with beautiful examples pointing to a powerful and detailed Creator. When it comes down to it, believing in evolution takes more faith than believing in creation. I guess you could say that I don't have enough faith to be an evolutionist or an atheist.

Removing God as Creator stems from the desire to remove accountability for our actions; if the universe is void of God, then we are in charge. Man becomes the true vine; the source of life, wisdom and morality. But if there is a God, then we are accountable to Him. We are the created and He is the Creator. There must be actions that please Him and others that don't.

Therefore, sin and righteousness exist. Because this is an uncomfortable feeling—to ponder divine scales of justice weighing our deeds—we dethrone the Creator by "scientifically" proving that we are at the evolutionary top of the heap. Now we get to make the rules of right and wrong.

Without God, there is no sin, just different choices; no need for forgiveness, just mistakes to sweep under the rug. Man is the decision maker, with his kingdom based on his preferences. Who needs God? What would a Savior save us from? Man's evolved sense of reason and his opposable thumbs have led us to place ourselves higher than God.

Our faith, which is encouraged by the evidence of a world created with design, leads us to the assurance that there is a God. He is a designing Creator with a special heart for man—yes, with an eternal sense of right and wrong but also a remedy for our sin through sending His Son to save. Now we can look at Jesus with new eyes.

We understand accountability because we believe in a Creator. Since it is His creation we have tainted, we trust in His Vine to forgive us. If there is a God, as we believe, then Jesus claims to be Him. He claims to be the True Vine, the Son of God, the Shepherd of our souls, and our Savior from sin. As believers, we have every reason to believe that He is speaking the truth. Truth will always be true. Therefore, the facts of the meticulous design of our world fill our heads in order to create deeper trust within our hearts. Truth becomes belief in Jesus, the True Vine. Again, the head leads to the heart just as the Creator leads to the Savior.

Clean Clips of the Gardener

I am the true vine, and my Father is the gardener. He cuts off every branch in me that bears no fruit, while every branch that does bear fruit he prunes so that it will be even more fruitful. You are already clean because of the word I have spoken to you. Remain in me, and I will remain in you. No branch can bear fruit by itself; it must remain in the vine. Neither can you bear fruit unless you remain in me. I am the vine; you are the branches. If a man remains in me and I in him, he will bear much fruit; apart from me you can do nothing.

JOHN 15:1-5

A gardener has a very scrupulous job. His role involves the clipping and pruning of individual branches so that the whole plant flourishes. With each changing season, the gardener has the best interests of the plant in mind. The Greek word used for "gardener" is *georgos*, the common word for "farmer."[5] He nurtures his crop as a shepherd cares for his sheep. Knowing the relationship of the gardener to the crop is crucial. For in this powerful metaphor, we see a picture of our faith. Jesus calls the Gardener His heavenly Father.

The gardener's role is essential to the health of the plant. Similarly, the Father's role in our lives is indispensable. Though He clips away, remember that He is our loving Father. Each clip and each trim is symbolic of His patient and edifying love for us. He trims so that we will look more like Jesus. The Father's role has the pointed goal of our bearing fruit. He has the end in sight, not just the comfort of the moment. The Gardener prunes our branches from a place of deep, eternal love for us. He sees beyond the fleeting moment of pain and looks forward to a day when we will bear more fruit as a result of the trim. God loves tomorrow's fruit more than today's leaves, so He clips.

Our human tendency is to compare the love of the heavenly Father with the love of our earthly father. Depending on your relationship with your father, this could have a negative or positive connotation. Perhaps you and dad have a great friendship, which encourages your walk with the Lord. The earthly love of a father has been a beautiful reflection of the heavenly Father's love in our life. Or maybe your story is totally different. Your relationship with your dad is strained or possibly nonexistent. Therefore, the love of the heavenly Father seems unattainable and fragile. Remember, the Lord's love for you is greater than any love a human could offer. Allow the disappointment with your earthly dad to turn to strength as you trust your heavenly Father.

Whatever your current or past relationship with your earthly father, we all agree that dads have strengths and weaknesses—but not our heavenly Father. Our Gardener only has strengths, and He showers His children with good things.

Which of you, if his son asks for bread, will give him a stone? Or if he asks for a fish, will give him a snake? If you, then, though you are evil, know how to give good gifts to your children, how much more will your Father in heaven give good gifts to those who ask him! (Matt. 7:9-11).

He has nothing but good things in mind for us.

Picture a beautiful red rose. Sometimes the Gardener prunes one petal at a time. One by one, red petals fall to the ground. Other times, He prunes the entire bud. When we lose a petal, sometimes we barely notice His gentle pruning. But when the entire bud topples over, we are prone to look to the Lord and wonder why. There may be a time in your life when you are standing there with an empty stem in hand. Grieve, cry, ache, but realize the magnitude of His love. Perspective is a wonderful thing, especially when the end result is looking more like Jesus.

In John 15:3, Jesus remarks that we are "already clean." He uses the same Greek word that Revelation 19:8 uses to describe the believer's robes in heaven. By His cross, we have been made clean—brand new—through the blood of Jesus. Pruning has nothing to do with losing or gaining our salvation, but everything to do with our sanctification—walking more in the power of Christ. The following verses illustrate that believers in Christ have been completely changed and cleansed (emphasis mine):

- Colossians 1:21-22: "Once you were alienated from God and were enemies in your minds because of your evil behavior. But now he has reconciled you by Christ's physical body through death to present you holy in his sight, *without blemish and free from accusation.*"
- Ephesians 1:4: "For he chose us in him before the creation of the world to be *holy and blameless in his sight.*"
- 1 John 1:7: "But if we walk in the light, as he is in the light, we have fellowship with one another, and the blood of Jesus, *his Son, purifies us from all sin.*"
- 2 Corinthians 5:17: "Therefore, if anyone is in Christ, he is a *new creation;* the old has gone, the new has come!"
- Isaiah 1:18: "Though your sins are like scarlet, *they shall be as white as snow;* though they are red as crimson, they shall be like wool."
- Revelation 19:6-8: "Hallelujah! For our Lord God Almighty reigns. Let us rejoice and be glad and give him glory! For the wedding of the Lamb has come, and his bride has made herself ready. *Fine linen, bright and clean, was given her to wear.*" (Fine linen stands for the righteous acts of the saints.)

The Father has made us clean in Christ. Our sins are forgiven and we have been made new. He takes a dirty heart and makes it brand new. Wherever you have been in your life, God will meet you there. He restores liars, cheaters and thieves. Big point to remember: We are not trying to become "clean" to gain salvation but "clean" because we have salvation. For those in Christ, you are clean, pure and forgiven. You are no longer classified as a sinner but as a saint, who sins on occasion. Pruning is the process of trimming to make us more like Jesus in our everyday steps. The Gardener is a loving Father who loves us and therefore prunes so that we would bear much fruit for our good and His ultimate glory. He is the True Vine and we are the pruned branches that abide to bear eternal fruit.

Abiding

Abide in Me, and I in you. As the branch cannot bear fruit of itself unless it abides in the vine, so neither can you unless you abide in Me.
JOHN 15:4, *NASB*

The alarm rang through the empty school hallways, bouncing off lockers and catching the attention of each focused classroom. Students straightened up in their seats. "Sweet! A fire drill to get us out of class!" Teachers, disgruntled at the inconvenience of another drill, gathered the attention of the class and proceeded to carry out the routine of the drill procedure. As the students filed into the hallways, they were astonished to see billowing smoke circling throughout the building. This wasn't a drill; this was the real deal—fire was making its way through the school. Chaos and frenzied emotions quickly mounted as the front lawn filled with students and faculty. They watched as flames engulfed the school. A quick head count revealed a startling reality—numerous students were unaccounted for. They were still inside the building.

After the incident, the school board met to determine the magnitude of the loss—not only the loss of classrooms and supplies, but also the tragic loss of life. It was soon discovered that the building was not equipped with a sprinkler system. In an effort to begin the healing and rebuilding process, the school board decided on a state-of-the-art sprinkler system that would be installed in the new school building. By the grand opening, the sprinkler system was in place and student life resumed to a new normal.

The school's janitorial staff paid close attention to every nook and cranny of the building. While making the rounds in the basement one morning, a janitor discovered a scandalous mistake in the new sprinkler system. It was state of the art, but never connected to the water source. It was a well-planned and constructed system without the only step that mattered—connection to the water source. Should a fire come again, the sprinklers would be useless. Connection to the source was key to its purpose.

The same can be said of our relationship with the Lord. If all the bells and whistles of Christianity are in place but without a connection to the Vine, it is for naught. We often lack connection with our true Source. Another way of saying "connecting" is "abiding." Abiding in the Lord brings nourishment to our lives in the same way that a branch receives nourishment from its source, a vine.

Intimately knowing the Gardener, our Father, changes the way we think about abiding in Him. His care gives us the reason and hope to abide. Different translations of the Bible use different terminology in John 15. Some use the word "remain" while others use the term "abide." Both terms hold similar meaning—to stay connected to a life-giving source. In our Christian walk, we as the branch often lack connection to the Vine. The sprinkler being connected to the water source was key. Similarly, our abiding relationship with the Lord is the power for life.

The Christian life is neither hard nor difficult; it is actually impossible without abiding in Christ. To abide in Christ means to have a desperate dependence and a restful residence in the Lord. I went with Kelly to a doctor's appointment as the due date for our son was approaching. Watching the sonogram, it was incredible to have a window into where God does His knitting. The sonogram was black and white, and yet suddenly, streaks of color began to pop up on the screen. The doctor pointed out that those colors were nutrients passing through the umbilical cord. Greyson was abiding in Kelly—desperately dependent on her for nourishment and yet resting peacefully. For me, it was a stunning picture of our abiding in the True Vine.

The call on our lives is not to bear fruit but to abide. If we abide, the fruit will take care of itself. Matthew 6:33 reminds us, "Seek first his kingdom and his righteousness, and all these things will be given to you as well." The question is not what we can do *for* Him but what can He do *through* us. Abiding dependently and restfully, not on our own efforts, is the route to bearing lasting fruit. The abiding life allows God to live through us. The Holy Spirit moves through believers as they surrender. We still prepare and plan, but we do so knowing that it is not our strength that brings the tipping point. We aren't the source; He is. A yielded and yet prepared heart is the place of strength.

As believers, we don't parent in our knowledge or personality. And it is impossible to walk through difficulties in marriage by willpower. We don't just grit our teeth during lonely times. We abide in the good and bad by resting in His care and call. Kelly and I ask our kids to give us space to spend time with God, saying, "Mommy is a better mommy after she has been with Jesus." "Daddy is a better daddy after he has been with Jesus." I'm also a better husband, friend and pastor. When I'm keenly aware of my true identity, I can better fulfill my roles. But if I focus on the roles of husband, father and pastor, I'll miss the joy of my identity as a Christian. I must abide in my identity in Christ to fulfill my roles on earth. The two can't be reversed.

The Lord's work through me is far more profitable in life and eternity than my own efforts. If we abide deeply, we will achieve eternally. Eternal value is found in abiding in the eternal I AM. Compare John 15:5 and 15:16: "apart from me you can do nothing" and "go and bear fruit—fruit that will last." Our choice is between "nothing" or "lasting." Abiding in the True Vine bears lasting fruit, while life in my strength amounts to nothing. I may be busy, but I will accomplish nothing for eternity unless I abide.

In this last I AM statement, Jesus is sending us out to live the Christian life. This seventh I AM vineyard illustration presents the diagram of a life in love with the Son, not just undertaking Christian activities for Him. We are all simply branches. Billions of branches have come before us and billions more will come after. We aren't called to produce the grapes but to abide in the Vine. If we abide deeply, we will achieve eternally. The heartbeat of the Savior will pulse through us. The following story from *ABC News* illustrates this truth perfectly.

Iowa Couple Married 72 Years Dies
Holding Hands, an Hour Apart

A devoted Iowa couple married for 72 years died holding hands in the hospital last week, exactly one hour apart.

The passing reflected the nature of their marriage, where, "As a rule, everything was done together," said the couple's daughter Donna Sheets, 71.

Gordon Yeager, 94, and his wife, Norma, 90, left their small town of State Center, Iowa, on Wednesday to go into town, but never made it. A car accident sent the couple to the emergency room and intensive care unit with broken bones and other injuries. But, even in the hospital, their concerns were each other.

"She was saying her chest hurt, and what's wrong with Dad? Even laying there like that, she was worried about Dad," said the couple's son, Dennis Yeager, 52. "And his back was hurting and he was asking about Mom."

When it became clear that their conditions were not improving, the couple was moved into a room together in beds side-by-side where they could hold hands.

"They joined hands; his right hand, her left hand," Sheets said.

Gordon Yeager died at 3:38 p.m. He was no longer breathing, but the family was surprised by what his monitor showed.

"Someone in there said, 'Why, then, when we look at the monitor is the heart still beating?'" Sheets recalled. "The nurse said Dad was picking up Mom's heartbeat through Mom's hand."

"And we thought, 'Oh my gosh, Mom's heart is beating through him,'" Dennis Yeager said.[6]

That's it! God's heart beats through us for the world to see. As we hold hands and hearts with the True Vine of Jesus, His pulse becomes ours and His life becomes ours. He is the Vine, we are the branches and His heartbeat is the fruit.

It is seamless. The final "I AM" statement of John leads us to the lifelong journey of abiding in Christ. The power is in Him, not us. The Good Shepherd's wisdom and leadership enable us to accomplish the tasks of eternity instead of aimless wandering. Abide deeply to achieve eternally.

A change of pulse changes actions as well. Seeing what Jesus does changes what I am to do. *I AM changes who i am*. His actions are to become my actions. His heartbeat becomes mine.

In John 14:12, Jesus says we will do even greater things than He did. Not greater in degree but in greater extent.[7] Jesus' earthly ministry was centered in Israel, while today, worldwide, abiding believers are carrying the message of Christ. From the Son of Man to mankind, throughout generations we shine His light. Abiding in your new identity as a clean, forgiven child of the Father is the root of miraculous living. Miracles are not the result of magic or sleight of hand, but connection to the highest Source. Read it out loud and sense its truth . . . *I AM changes who i am*.

He flows; I yield. He speaks; I listen. I grasp His hand and He becomes my pulse. He is the Vine, I am the branch, and my life bears His fruit. Grapes on the vine are not exhausted by effort. Instead the grapes trust in the vine's nutrients. Christians who rely on Christ trust the growth to come through Him. Therefore, abide. Rest in Him. This is the journey of faith and the call of the final I AM statement of John.

Abide—look to the design of the Creator of the universe, connect the sprinkler system, see the sonogram, feel the heartbeat, and dependently rest in the True Vine. The fruit will come in season. Abide deeply to achieve eternally. That's the Christian life.

FOR FURTHER REFLECTION AND DISCUSSION

The "I AM" Playlist Pick

Song	Artist	Album
"Strong Enough"	Matthew West	*The Story of Your Life*

1. How does our head influence our heart when it comes to worshiping God?

2. Why is belief in creation so important? Which fact of our world's design was the most significant to you?

3. God is the Gardener of our lives. What has He recently pruned in your life? What is He pruning now? How will He use this to bring more fruit?

4. What does it mean to abide? How is this refreshing to our effort-driven mentality?

5. Discuss the phrase "abide deeply to achieve eternally."

6. How can God's pulse beat stronger through you? How can abiding deeper make this possible?

Contrasts Create . . .

We started this book with a statement: "Contrasts create impact." I sat with football players realizing the contrast; the clear difference between us was encouraging and intimidating at the same time. The same could be said of the ground we have covered since then. More than a middle line-backer, we have seen the Miraculous Messiah. His miracles and "I AM" statements have built upon one another, cumulating in His resurrection. Jesus rose again, declaring He was the miraculous Messiah and reigns over death. Christ is completely "other" when compared to us—but that contrast creates the impact. The miracles drop our jaws and the I AMs blow our minds. These all combine to show He is the Son of God and will change our hearts. *I AM changes who i am.*

The clarity and power of the seven miracles and seven statements of identity are like a good meal. Different textures, tastes and types of food, but all headed to the same goal of filling and nourishing our bodies. Equally, our meal throughout this book has been to fill and nourish our souls. The miracles are different—toasting a glass of heavenly wine at a wedding is poles apart from unwrapping Lazarus's grave clothes in a cemetery. And each I AM is different too. But the contrasts are forever pointing to the same impact. The Messiah has arrived! Jesus is here, and He knows He is the I AM, the self-existing, past, present and future God who commands creation and changes lives.

Seven Miracles of Jesus

1. Turning water into wine (JOHN 2:1-12)
2. Healing the nobleman's son (JOHN 4:46-54)
3. Healing of the lame man (JOHN 5:1-17)
4. Feeding the 5,000 (JOHN 6:1-13)
5. Walking on water (JOHN 6:16-21)
6. Healing the man born blind (JOHN 9:1-41)
7. Raising Lazarus from dead (JOHN 11:1-45)

Gregg Matte

Seven I AM Statements of Jesus

1. I AM the Bread of Life (JOHN 6:35,48,51)
2. I AM the Light of the World (JOHN 8:12)
3. I AM the Door/Gate (JOHN 10:7)
4. I AM the Good Shepherd (JOHN 10:11-14)
5. I AM the Resurrection and the Life (JOHN 11:25)
6. I AM the Way, the Truth, and the Life (JOHN 14:6)
7. I AM the True Vine (JOHN 15:1)

With these truths swirling in our hearts and heads, we conclude and continue our journey. The conclusion is the comma between you as the reader and me as the author. It's funny how we can become friends through the pages of the written word. Thanks for allowing me to walk with you. I pray that the journey was full of impact. When you put this book on the shelf or hand it to a friend, we'll conclude until I write and you read another time.

But more than a conclusion, there is a continuation! God now wants both of us to live in His miraculous power. He longs for both of us to know the I AM of Jesus living inside of us. Through the Holy Spirit who indwells every believer, we will continue to see miracles; and with every miracle, we will know Him better. From here, let's walk with God. Let's pray for the miraculous and press on to know the I AM more intimately. Let's go together, leaving these pages to run with God and be on the lookout for the miraculous in our homes, schools, offices and churches. He is still at work and wanting to change who we are and what we do. Let's live in God's power to be a miracle for someone in need. Then we'll simply point to Jesus the miraculous Messiah, the I AM who still changes lives.

Say it out loud one more time . . . *I AM changes who i am!*

Thoughts on Drinking

The miracle of water turning to wine is troubling to some Christians because they would have much preferred to see Jesus turn wine into water. The discomfort with the miracle is a symptom of the confusion we have with the subject of drinking in general. So let's talk it through, not from a place of judgment or legalism, but in a desire to think. Engaging our brains will lead to engaging our hearts and our steps.

Believe me, I have done it all in regard to drinking. Here's my journey: "I was so wasted, I did what? . . . No, thanks, I don't drink . . . Sure, a glass of wine with dinner would be nice . . . No, thanks, I don't drink." Drunk, buzzed, as a social act, abstaining from—I've done it all. So let's talk this topic through in bullet points.

- **First of all, everyone agrees that drunkenness is wrong.** To say that someone "drinks" is never meant as a compliment, but always as a negative or a concern. We all concur that drunkenness is not right in the eyes of the Lord or man. Truly, it has to be bad if both God and man agree.

  Wine is a mocker and beer a brawler; whoever is led astray by them is not wise (Prov. 20:1).

  Woe to those who are heroes at drinking wine and champions at mixing drinks (Isa. 5:22).

  And envy; drunkenness, orgies, and the like. I warn you, as I did before, that those who live like this will not inherit the kingdom of God (Gal. 5:21).

  Be careful, or your hearts will be weighed down with dissipation, drunkenness and the anxieties of life, and that day will close on you unexpectedly like a trap (Luke 21:34).

Do not get drunk on wine, which leads to debauchery. In-stead, be filled with the Spirit (Eph. 5:18).

The first biblical account of drinking is found in Genesis 9:20-22: "Noah, a man of the soil, proceeded to plant a vineyard. When he drank some of its wine, he became drunk and lay uncovered inside his tent. Ham, the father of Canaan, saw his father's nakedness and told his two brothers outside." In addition to the biblical injunction against drunkenness, note the following:

> Drunk driving is against the law in all 50 states in the United States.
> Half of all traffic fatalities and one-third of all traffic in-juries are alcohol-related.
> Drunks in a social environment are disdained, pitied, laughed at and, at the most, tolerated, but never admired.
> To say someone is drunk is never a compliment.
> Drinking is always referred to as a problem, not a quality.
> 67 percent of all murders are alcohol-related.[1]

· **Why do people drink?**

1. *To fit in or relax:* Alcohol helps us feel relaxed and gives us confidence in conversation.

2. *For possible health benefits:* Some studies have shown that a moderate intake of alcohol (usually wine) has health benefits.

3. *As a hobby:* People enjoy collecting bottles of wine, or for the less affluent, bottle caps of beer. There are connoisseurs who know the ins and outs of creating the drink and appreciating it.

4. *To numb pain or bolster insecurities:* Sadly, we must admit this is a huge reason for drinking. The feeling it brings helps us cope with life. I've been there and have compassion for those who are there now. There is lots of pain in our society; therefore, there is lots of drinking in our society.

5. *Because it looks "cool":* Let's be honest, it is a beverage that people proudly tote. The beer bottle makes men feel tough and the wine glass makes women feel beautiful. Cool is the key.

· **Why do people choose not to drink?**

1. *Witnessed addiction and destruction of lives:* We all know someone whose life has been ruined by alcohol.

2. *It looks like the world:* Since the vast majority does drink, and the younger crowd mostly drinks to excess, abstaining gives an opportunity for a Christian to look different from the crowd. Hopefully, this differences draws people to ask why. I remember the first time I stopped drinking. The shock that I wasn't like everyone else resulted in my being able to share Christ countless times.

3. *It supports a destructive industry:* A portion of the money spent on alcohol by a well-meaning social drinker ultimately ends up funding a drunk-driving accident, domestic violence and other crimes.

4. *It seeks to provide what only Jesus can:* Relaxation and courage are to be found in the Holy Spirit's power.

5. *It impairs decision making:* Dr. Richard Strain has stated, "As a brain surgeon I have yet to meet a moderate drinking colleague who would like me to operate on his son after I 'had a few.' No one does his best after drinking. He may think he does, but his judgment is defective. . . . Moderation is a terrible fallacy."[2]

· **How should a Christian respond?** Ask yourself three questions:

1. *Does drinking hurt my walk with Christ?* Am I trying to find something Jesus intends to provide (acceptance, courage, peace) and, therefore, hindering my faith in Him? Are we looking to the bottle to find what should be found in the Bible? The Lord wants us to trust Him for the things we need. "Do not get drunk on wine, which leads to debauchery. Instead, be filled with the Spirit" (Eph. 5:18).

2. *Does drinking hurt my witness for Christ?* If we look the same as everyone else on the outside, they might assume there is nothing different on the inside.

3. *Does drinking hurt anyone else's walk with Christ?* Who is watching you? As known believers, many eyes are watching us with

respect. They are looking for clues for how to live life. Drinking may be a stumbling block or increase the temptation for them by seeing someone they respect in Christ with a Bible in one hand and a Bud Light in the other.

Most importantly, those with children under 21 in the house, and especially those with young children, need to understand that little eyes are watching. Parents and grandparents alike, our influence is tremendous in the area of drinking. Kids are looking for rites of passage to adulthood. This is why they want cell phones, purses, pierced ears and driver's licenses. They are seeking ways to look like an adult. Drinking and sex are the two activities that every media outlet is proposing to do the trick of looking like a grown up.

I remember growing up hearing certain glasses referred to as being filled with an "adult drink." So when I was a teenager wanting to act like an adult, do you think I would have a Coke or a beer? Understand it as clearly as I can say it—flat out, there is no such thing as responsible drinking for high school or college students. At best, it is a crime, and at worst it is kids getting intoxicated and making horrible decisions as a result.

Now, I've been around the block enough to know that just because the parent chooses not to drink doesn't ensure the teen is a teetotaler. I'm saying we have to understand they want to be adults before they are ready, and they are looking to us to find out what an adult is. My advice is this: Don't drink in front of children. Kids see things differently. A glass of wine each evening at dinner may be remembered as, "My dad drank a lot." Adult drinks send the wrong clues of what it means to be an adult. "It is better not to eat meat or drink wine or to do anything else that will cause your brother to fall" (Rom. 14:21). (Romans 14:15-21 is a good guide in its entirety.)

· **Let's ask a couple of questions:**

  ➢ Are there people who love the Lord and are walking with Him who drink alcohol? Yes.
  ➢ Are there people who love the Lord and are walking with Him who do not drink alcohol? Yes.

· **Here's the bottom line:**

> ➤ *For the believer in Christ, drinking is a prayerful decision to make before the Lord.* Take your decision to the Lord in prayer. Search the Scriptures, asking not what is permissible but what is best. First Corinthians 10:31 tells us, "Whether you eat or *drink* or whatever you do, do all to the glory of the Lord" (emphasis added).

> ➤ *Finally, know that Jesus is your peace.* "You have filled my heart with greater joy than when their grain and new wine abound. I will lie down and sleep in peace, for you alone, O LORD, make me dwell in safety" (Ps. 4:7-8).

Why Is John 5:4 Missing in the *NIV*?

As you read through John's account of healing in chapter 5 of the *New International Version,* you may notice the fact that verse 4 is entirely left out of the passage. Perhaps you consider it as nothing more than a typo. However, it was left out intentionally. Other translations of God's Word include verse 4, which states, "From time to time an angel of the Lord would come down and stir up the waters. The first one into the pool after each such disturbance would be cured of whatever disease they had." The inclusion of this verse is often controversial, as we just can't put practical reasoning behind it.

When things really don't make sense in Scripture, it is important to know how to wade through the waters of confusion. A lack of understanding can cause great division. Churches can split over controversy around one particular passage. It's easy to ignore the verses that don't make sense to us, but then we are missing part of God's Word. Learning how to tackle tough passages of Scripture can be a tremendous blessing to our walk with the Lord. The more we understand how to interpret Scripture, the more we can understand who God is.

A confusing Scripture brings us to a decision point. We can ignore the part that doesn't make sense; but that only leaves us with partial understanding. Or we can dig deeper.

1. The oldest and best manuscripts we have of the Bible do not include verse 4. In fact, it was not added to the Bible until AD 400. Part of understanding Scripture is a willingness to dig for more clarity. When things don't line up, we can be confident that God is not inconsistent. Instead, His Word is perfect. He did not make a mistake by including one verse or excluding another one. Every word is in Scripture with great intentionality. Being confident of this, when things don't make sense, the first step is to dig deeper. God's Word can withstand our

poking and prodding. It can weather the deepest investigation. When we are seeking a deeper understanding of His Word and we faithfully pray for clarity, we can be sure that the Lord will reveal Himself in new ways. Another step in understanding a difficult passage of Scripture is to look at the bigger picture. By looking at the bigger perspective of what God is doing in Scripture, we can make sense of a single verse.

2. When we examine verse 4, we see that it doesn't line up with the big picture of Scripture. In the rest of the Bible, we do not see angelic healings or general water healings. So this particular verse does not line up with the big picture of God's Word. Finally, when you are wrestling with a confusing passage, it is good to ask the questions who, what, when and where. By breaking down the passage and answering these questions, we can bring clarity out of confusion.

3. Verse 4 indicates that the water has the healing power. However, the Gospel of John makes it clear that the man is not healed by the water of the pool, but by the very word of God. Jesus does not help the man to the water to be healed. He says, "Get up! Pick up your mat and walk" (John 5:8). When we take time to understand tough areas of Scripture, we often reap great benefits. We can approach God with confidence, knowing that He will bring clarity as we battle to understand His written Word.

Tips for Small-Group Leaders

Leading a small group can be a daunting task. But rest assured, God will lead you. You will have the blessing of watching water turn to wine right before your eyes each week. My desire is to give you a few helps, which is why I have concluded each chapter with discussion questions. Use them as you see fit and feel free to add your own in order to connect more specifically with your group.

The best length of study is six to eight weeks. Below is the outline for an eight-week study. This will keep you moving. Take it at your own pace.

Week	Material
1	Introduction and Chapter 1
2	Chapters 2 and 3
3	Chapters 4 and 5
4	Chapters 6 and 7
5	Chapters 8, 9 and 10
6	Chapters 11 and 12
7	Chapter 13
8	Chapters 14, 15 and Conclusion

For a six-week study, combine weeks 2 and 3 (chapters 2 through 5) and weeks 6 and 7 (chapters 11 through 13).

Remember, your job as the leader isn't to preach but to shepherd the flock. Don't feel like you have to ensure that the group answers every question, but instead engages in discussion of how the miracles and I AM statements bring life change and application. You are a guide on a journey, not a professor checking the boxes of completing each question. Pray for each person by name during the week and check on him or her via email, text or phone when possible. The personal connection will go miles for group members' hearts being open during the study.

As you lead, you will find that some people will talk too much while others will talk too little. It is acceptable for personalities to show, but don't let one person dominate the discussion. Here are a few sentences to put in your pocket that might help bring out the shy and temper the talkative:

- "On this next question, let's hear from someone who hasn't shared yet."
- "Sally, what are your thoughts?"
- "Dominant Dave, shush!" (Well, maybe pull him aside first and say, "Dave, I need your help on something. You have great answers. Next week, work with me to help create space for some of our quieter friends to share.")

Another thing that will help meetings are occasional surprises, using visual aids or doing group projects. Here are a few creative ideas:

Week	Material
1	At the end of the session, give every person a bottle of water to place on their nightstand as a prayer reminder of the changes God wants to make in them during this study. Encourage them to pray, "Lord, change me as I walk in faith" each time they see the water bottle.
2	Divide the group to share prayer requests and then write notes of encouragement to the person prayed for. Bring paper and pens to write the notes.
3	Ask someone to volunteer to bring Bubble and Squeak as a snack for the next week: http://allrecipes.com/Recipe/bubble-n-squeak/detail.aspx. Or buy a loaf of bread for each person and stack them in the middle of the table. Tell them to eat as much as they want, then tie it into the abundant provision of Jesus.
4	Have the group sing "Row, Row, Row Your Boat" to start the session.
5	Bring blindfolds and make the group wear them for part of the meeting. Ask them what it was like to lose their sight.
6	Ask three group members to make noise and distract the group as the session begins in order to illustrate the noise of our world distracting us from hearing the voice of the Shepherd. (They can use a cell phone ringing, coughing loudly or rearranging chairs.) Or give each person a green crayon to remind them to not fall for the age-old lie that the grass is greener on the other side.
7	Choose two obituaries from the previous week's newspapers to read, highlighting the fact that we all will die one day. How would the family react to have the person back? Pray for the families from the obituaries.
8	Bring grapes to the meeting as a snack to kick off the session. Use it as a conversation starter on the taste of good fruit. Or upon arrival, ask every person to remove one shoe at the door (even if you are meeting at church ☺). Then discuss how they adapted to hobbling and how Jesus can restore our walk with Him.

Music moves us. So I put together an "I AM" playlist for you and your group to download. The songs will encourage you in between times of reading. Also use them to close your group's discussion time. Ask everyone to listen, and then end in prayer. Enjoy!

The "I AM" Playlist

Song	Artist	Album
"Our God"	Chris Tomlin	*And If Our God Is for Us*
"Life Light Up"	Christy Nockles	*Life Light Up*
"Healing Is in Your Hands"	Christy Nockles	*Passion: Awakening*
"When the Saints"	Sara Groves	*Tell Me What You Know*
"Walk on the Water"	Britt Nicole	*The Lost Get Found*
"I AM"	Mark Schultz	*The Best of Mark Schultz*
"I AM"	Kirk Franklin	*Hello Fear*
"Jesus Messiah"	Chris Tomlin	*Hello Love*
"I AM"	Nicole C. Mullen	*Redeemer*
"I AM"	Ginny Owens	*If You Want Me To*
"Jesus"	Kirk Franklin	*The Fight of My Life*
"Jesus Savior/Doxology"	Breakaway Ministries	*Breakaway/Live*
"Strong Enough"	Matthew West	*The Story of Your Life*

Finally, when you have two weeks left in the study, if you sense the group would like to continue meeting together, I would suggest studying my previous book *Finding God's Will*. Since the group is familiar with my writing style and questions, it will be an easy transition. *Finding God's Will* is based on the life of Moses and how the discovery of God's will led him from being a vagabond felon to becoming the leader of the people of God. God's will is something we all desire and need, and the book will help your group continue their journey with Christ. Ask the group if they would like to continue meeting and learn about *Finding God's Will*.

Thanks for letting the Lord use you and trusting my book to lead you. Let me know how things go and how I can pray for you and your group, pastorgregg@houstonsfirst.org.

Because I AM changed who i am,
Gregg

ENDNOTES

Chapter 1: H₂O to Merlot

1. See Appendix I for more on how Christians view drinking.
2. J. D. M. Derrett, *Law in the New Testament* (London: Wipf & Stock Publishers, 2005), p. 238.
3. For more information, go to www.breakawayministries.org.

Chapter 2: Behind the Blinking Light

1. Layne was more like a big brother to my wife, though he was officially her cousin. He and his brothers would spend summers stomping corn and swimmin' in the creek on their family's ranch. Layne's wife, Erin, was my assistant at Breakaway Ministries. Kelly and I take full credit for setting Layne and Erin up. We double dated to see *Meet the Parents*. He told me at the popcorn stand about Erin, "She's beautiful!" Love at first sight. Oh, yeah, Layne's mom came too. No, really, it was the five of us. He was a great man. I still miss him. For more information, see http://www.caringbridge.org/visit/laynecole.
2. James Jarrett, "Healing and Love," April 14, 2001. http://prayforlucy.wordpress.com. Lucy Jarrett is a chronically ill heart patient. Her parents, James and Katie Jarrett, write this blog.
3. David Dickson, *The Elder and His Work*, George Kennedy McFarland and Philip Graham Ryken, ed. (Phillipsburg, NJ: P&R Publishing, 2004), p. 58.
4. The distance from Cana to Capernaum is approximately 20 miles (see John 4:46).
5. Charles Haddon Spurgeon, *An All-Around Ministry* (Edinburgh, UK: Banner of Truth, 1960), p. 384.

Chapter 3: When 2 Plus 2 Doesn't Equal 4

1. Did you notice that verse 4 is missing in this quote from the *New International Version*? Appendix 2 explains why.
2. See Isaiah 53:5.
3. J. C. Ryles, "Sickness," taken from Brian Croft, *Visit the Sick* (Leominster, UK: Day One Publications 2008), pp. 84-85. (FYI, "Sickness" is a paper worth reading in its entirety.)
4. Ibid., p. 89.
5. Historian Daniel J. Boorstin, 1988. This is in reference to President Kennedy and is one of the first quotes you read when entering into the Sixth Floor Museum of the Texas School Book Depository in Dallas, Texas.
6. Ryles, "Sickness," from Croft, *Visit the Sick*, p. 90.

Chapter 4: Don't Just Bubble and Squeak By

1. As a kid, one of my favorite records (yes, records) was the *Urban Cowboy* soundtrack complete with John Travolta on the cover. "Lookin' for Love in All the Wrong Places" by Johnny Lee was one of my favorites . . . uh, as an eight-year-old. Weird, I know.
2. P. L Tan, *Encyclopedia of 7700 Illustrations: A Treasury of Illustrations, Anecdotes, Facts and Quotations for Pastors, Teachers and Christian Workers* (Garland, TX: Bible Communications, 1996).
3. Legacy 685 is based on Psalm 68:5-6: "A father to the fatherless, a defender of widows, is God in his holy dwelling. God sets the lonely in families." For more information, visit www.houstonsfirst.org/legacy685.

Chapter 5: If We'll Add, He Will Multiply

1. "*A Dictionary of the English Language,*" Wikipedia.org, http://en.wikipedia.org/wiki/A_Dictionary_of_the_English_Language; see also http://www.archive.org/stream/dictionaryofengl02johnuoft#page/n205/mode/2up.
2. Mona Stewart, "Bread and Bread Making in the Ancient World," *Biblical Illustrator,* Fall 2011, vol. 1, no. 1.
3. Mariano Rivera, the Yankee closer, was paid a salary of $14,911,701 in 2011 according to ESPN.
4. P. L. Tan, *Encyclopedia of 7700 Illustrations: A Treasury of Illustrations, Anecdotes, Facts and Quotations for Pastors, Teachers and Christian Workers* (Garland TX: Bible Communications, 1996).

Chapter 6: Time to Sail

1. A. J. Kostenberger, *John: Baker Exegetical Commentary on the New Testament* (Grand Rapids, MI: Baker Academic, 2004), pp. 204-205.
2. Wayne Cordeiro, *Leading on Empty* (Grand Rapids, MI: Bethany House, 2009), p. 73.
3. C. B. Larson and B. Lowery, *1001 Quotations that Connect: Timeless Wisdom for Preaching, Teaching, and Writing* (Grand Rapids, MI: Zondervan, 2009), p. 205.
4. C. S. Lewis, *The Problem of Pain* (New York: HarperOne, 2000).

Chapter 7: Pink Canoes and Barbie Dolls

1. Salvation is not obtained through church attendance or doing good things but through the belief that the holy God sent His perfect Son to die on sinners' (our) behalf and rise again (see Eph. 2:8-9).
2. "Capsized Man Phones for Help 3,500 Miles Away," Reuters News Agency (September 11, 2001).

Chapter 8: Show, Then Tell

1. Andreas J. Kostenberger, *John, Baker Exegetical Commentary on the New Testament* (Grand Rapids, MI: Baker Academic, 2004), p. 35.
2. R. C. Sproul, *John, St. Andrew's Expositional Commentary* (Lake Mary, FL: Reformation Trust Publishing, 2009), pp. 269-272.
3. Charles Spurgeon, "Faith: What Is It? How Can It Be Obtained?" cited in Frederick M. Baron, comp., *One Hundred Revival Sermons and Outlines* (New York: Hodder & Stoughton, 1906), p. 339.
4. Illustration from Quintin Morrow, September 2002. http://www.sermoncentral.com/contributors/quintin-morrow-sermons-6770.asp.

Chapter 9: Flip the Switch

1. Bob Deffinbaugh, "The Light of the World (John 8:12-30)," Bible.org. http://bible.org/seriespage/light-world-john-812-30.
2. P. L. Tan, *Encyclopedia of 7700 Illustrations: Signs of the Times* (Garland, TX: Bible Communications, Inc., 1996).
3. From the poem "God Knows" written by Minnie Louise Haskins, Bristol, England in 1908, as revived by King George VI during his World War II broadcast.
4. Thirty pieces of silver was the typical price of a slave in that day. Jesus' death would buy us back from our slavery to sin.
5. Memorial Park was originally Camp Logan, where the U.S. Army trained for World War I. It is now named in their honor.

Chapter 10: See!

1. Paul Sims, "Blind Man Sees Wife for First Time After Having a TOOTH Implanted into His Eye," Mail Online, July 4, 2009. http://www.dailymail.co.uk/news/article-1197256/Blind-man-sees-wife-time-having-TOOTH-implanted-eye.html.
2. Find more information about As Our Own's work in India in the back of this book and at asourown.org.
3. J. M. Boice, *The Gospel of John: An Expositional Commentary* (Grand Rapids, MI: Baker Books, 2005), pp. 689–692.
4. Edward, Duke of Windsor, quoted in *Look* magazine, March 5, 1957. http://simple.wikiquote.org/wiki/Edward_VIII_of_the_United_Kingdom. A few parenting books I recommend: John Rosemond, *Parenting by the Book* (New York: Howard Books, 2007); Walker Moore, *Rite of Passage* (Nashville, TN: Thomas Nelson, 2008); Joe White, *Faith Training* (Carol Stream, IL: Tyndale House Publishers, 1998).
5. Max Lucado, *God Came Near* (Sisters, OR: Multnomah Press, 1987), p. 13.

Chapter 11: Some Sheep and a Gate

1. Funny story on this verse: One time when a nine-year-old boy asked me to autograph *Finding God's Will*, I signed my name and meant to write the reference of this verse, but instead I wrote Hebrews 3:10, which says, "That is why I was angry with that generation." So I'm sure he wondered why his pastor was so angry with his generation.

2. "Discipline," Bing Dictionary. http://www.bing.com/Dictionary/search?q=define+discipline.

3. I learned so much of my new deepest desires from my former pastor, Dwight Edwards. Dwight was my pastor at Grace Bible Church in College Station, Texas, for many years. I was in a study group of three young ministers, and Dwight took us through the manuscript of his book *Revolution Within,* published by WaterBrook Press in 2002, before it was printed. It was life changing for me.

4. Augustine, *The Confessions of Saint Augustine* (B&R Samizdat Express, 2008), p. 1.

5. See http://www.campolympia.com/.

6. C. W. Cranford, *Cups of Light: And Other Illustrations* (Willow Grove, PA: Woodlawn Electronic Publishing, 1988).

Chapter 12: "Baa" Means Good

1. C. B. Larson and P. Ten Elshof, *1001 Illustrations that Connect* (Grand Rapids, MI: Zondervan Publishing House, 2008), pp. 111-112.

2. Gregg Matte, *The Highest Education* (Nashville, TN: Lifeway, 2000), p. 15.

3. Dallas Willard, quoted in C. B. Larson and B. Lowery, *1001 Quotations that Connect: Timeless Wisdom for Preaching, Teaching, and Writing* (Grand Rapids, MI: Zondervan Publishing House, 2009), p. 236.

4. Wayne Cordeiro, *Leading on Empty* (Grand Rapids, MI: Bethany House, 2009), p. 14.

5. J. M. Boice, *The Gospel of John: An Expositional Commentary* (Grand Rapids, MI: Baker Books, 2005), pp. 759-764.

6. Clint Council, cited in Aimee Herd, "A Young Mother's Sacrifice, and Her Husband's Inspiring Faith," May 2, 2001. http://www.breakingchristiannews.com/articles/display_art.html?ID=8891.

Chapter 13: Dawn of the Dead Living

1. Katie Couric, cited in Cable Neuhaus, "Whatever Katie Wants," *AARP,* November–December 2005.

2. Jack Nicholson, cited in Dotson Rader, "I Want to Go On Forever," *Parade* magazine, December 9, 2007.

3. C. S. Lewis, *Mere Christianity* (New York: Macmillan Publishing Company, 1952), p. 104.

4. I heard this thought in a message given by Walt Baker of Dallas Theological Seminary at Grace Bible Church during the GO! Missions conference.

5. Peter Kreeft, *Love Is Stronger Than Death* (San Francisco: Ignatius Press, 1992), pp. 22,25,35. This book is a great read on death, and I highly recommend it. But know that it is a difficult and very thought-provoking book as well.

6. Ibid., pp. 22,25,35.

7. Brian Croft, *Visit the Sick* (Leominster, UK: Day One Publications, 2008), p. 88.

8. *Embrimaomai,* Heartlight's Search God's Word, Strong's #1690. http://www.searchgodsword.org/lex/grk/view.cgi?number=1690.

9. Jesus raised the son of the widow of Nain from the dead (see Luke 7:11-15); the daughter of Jairus from the dead (see Luke 8:41-42,49-55); and Lazarus from the dead (see John 11:1-44).

10. Elizabeth Kübler-Ross, cited in R. B. Zuck, *The Speaker's Quote Book: Over 4,500 Illustrations and Quotations for All Occasions* (Grand Rapids, MI: Kregel Publications, 1997), pp. 180.

11. C. B. Larson and P. Ten Elshof, *1001 Illustrations that Connect* (Grand Rapids, MI: Zondervan, 2008), pp. 361-362.

12. Edd and Nina Hendee are the owners of a wonderful restaurant in Houston that even does mail orders! See www.tasteoftexas.com.

13. M. P. Green, *Illustrations for Biblical Preaching: Over 1500 Sermon Illustrations Arranged by Topic and Indexed Exhaustively* (Grand Rapids, MI: Baker Book House, 1989).

14. R. B. Zuck, *The Speaker's Quote Book: Over 4,500 Illustrations and Quotations for All Occasions* (Grand Rapids, MI: Kregel Publications, 1997), p. 100.

15. Peter Kreeft, *Love Is Stronger than Death* (San Francisco: Ignatius Press, 1992), p. 63.

16. "Our Daily Bread," Sunday, May 27, *10,000 Sermon Illustrations,* Galaxie Software, 2002.

Chapter 14: Partridge Family Praise?

1. See http://www.partridgefamilytemple.com/.

2. P. P. Enns, *The Moody Handbook of Theology* (Chicago, IL: Moody Press, 1997), p. 218.

3. In the *Encyclopedia of Biblical Prophecy: The Complete Guide to Scriptural Predictions and Their Fulfill-ment* (New York: Harper & Row, 1973), Dr. J. Barton Payne, former professor at Wheaton College, Illinois, lists 91 prophecies; in *The Life and Times of Jesus the Messiah* (1883), Alfred Edersheim, a Jew-ish convert to Christianity and a biblical scholar, cites 400.

4. Two of the best Old Testament "prophecy places" are Psalm 22 and Isaiah 53.

5. William Evans, *The Great Doctrines of the Bible* (Chicago: Moody Press, 1998), p. 60.

6. Laura Sheahen, "The Resurrection of Jesus: An Interview with Lee Strobel," BeliefNet. http://www.beliefnet.com/Faiths/2005/05/The-Resurrection-Of-Jesus-An-Interview-With-Lee-Strobel.aspx?p=3.

7. R. C. Sproul, *John, St. Andrew's Expositional Commentary* (Lake Mary, FL: Reformation Trust Pub-lishing, 2009), pp. 269–272.

8. I heard Robert Jeffress, pastor of First Baptist Dallas, on a *FOX News* interview say, "People don't go to heaven in groups but through their individual decision to trust Christ as Savior." See www.firstdallas.org.

9. "Concern," Sermon Illustrations, from *Bits and Pieces*, December 1989, p. 2. http://www.sermonillustrations.com/a-z/c/concern.htm.

10. Chuck Colson, "Why Harvard Can No Longer Teach Business Ethics 2010," Business Ethics Con-ference, June 12, 2010.

Chapter 15: Sprinklers, Pulses and Vineyards

1. "Top 10 Tabloid Headlines," City Newstand, Spring 2008. http://www.citynewsstand.com/TopTen.htm.

2. Charles Swindoll, *Swindoll's New Testament Insights on John* (Grand Rapids, MI: Zondervan 2010), p. 256.

3. The movie *Expelled* (2008) with Ben Stein does a wonderful job discussing the battle taking place in today's universities of design versus chance.

4. Frank Harber, *Reasons for Believing* (Green Forest, AR: New Leaf Press, 1998), pp. 39-40.

5. K. O. Gangel, *Holman New Testament Commentary*, vol. 4, John (Nashville, TN: Broadman & Hol-man, 2000), pp. 282–284.

6. Christina Ng, "Iowa Couple Married 72 Years Dies Holding Hands, an Hour Apart," *ABC News*, October 19, 2011. http://abcnews.go.com/US/iowa-couple-married-72-years-dies-holding-hands/story?id=14771029#.Tt-Js3M4NL4.

7. J. Hampton Keathley, III, "Help for Troubled Hearts," Bible.org. http://bible.org/article/help-troubled-hearts-john-1331-1431.

Appendix I: Thoughts on Drinking

1. K. O. Gangel, *Holman New Testament Commentary*, vol. 4, John (Nashville, TN: Broadman & Hol-man, 2000), pp. 41-42.

2. Dr. Richard Strain, cited in Willard Collins, "Facts Which Must Be Faced," *Gospel Advocate*, Feb-ruary 4, 1965, p. 71.

as our
own

As Our Own rescues children in India from lives of slave labor, such as organized begging and the sex trade. The rescued children are welcomed into the As Our Own family where they receive loving, lifelong aftercare, including nurture, education and guidance. The children do not graduate . . . ever. They are family. The girls have been adopted as daughters—considered "as our own"—for life. To prevent ongoing patterns and cycles of exploitation and enslavement, As Our Own actively engages the Church in India to bring transformation to broken communities, where predators cannot prey on the innocent anymore.

To learn more about the rescue, aftercare and prevention work of As Our Own, visit AsOurOwn.org.

A portion of the author's royalties will be given to help the work of As Our Own.

ABOUT THE AUTHOR

Gregg Matte was born and raised in Houston, Texas, and trusted Christ as his Savior at the age of 16. Since then, God has done a tremendous work in him and through him. In 1989, as a Texas A&M sophomore, Gregg and his roommates started a small Bible study named Breakaway in their apartment. Under Gregg's leadership, Breakaway exploded, reaching more than 4,000 students each week. In 2004, God called Gregg to become the pastor of Houston's First Baptist Church. Today, this great church has grown tremendously and is impacting the world as never before. Gregg holds a marketing degree from Texas A&M and a master's degree in Christian Education from Southwestern Baptist Theological Seminary. He is the author of *Finding God's Will: Seek Him, Know Him, Take the Next Step*. Most importantly, Gregg is married to Kelly and is a father of two: Greyson and Valerie.

Contact Gregg Matte at
pastorgregg@houstonfirst.org

Twitter: **@GreggMatte**

Check out his website at
www.houstonsfirst.org

God's Will Is What Happens
When You Seek Him

"Gregg Matte is a great Bible teacher and no one can illustrate a point more masterfully."
BETH MOORE
New York Times Bestselling Author

FINDING GOD'S WILL

Seek Him, Know Him, Take the Next Step

GREGG MATTE

Finding God's Will
Gregg Matte
ISBN 978.08307.56582
ISBN 08307.56582

If you are praying for God's direction in a significant area of your life, you may wonder how you will know when He is guiding you. You may even wonder if He is guiding you . . . and that's okay! God's followers have wrestled with what it means to seek His will since time began. Take Moses, for example. When he met God for the first time, in a burning bush on the backside of a mountain, Moses had no idea what the Lord had in store for his life. How did he figure out that he was called to lead the Israelites out of slavery in Egypt? Where did he find the confidence to stand firm on the shore of the Red Sea instead of turning tail or surrendering to Pharaoh's army? All Moses knew in the face of that blazing shrub was that he should remove his sandals—he was on holy ground. Drawing close to the Almighty One, Moses discovered, as you can in *Finding God's Will*, that the will of God is not a single event to be experienced but a process to live. Are you ready?